THREE STRIPES A

One may wonder whether this

of Dunkirk to add to the already swollen list, just another series of anecdotes and reminiscences to come out of the Second World War — now distant from us by almost fifty years. At first, glancing through these pages, one would think so.

But it does not follow this pattern entirely.

We have been regaled by stark revelations of war in the air, and on and under the sea; held enthralled by gripping yarns of ex-prisoners of war and escapees — but this is a Gunner's tale, the tale of a Field Gunner in the Royal Regiment of Artillery, a branch of the service which appears to have been neglected. Or is it that Gunners are more reticent?

Be this as it may, J. E. Bowman begins his tale with his enlistment in 1939 and tells how, over a prolonged period, he becomes the servant of the Gun. Emerging at the end of the war somewhat mauled and older than his years, he is surprised to find that he is still alive.

There is also a love-story interwoven, for, in a world where moral values are fragile and where marriages tumble in ruins, he finds a girl who remains loyal and devoted to him when he needs her most.

THREE STRIPES AND A GUN

A YOUNG MAN'S JOURNEY TOWARDS MATURITY

J. E. Bowman

MERLIN BOOKS LTD.
Braunton Devon

First published in Great Britain, 1987

ISBN 0 86303 335-0
Printed in England by Antony Rowe Ltd., Chippenham, Wiltshire, England.

CONTENTS

ILLUSTRATIONS

PREFACE

It must be understood that this is a gunner's tale, as opposed to that say of a signaller or driver or a member of the Command Post Staff. Each would tell a different story, for each would see a specific situation in a different light from me. I would expect the account of a commissioned officer, for instance, to be more organized, more terse and more restrained than mine in its emotional content.

Futhermore, it is not the story of any gunner or all gunners. The experiences are mine alone, and although many were shared by my comrades they will have viewed them from different angles and may disagree with me on specific issues. I can only hope that the points of dissension will be few in number.

As far as I am able I have tried to be accurate with my details. But after forty years there must surely be errors and omissions, though hopefully not many, and for these I apologize in advance.

It is fashionable in this lax age to throw in the 'four-letter' word with such abandon that it has become commonplace. I wish to make it clear that I do not subscribe to this custom. It is only after much internal debate that I have decided to include it in the text where I consider it to be necessary, in order to accentuate the realism which, because of the subject of the book, is sometimes of a coarse nature. In doing so, in no way do I pander intentionally to current trends.

J. E. Bowman

ACKNOWLEDGEMENTS

I extend my grateful thanks to Colonel P. R. R. de Burgh, OBE, of The Royal School of Artillery; and to two officers, formerly of 22nd Field Regiment, RA, Brigadier A. R. Babington, MC, and Lieutenant-Colonel D. S. Lucas, OBE for their courtesy, kindness and painstaking assistance. I feel that I have drawn upon their time and expertise in a most inordinate fashion. It has been made clear to me, very poignantly, that 'Once a Gunner, always a Gunner' is no mere hollow phrase.

The book was almost completed when I was fortunate enough to glean further corroboration from Doctor W. H. M. Wilson and from two members of my Battery, Battery Sergeant-Major C. E. L. Prior and Sergeant J. M. Stoker, and to these also I express my thanks.

Mrs Agnes Greenbank, who has performed the difficult task of typing my manuscript deserves a special kind of praise. As if the unusual technical terms were not enough, she has had to grapple with my handwriting which started badly and went from worse to worse.

I am also obliged to Dr Chris Ankcorn for drawing attention to the article on penicillin, and for his persistence in insisting that the book should be completed.

To my own family I am indebted in various ways, to all of them for their continuous support and forbearance; to my mother, now passed away, who undoubtedly suffered much during the war without complaining; to my dear wife Joan, or if she prefers it, Bid, without whom this book would not have been written at all; to our elder son, Geoffrey, for his advice on the format, especially in the difficult preliminary stages; to our son, John, for preparing the maps and graphics, to our daughter, Susan, for supplying certain details of a clinical nature, and assistance in final presentation.

The book has, of course, been written primarily for my immediate family and hopefully, for subsequent generations who may find some interest in the trials and escapades of ancestors who survived in an age which to them will seem quaint and archaic. There is also my other family for whom I have written, my comrades of the Royal Regiment of Artillery, for it was they, with whom I shared an important part of my life, who did so much for me in the formative years.

EXTRACT FROM GUN DRILL FOR Q.F. 25-POUNDER MARK II ON CARRIAGE 25-POUNDER. MARK I
(WAR OFFICE PUBLICATION 9TH OCTOBER, 1944)

The following summary of principal duties is not a comprehensive list, but is intended as a guide to Nos. 1 and instructors.

DUTIES OF 1:
1 is in command of the detachment and is responsible for the entire service of the gun. Normally he acts directly on the orders of the G.P.O., but during the engagement of tanks, he is responsible for fire control after the G.P.O. has ordered "Engage".
During programme shoots, 1 controls the fire of his gun in accordance with the written detail of the gun programme, but acts immediately on any verbal orders from the G.P.O.
1 is responsible that his equipment is in all respects serviceable. He will make members of the detachment responsible to him for the completeness and serviceability of the parts and stores which they examine at examination of equipment.
He is responsible that his gun is at all times laid at the correct line and elevation.
He supervises the preparation and supply of ammunition and reports any unserviceable ammunition to the G.P.O.
He orders the gun to be loaded and fired.
He is responsible that the maximum protection is provided for his detachment, consistent with efficient service of the gun.
During firing he watches the action of the recoil mechanism and corrects any faults.
During pauses in firing he supervises the maintenance of the equipment and directs the clearing up and collection of salvage.
He arranges reliefs. He may order any numbers to "Rest" if he considers that the service of the gun can be maintained without them.
He is responsible for the following miscellaneous details:

(a) Arranging camouflage as ordered by the G.P.O.
(b) Recording details of the ammunition fired in each series.

QF 25pdr Mk 2 on Carriage Mk 1

showing main parts mentioned in text.

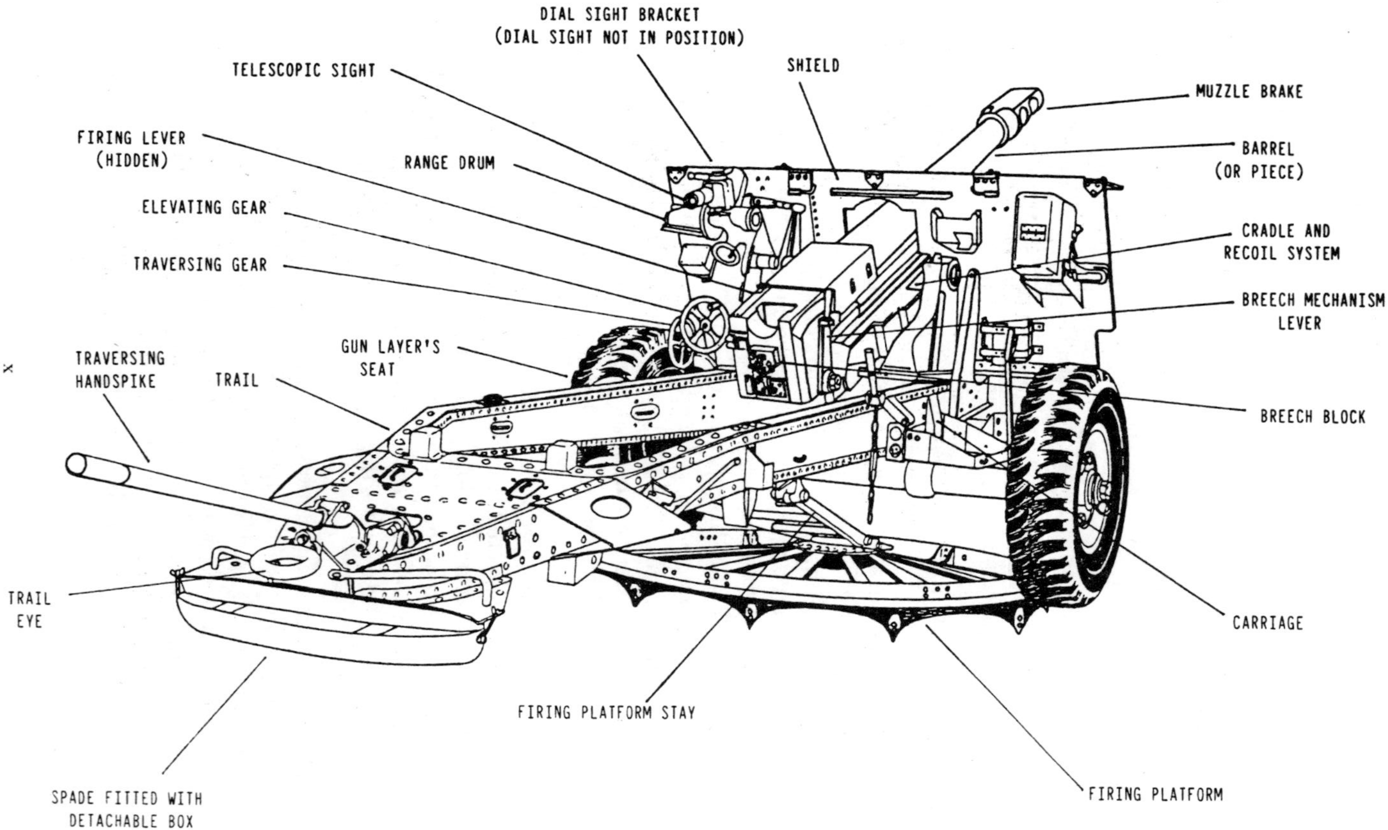

Principal Operators of the gun

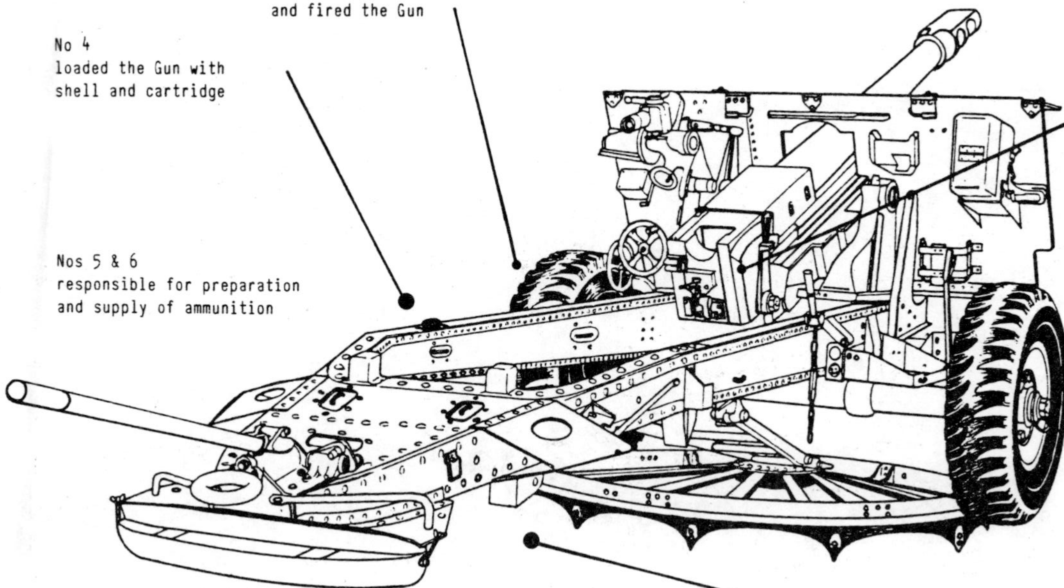

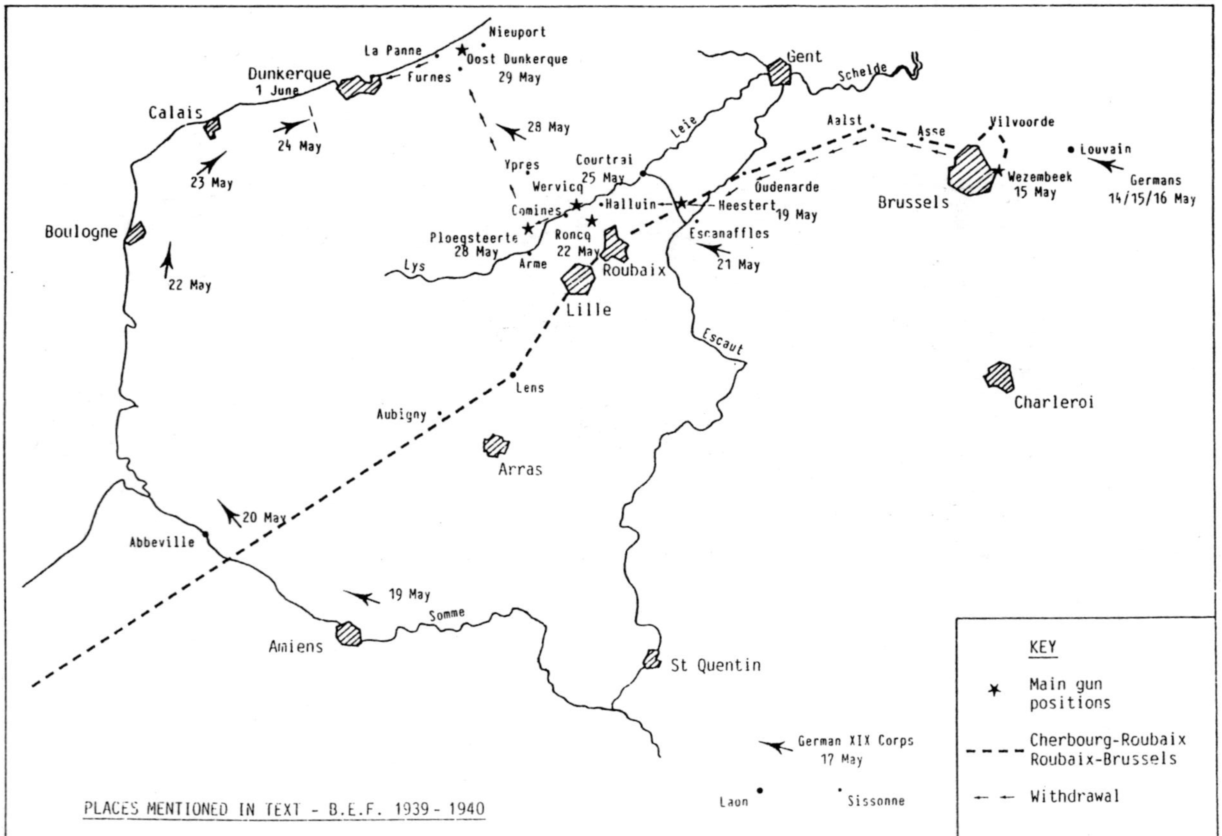

PLACES MENTIONED IN TEXT - B.E.F. 1939 - 1940

PLACES MENTIONED IN TEXT - NORTH AFRICA AND EGYPT

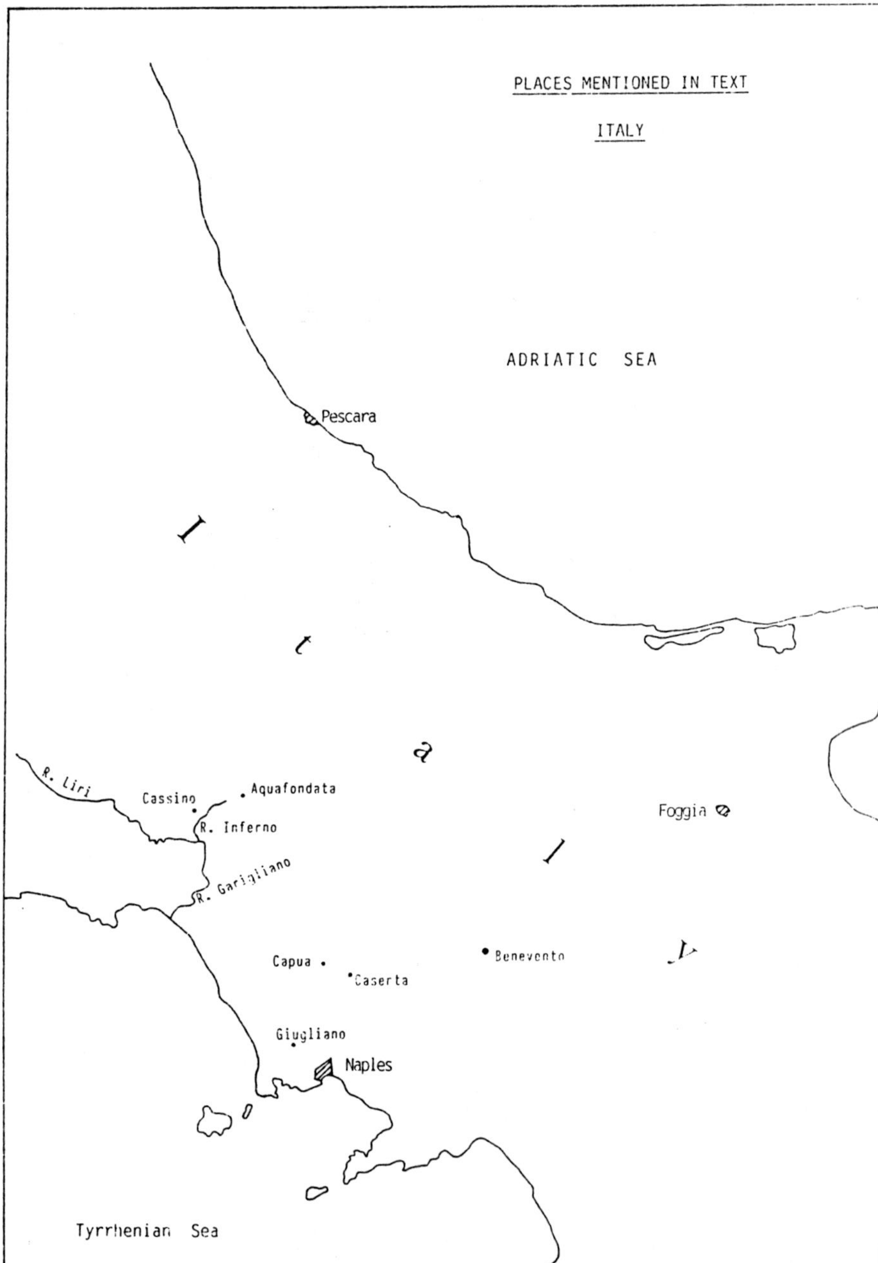
PLACES MENTIONED IN TEXT
ITALY
ADRIATIC SEA
Pescara
I t a l y
R. Liri
Cassino
Aquafondata
R. Inferno
R. Garigliano
Foggia
Capua
Caserta
Benevento
Giugliano
Naples
Tyrrhenian Sea

PART ONE

Home 1939

Oh! I recall the time when I enlisted on the spree,
To be a gallant gunner in the Royal Artillery,
And my heart is an-aching and a-breaking,
To be in Civvy Street once more.

CHAPTER I

No villagers lined the roadside of Hambleton, near Blackpool, in the Fylde; no flags waved to bid me Godspeed as I hurtled down 'the village' as we called it, and turned right on to the main road and headed towards Preesall and the Lancaster Road.

It was a grey morning in February, 1939. A few days previously I had taken a most drastic plunge. I had enlisted in the Royal Regiment of Artillery. There are several branches of the Regiment, but I had chosen the Field Branch, originally called the Royal Field Artillery. It was not just for a long weekend, but for six years with the Colours and a further six with the Army Reserve. I was soon to refer to this contract as 'six and six'.

The Army was considered a lowly profession for the ranker and by my action I had placed myself in the company of ne'er-do-wells, those of limited intelligence and those who shirked 'an honest day's work'. What was even more incomprehensible was that I had taken this step entirely of my own free will.

The inhabitants of this, the Village of My Birth, those who had given me more than a passing thought, must have considered me an unstable young chap. There were times when I came near to agreeing with them. Even the most generous and favourably inclined would see me as a devil-may-care fellow with small regard for responsibility. There was a lot of truth in this, for I had little time for convention and a recklessness towards danger which is a common characteristic of the very young male of any species.

As I was not quite nineteen and thus very naïve, having been brought up in this secluded and sheltered village, it took me some time to realize when I began to rub shoulders with other strata of society that I had several good points in my favour.

First of all, I had no domineering parents to insist that I should stay with them to take over the family business or farm in fifty or sixty years' time when they had died. I lived with my mother and grandmother in a cottage, and my mother, although it must have been a tremendous wrench for her, had known for some time that I must spread my wings eventually. Apart from being committed to help my small family I was free. My Uncle Ben, for whom I had much affection, lived near by in the village, but he was fully occupied in raising a young family on very slender means, and I could not and would not lean on him.

My attitude to freedom was a vexed question. The general view must have been that I had undertaken to serve what amounted to little less than a prison sentence, but it must be obvious already that I took a very different view.

There was no one to whom I could turn for money; no one who was ever going to leave me any. Unlike some young folk round me who could expect help and eventually a tidy little sum in a will, I had nothing. If I wanted to succeed I should have to do it for myself. If I looked for security and comfort, neither of which I cared much about, I should have to collect them for myself.

Nor was I concerned that I had put myself out of the marriage market, for I had never really been in it. No watchful mummy, and most mummies are watchful, would have allowed her daughter to walk out with one who had no prospect of a farm or even a smallholding or, failing these, at least a nice settled job. I was safe from the onslaughts of scheming mothers. Quite soon when I knew my Kipling better I would quote to my mother these lines in order to reinforce my adverse attitude to marriage.

A fool there was and he made his prayer
(Even as you and I!)
To a rag and a bone and a hank of hair
(We called her the woman who did not care)
But the fool he called her his lady fair —
(Even as you and I!)

To sum up, I was healthy, fit and young with no material possessions to speak of, and I was single and unattached. The world was my oyster. What other benefits could there be?

Well, there was one more which was to prove to be very valuable. Thanks to my mother's wisdom and sacrifice and my own ability in gaining a County Scholarship, I had been given a good education at a sound and long established provincial grammar school. What subversive influence was it which overthrew such splendid schools? People can say and think what they like, but their destruction has caused shattering repercussions in several different directions.

I had left Baines Grammar School, Poulton-le-Fylde when I was in the second year Sixth, as I thought that it was time to help out at home. Although I respect my old school for having given me such a good grounding, I can criticize it for not pointing out the possibility of scholarships. I would have worked better had there been a challenge. The students who went on to be teachers and doctors seemed to have private means at their disposal, so I never investigated any further, and no one else did.

About the time that I left school at the age of seventeen, I had been interviewed for a post as a clerk in some local government department in the County Offices, Preston. This kind of position was much sought after for its security and for the 'collar and tie' image.

I was interviewed unofficially at the home of a Very Impressive Person, a kind of latter-day, diminutive Pooh-bah, who lived at Knott-End-on-Sea in a big house, and who had a most important position and a lot of influence. My mother had a very serf-like attitude to folk who kept servants and lived in big houses, for she had worked in service herself. People in lowly positions did a lot of forelock pulling in those days, partly through centuries of tradition, mainly because there were no rent rebates and social benefits if jobs were lost through lack of deference to pompous, overbearing employers. I was reared on good manners, for which I am duly grateful. My cap was lifted constantly, but conscious humility was alien to my nature and the indoctrination which had been handed down through many generations like a treasured heirloom, passed me by.

I was ushered in to meet my possible patron. Repulsively fat, short of breath and small of stature, he leant against his huge highly polished mahogany table and assessed me with his small, porcine eyes. I was just short of six feet, lean and trim in my neat navy blue suit. Did he resent me because I had youth and he was on the way out? He was obviously as unimpressed by me as I was, though not quite so obviously, unimpressed by him. I gave him the 'good manners' treatment but I offered no deference. He expected me to make suitable signs of servility but I made none, and lost the job. How fortunate for me, for I should never have found myself and would have been bored for a whole lifetime. The Very Impressive Person was not really very good at assessing people, for the County Officers lost a willing lad, at least for the time being. I might add that an ingratiating approach was no good where I was going. It would have met with no success at all.

My second venture at earning my living met with little success. I worked for a photographer in Blackpool for two whole days. Photography, I discovered, was just not my vocation. One foray to capture on film a group of idiotic-looking holiday-makers posed outside a large hotel at South Shore was enough for me. I made a fumbling attempt to set up a tripod, a thing which I had never had cause to handle or even seen before. My superior, an unkempt little man who looked as if he should have been wearing a dirty raincoat even if he wasn't, and who resembled a bedraggled bassett-hound, was boringly officious and became very testy. There was mutual relief at our parting and I trod heavily on the pedals of my Raleigh bicycle all the seven miles back to the Village of My Birth.

I went to work on a farm owned by my relatives at Land Hill, after I had spent a marvellous harvest-time at Crane Hall Farm at Rawcliffe, with the Critchley family. At Land Hill I was at home as one of the family and my cousin Arthur was like a brother. I was received into the Critchley family also during that late summer of 1937, and I shall always be grateful to them for their kindness and consideration. Farm work was enjoyable and I revelled in my strength and endurance. But for my mother's sake and for my own I took the step which I did.

In that last year prior to my enlistment I had read and reread F. Yeats-Brown's *Bengal Lancer* and *Lancer at Large*. I was given Gilbert Frankau's *Royal Regiment* as a Christmas present. I read about the North-West Frontier of India. There was more than a little of the romantic in me — probably still is. Gary Cooper, resplendent in the uniform of a 'Bengal Lancer', stood on my bedside table. Nowadays in this strange incomprehensible society such an attachment would be considered 'kinky' or 'queer'. Oh! brave new world?

I had passed my medical and signed my contract at Lancaster Barracks on 8th February, and I was given four or five days to settle my affairs (*sic*) and make my farewells. It was as if I were going to another planet. I met remonstrations, exhortations and even some good wishes, though these were mingled with ominous forebodings. I cannot remember anyone envying me, which I thought odd for I was looking forward to my chosen profession. The attitude I took was that if they were going to break me, they presumably being a group of sadists reared by the Army and specially chosen, I would give them a bloody good run for their money.

The break was bound to be severe. I had never travelled more than a few miles from home, and apart from having slept at Land Hill Farm, a few minutes away over the fields, I had rarely forsaken my own feather bed.

There were no half-measures about my departure. Ronnie Critchley, my mate at the time, drove me hell-for-leather on his high powered motor cycle to Lancaster Barracks. The French have a saying for it — *comme si le diable était à ses trous* — 'as if the devil were at his heels'.

In the twinkling of an eye I had picked up my travel warrant and papers, caught the London train, and still wide-eyed with wonder and with invisible straw sticking out of my hair, managed to conquer the Underground system sufficiently to find Charing Cross Station, from where I went on to Woolwich.

It was a dark wet evening when the train pulled into Woolwich Station. I suppose it must have been between seven and eight o'clock. When I emerged into the street the wetness was reflected by the street lamps. It was as if I had stepped into one of those sombre sepia prints showing one of the more depressing scenes of Victorian London.

There was no one in sight. Or was there a solitary figure yonder, standing under a street lamp? As I drew near I saw that indeed there was a soldier there, wearing a red and blue side hat pulled well forward in flamboyant style over his right eye. His face was very lean and in this light it was the colour of very dark oak.

His overcoat (greatcoat in actual fact but I did not know the correct name then) hung loosely on his thin frame and the big collar was pulled well up round his neck. He looked cold.

"Excuse me Sir," I said very tentatively, "excuse me, but could you please direct me to the Artillery Barracks?"

This impressive uniformed figure, still and melancholy as a heron, paused from his gazing at far distant horizons and his inscrutable eyes favoured me with a long, slow, appraising look.

"What are you on, son?" he asked. I did not know what he meant, but my intuition must have told me. I replied that I was reporting for duty as a recruit with the Royal Artillery. His answer was unexpected and forthright.

"For f . . . 's sake go home before it's too late," he said.

Then he peered once more into untold mysteries. He did manage to return to my own plane, briefly, to point to the gates of the Lower Barracks, a stone's throw away.

Such was my introduction to my new career. I thanked him and slid away, for this strong silent approach was completely new to me. He passed out of my life forever. I suspect that he had returned that very day from India, for a draft had just come off the boat. Had he been in a talkative mood he would probably have told me that he had done 'six tomato seasons' and a 'tora buckshee' — a little bit extra for the King. Six years or more in that hot and distant land brought about great changes in a man. These old Indian soldiers were fond of saying that their unusual behaviour on occasions was due to 'long service in bad stations', which encapsulated the boredom and frustration spent in a hot climate in one terse, telling phrase.

There was no drawback to my admittance to the Barracks. I joined a most motley crew of young men, and others arrived at intervals. We could all have worn the cap and bells in any medieval court in Europe. I was sartorially elegant, comparatively, in my navy serge suit from the Co-op, with its matching shirt and tie. Not so with some of my comrades. There were one or two who approached my dress, but the rest looked as if they had been transferred from a Dr Barnado's soup kitchen in the late nineteenth century. None was devoid of footwear but some of it was in a dire state of disrepair. Poor devils! Little did I know that they had joined up out of sheer desperation. I thought that I was poor, but compared to some of these I had been reared in the lap of luxury.

We were told to undress and have a bath. This bath, if I remember correctly, was a great stone or concrete structure into which several of us were turned at a time. The water was hot in this communal bath, and each of us was given a slice off a large block of carbolic soap. As soon as we were dressed again, still in our 'civvies', we went to a small, bleak dining-room for our supper. No other barracks ever seemed afterwards to be as austere as this section of the Lower Barracks. Was it really so bare in comparison with others, or did I adjust quickly to spartan conditions?

The food was ample but plain. We were given thick slices of bread with marge, and either jam or cheese, or both. One could depend on there being plenty of hot, sweet tea or cocoa, drunk out of white pint mugs.

My first barrack room, one of many in the years to come, was a forbidding, sterile, empty place. It was painted dark green to half-way up the walls. The rest was in a lighter shade. Folded metal bedsteads were ranged on either side, stretching the whole length of the room. Had these bedsteads been changed to stalls it would have won the highest award for the best presented and most hygienic cow-shed in an Ideal Cow-shed Exhibition. I should know, for I had spent a lot of time in cow-sheds.

On each bed were blankets and sheets neatly folded, as well as a pillow. There were also the three square, solid 'biscuits', which, when laid side by side formed a mattress. Very quickly and efficiently, we were shown how to make our beds. All was so clean, so ordered. There had been no shouting whatsoever.

I had peeped into an adjoining barrack room in which was a draft from India, awaiting discharge or posting to another station. My assessment had been brief, for as soon as I had put my head in at the door I was greeted with loud ribald remarks which made me withdraw very hastily. I had seen enough though. How snug and homely it was, with uniforms, belts, solar topees (standard tropical equipment still) bulging kitbags and trophies scattered about. Animated chatter and banter filled the room.

An old soldier, I found, can make his tiny bed-space his home in a minute or two. The recruit is completely at a loss. We made up our beds in silence and crept into them without much exchange of conversation. There was nothing with which to fill up this bare, resounding space; there was certainly no laughter or the friendly jostling of lusty young men. It was as if we had been sealed in a germ-free plastic cocoon, away from all mankind. I sat on the edge of my bed for a short while, before getting into it. It was only a short while for we had been warned that it would soon be 'lights out'.

They were right I thought. All those dreadful prophecies and warnings issued by people in the Village of My Birth had been well founded. I had acted in a thoroughly irresponsible manner.

It was possible, I knew, to 'buy oneself out'. For a certain sum, twenty pounds I believe it was then, one could cancel one's contract with the Army. But I was only to earn fourteen shillings a week, and much of this was to be sent home. I calculated that I should have served my six years well before I could amass the sum required. I was concerned.

Later, on talking about this first night with some of the others I found I was not alone in thinking like this. There was a saying which ran:

> 'Dear mother, it's a bastard,
> Sell the pig and buy me out.'

The rejoinder was:

'Dear son, pig's dead.
Soldier on. So are you.'

I longed with a deep, deep longing for my small, secure comfortable bedroom with its feather bed. I thought of Gary Cooper, resplendent still on my dressing-table, but somehow the glamour was not as strong. There was certainly no glamour at all where I was.

There was one hopeful sign. None of our mentors had shouted or behaved abominably. None had shown signs of pique or temper. There was firmness without fuss, authority without pomposity. Maybe it would turn out all right I said, with that resilience which is probably the most wonderful possession of youth.

Would I, given the opportunity at this point, have gone back home? I think not.

I curled up in a foetal position under my blankets and went to sleep. Occasionally the unfamiliar chiming of a clock awakened me, and I felt a slight panic when I realized where I was.

Next morning, very early, long before it was light, I was awakened by the trumpeter sounding 'Reveille'. 'Rise and Shine'.

My first day with the Royal Regiment had begun.

CHAPTER II

After breakfast we were taken to the quartermaster's store, subject of a very famous song, where everything was ready for us, you could be sure. In a brief operation we were issued with our kit. Drawers woollen, long 2 — vests, woollen, 2 — the list was reeled off, and as we went along the counter, polished by generations of kit issues, the assistants slapped articles at us with lightning speed and precision.

We got two vests, two pairs of long pants, two shirts, two pairs of socks, two boiler suits and two pairs of boots. There was a wide leather belt with a metal buckle, a peaked cap of khaki which we called a cheesecutter, and a chin-strap and badge. Towels, knife, fork and spoon, a pint mug, shaving kit, boot brushes, everything we needed was here. There was even a housewife containing needles and thread.

In a corner of the square near the stores, out in the open with a shrewd winter wind blowing, we stripped off our civilian clothing and put on vest, pants, shirt, socks, boiler suit and boots. We wore the cap, as yet unadorned by chin-strap and badge. All surplus kit we put in our kitbags. It did not take long, for an air of urgency had sprung up from nowhere and from now on it was to condition everything we did. Just enough time was allotted for a task or a duty or a new skill, but to perform it one had to move, move, move!

After a few days, when we had passed another medical and received inoculations and vaccinations we were transferred to the Top Barracks — the RA Barracks.

In our new brown boiler suits, peaked caps and new, stiff boots we 'marched' up the hill in some attempt at formation. What an extraordinary, motley collection of non-soldiers we must have presented to the inhabitants. No doubt they took such ragtag and bobtail visitations as part of everyday life, it being a garrison town.

For six weeks we were to wear the 'uniform' we had so recently donned. We changed our underclothes and boiler suits every week, so there was always 'one on and one in the wash', but the outward appearance was always the same. We were not to set foot outside

Barracks except when we were taken on 'fatigues'. No smart khaki uniforms were issued until a period of about six weeks had elapsed, when hopefully we ourselves would have acquired bearings sufficiently soldier-like to do justice to them.

Boiler suits (or overalls) became more faded week by week, and shrank with constant washing, as did our socks. After three months quite an expanse of 'long john' was visible for one item of clothing went upward and the other receded into the tops of our boots.

The RA Barracks, the Depot, was and still is the home of the Regiment. I think there were two squares in my day, round each of which ran the barrack blocks housing about 3,000 men, and the administrative buildings. The Main Entrance, the Main Guardroom and the Officers' Mess overlooked the great expanse of asphalt which was the Front Parade. Across from the Main Entrance, on the opposite side of the Parade, stood an impressive array of venerable cannon, trophies of wars fought long ago and now forgotten by most.

In our square the ground floor buildings were stables, now mainly deserted, for most branches of the artillery had been mechanized. The barrack rooms were on the second floor, and were approached by flights of wooden stairs leading on to verandas. Actually during our training we did move barrack rooms several times, but I remember best the ones on the verandas.

Above my bed-space in my new home hung a metal holder in which was a card. It is rather faded now. Below the regimental crest was my new status:

885017 Gunner Bowman J. E.
2/7/39 Squad
Squad Sergeant. Sgt. Hardy.

We were in one of the three batteries of 1st Training Regiment, RA. Sergeant Hardy was of medium height and was lean and very alert. As one would expect, he was always impeccably turned out, for it was he who had to set a good example at all times to us his disciples. His lean face had that deeply-engrained light-oak colour which I came to associate with the 'Ponki-Wallah', the old Indian soldier, though in his case I cannot be certain. He was a very humane man, devoid of malice or sarcasm. He expressed no favouritism. Very quickly he gained our respect and we obeyed his slightest wish. We had no option, I know, but his firm but fair manner, coupled with his efficiency, encouraged us to work together as a unit, as well as individually.

Everywhere we went was as a squad of about a couple of dozen men. We started off with the old 'fours' drill, but we soon changed to a formation of 'threes'. We fell in on the square for 'Roll-Call', in the darkness at this time of year. We were washed and shaved with our boots, belt, buckle, chin-strap and badge polished the night before. A quick flick with a duster was all that was needed. After inspection (there was always inspection, all the time) we moved to the right in threes, our right arms swinging, our left hands clenching knife, fork, spoon and mug, pushed up well behind our backs, and went to breakfast.

A normal day's training began when we rose at 06.00 hrs. Before breakfast parade at 06.40 hrs, which meant 06.35 hrs for 'a good soldier is always on parade five minutes before time', we made up our beds, laid out our kit for inspection and washed and shaved.

At 08.15 hrs there was 'training as per programme' until 12.15 hrs, with a short break or two between. Dinner break ended at 13.45 hrs when we continued our training until 16.15 hrs. This was followed by Tea Parade. Supper was at 19.00 hrs, and Lights Out at 22.15 hrs.

According to our timetable, Thursday and Saturday afternoons and Sundays after Church Parade were free, but it did not always work out like that.

Often we ran, or double-marched. We doubled to the gym, then on to school, after which we might go straight on to the square for marching drill, 'stick' drill or later, rifle drill. We had to anticipate our routine and select the right kit to take with us, and woe betide us if we forgot. Extra drills or fatigues were meted out without ceremony, and we could ill afford the time, for it meant that we would have all our polishing and preparing to do late at night.

We doubled back and forth interminably for haircuts. The Depot had special fetishes for urgency, training, hygiene and above all it seemed, haircuts. Whatever straw remained in my hair from my previous existence as a peasant disappeared completely, never to return.

At school I was excused all tuition save in map reading and Regimental history. A gunner never leaves his gun in action, save on a stretcher, I was told. I learnt about Bull's Troop, Mercer's Troop and the action at Le Cateau. Of course we were indoctrinated. We were Gunners, after all, or were going to be, and the sense of loyalty we were assimilating could prove vital to our survival.

In the huge gymnasium, which was very well equipped, we were never given a spare second — not that we were anywhere else, but it was here that it seemed even more hectic. We flung ourselves about, we flung heavy balls about, we did press-ups and then leapt on and off the wall bars. Always the Instructors incited us to even greater efforts. It was never like this at school, and I wished that it had been. There were other devices like boxes and horses over which we sprung and were caught, more often than not, by our trainers. Occasionally to show their displeasure they would let us fly past them unaided.

If we were late in arriving or in dressing or undressing, or if there were sweat marks round our ankles where our socks had been we had to report for extra gym. I had to make my way there in the evenings a couple of times because I did not spring hard enough and failed to clear the 'horse' which was set high.

The Instructors, or 'gym-busters' wore red and blue striped jerseys when they were not giving us a work-out. One impressed me particularly with his expertise. He was quite short and dapper with the build of an Adonis. He moved with the grace of a ballet dancer and had the features attributed to Mephistopheles. The fact that he had a gap in his front teeth gave him an even more devilish appearance.

In the early days of our training one of our number showed resentment at being allegedly pressed beyond his limits. He was a big, strapping lad, but it made no difference. The dapper mephistophelean figure produced two pairs of boxing gloves and we all stood round whilst he gave our colleague a very sharp, short lesson in good manners. There were no more signs of sullenness after that, from anyone.

I also tried my hand with the gloves on. On 25th April when we were well into our training I wrote home, 'I have just been boxing again against another squad with six other blokes from 2/7 Squad, but we got the worst of it this time. I was slammed round the ring, but I have survived with no injuries whatsoever.'

This, being for home consumption, was not strictly true. My opponent was a short, stocky chap and I thought that with my greater reach it was a walk-over. He was no stranger to the ring. He sparred with me for a couple of rounds, even allowing me to get in a blow or two. Then he struck me squarely in the mouth. I saw the statutory collection of stars, sank to my knees, spat blood but fortunately no teeth, and felt raw at the back of my nose for a month. For two or three days with the help of a bit of black cork I could have passed for Al Jolson. My mates greeted my swollen lips with snatches of 'Mammy', complete with characteristic arm waving gestures. "Hard luck chum. You shouldn't have joined."

I had learned two things. Never complain — and watch out for short, stocky men.

The gym-busters were splendid looking fellows, not without self-admiration. On fine days in spring they would install their apparatus in the open air and would gyrate on the bar, drawing the admiration of us clownish lumpish creatures as we trotted past on our next mission.

Sometimes we ourselves did some punishing or reproving. If one of us was not up to standard and we were all getting into trouble for it, we soon let him know. Once, without any extraneous prompting we took up and flung one of our comrades into a horse trough filled with icy cold water. His personal hygiene just was not good enough, but there was a dramatic improvement after that.

There was a more serious incident which was solved by a corporate act. There was this bad tempered Scotsman who started to throw his weight about with a couple of our squad. He tipped them out of bed, disarranged their kit and threatened them with violence. We staged a crusade designed to protect the weak against the strong. One night after 'Lights Out' — it must have been late rather than earlier in our course — three of us fell on him from above as he came in through the door. His rage then was mild to that which he showed when he went to his bed-space and found that his bed wasn't there. It took him some time to discover that it was hanging out of the window, 'biscuits' as well. We all fell on him, dragged him downstairs and gave him the 'horse trough' treatment. No one came out to reprove us for being naughty boys. The disturbance was never mentioned, but you can be sure that it had not gone unnoticed. Though our Scotsman remained an unlovely character he gave no further trouble and our communal life went on undisturbed.

Up and down — up and down on the square we marched. In three months I wore out two lots of heavy studs on my boots. We moved to the right in threes, about turned, performed every conceivable manoeuvre. We slow marched, quick marched, broke into slow time again. If, when we stood at ease our feet were not spaced wide enough apart we were informed that we should not be afraid to separate them more. We were not NAAFI tarts, and our guts would not drop out. We did complicated drill with canes, as later we did with rifles. We saluted on the march or at the halt, with or without our canes, we shouldered, ordered and presented arms and marched with them at the short trail. At first we counted all our drills, all together, out loud. One — two — three, — up — two three, — down — two — three, — out. Later we stopped using our voices, but the counting still went on in our heads.

On and on we went, until our movements were well known and co-ordinated. I would not say they were mechanical, which implied that mental effort was no longer required, for such precision as we were achieving needed considerable concentration.

Our boiler suits, one on, one in the wash, became shorter and shorter in the legs, and paler and paler in colour. New recruits were easily distinguishable from those in the final stages of training.

A miraculous transformation was taking place. The pack of vagrants which had lumbered up the hill to the Grand Depot a few weeks before was now a team of very presentable soldiers, almost as alert as Sergeant Hardy himself.

I was enjoying this busy life and I was also reacting favourably to the challenges. Furthermore, I found my squad mates a very likeable lot on the whole and I was forming friendships.

Our barrack room was no longer bleak and bare. Our kit filled up the space. Each had a locker above his bed, each a chest at the foot of his bed for his personal belongings, although we had few of these to speak of. Every morning our metal bed frame, which was in two halves, was pushed in, the biscuits were arranged with blankets and sheets folded and arranged just so. Kit was displayed in and on top of the locker 'according to the book'. The barrack room was inspected every morning.

The floor of wood, highly polished already, was 'bumped' and repolished every day. For this we used a weighted appliance called a bumper which we swung to and fro, sometimes with a piece of old blanket wrapped round it for an extra shine. On Thursday mornings there was a big inspection with an officer present, so on Wednesday nights we laid out our kit, stitched a name tab on our blankets, bumped the floor, put down newspaper where we had to walk to the ablutions and slept on the floor by our beds. What ridiculous devotion? It did us no harm and no grievance was voiced except in fun.

The coal-burning stove was allowed to go out for this inspection. Then we treated it with blacklead and whitened the surrounds.

"Stand by your beds." All was ready for inspection. Should we be found wanting in any respect there would be another one the next day, even more searching if possible than the previous one.

As soon as we came off the square, or from our meals, we polished. We polished our belts, chin-straps, badges, boots. We treated our boots with Cherry Blossom rubbed in with a toothbrush handle, after the rough leather had been smoothed down with a heated knife. This process was tricky for the leather could soon be damaged. It was also forbidden, but everyone did it. As we rubbed we spat frequently on to the surface. Our boots shone like glass. Spit and polish was no stranger to us. We brasso-ed the metal heel-caps and the studs of our best boots which we reserved for special parades and which were usually in position on top of our lockers.

On 25th April we sent home our 'civvies' which had been in store. We marched down to the station with our parcels under our arms, and saw them on their way. Some of our parcels were constructed so crudely that days were spent wondering whether they had arrived intact. Mine managed to limp home safely.

Having been measured for our uniforms during the first month, we were issued with them about this time, after a fitting and, of course, a searching inspection. Those regimental tailors were supreme masters of their craft. A few deft moments with a tape measure, a preliminary fitting for final, small adjustments and the garments rested on one like a kid glove.

We now had shoulder badges and buttons to keep clean. For the buttons we had a metal device called a button-stick, which slipped behind them and kept the polish off the material. There was also a lanyard to 'blanco'. We wore our uniforms on the square more and more as we became more presentable as soldiers, but again one of the two uniforms was kept for ceremonial wear.

On alternate weeks I bought a tin of Brasso or a tin of boot polish, stamps or notepaper and envelopes. As I drew half a crown a week whilst I was in training I had just enough, if I managed carefully, to buy a 'char and a wad' — a cup of tea and a cake. As was customary there was a well-appointed NAAFI, but unfortunately I could not afford to spend much in it. My means were slender so my life-style was frugal. I was paid fourteen shillings a week, but I sent some home and saved a little for when I went on leave.

In spite of the constant comings and goings, the hectic preparations and the all-pervading urgency, our barrack room became a very snug place later in the evenings or at weekends, in the afternoons. With the stove glowing red, we might lie on our beds and talk to each other or we might indulge in a bit of good-natured ragging. I liked to have a read for a while before the Trumpeter sounded 'Lights Out', but there were only rare occasions when I could indulge myself during the week. Solitude could be found in the Writing Room or the Recruits' Library. I remember them, rightly or wrongly, as panelled rooms furnished with good, solid wooden chairs and tables, such as are found in ancestral homes.

Sometimes I would be approached and asked to read a letter, and even occasionally to answer one. Once I gave rein to a roguish inclination in a reply to a Welsh maiden called Blodwen. 'Dear Blodwen,' I wrote, 'your epistle arrived like a shaft of radiance in a week of gloom . . . . ' and went on to add that she 'had eyes which would make the dog-stars weep'.

I was ignorant of the meaning of 'dog-stars', as I imagine Blodwen would be, for I had lifted the quotation from a book. I never knew whether the romance with Blodwen blossomed or shrivelled because of my letter. Could she really have eyes like that? I fantasized on Blodwen as I dropped off to sleep.

From morn till night at precise times the trumpets rang out their messages.

'Come to the stables, ye men that are able
To water your horses and give them some corn,
Don't give them too much or they'll get the f . . . . n' horn.'

Alas! 'Water and feed' was an anachronism, for no longer were six-horse gun teams used to draw the guns.

There was still 'Cookhouse' — the call to meals:

'The officers' wives get pudding and pies,
The soldiers' wives get skilly.'

What on earth was skilly? How old were these doggerel verses which more often than not contained some crude comment or other? Here was another legacy, passed down through successive generations.

Strange new words began to enter into my language. They were not only those which were considered unsuitable in the presence of ladies, but ones which came mainly from India or Egypt. The result was a language only understood by servicemen, or even in our case, by artillerymen. We could hold a conversation among ourselves which only we could understand. We had our own anecdotes and exchanges and they could be very witty.

Stationed in the Lower Barracks, sometimes called Red Barracks, were the boy soldiers or trumpeters. They were called 'Badgies', for it was here that they earned their first badge, after undergoing their recruit training. Every day they played 'Pedro the Fisherman' as they marched up and down the square. The sound of their trumpets carried up the hill and over the buildings on to our own square, where we ourselves were marching and swinging our arms, heads erect under our peaked caps. We were intent on catching the command of Sgt. Hardy, now about two hundred yards away and receding rapidly — "Squa — ad — Halt" — or "Squa — ad — About — — Turn". Should we fail to hear his orders we should march straight into the wall with a terrific thump and a pile-up.

When I joined my service unit and the reservists were mobilized I was given 'Badgie' as my nickname, for although technically not entitled to it I was one of the youngest members. 'Badgie' I became and 'Badgie' I remained during the whole of my service with that unit.

The Army has a name for the odd jobs it calls upon its soldiers to perform on the side. It is called 'fatigues'. Once or twice I went outside the Barracks in my boiler suit to a rubbish dump where I spent a morning levelling out the refuse which had been tipped there. It was not a very exacting task for I was on my own and my shovel was small. I had been used to a much larger one when I cleaned out the cow-sheds back home. One Sunday morning I scrubbed out the gymnasium in the company of several others. The best 'fatigue' I was sent on was to scrub the tiled floor of the kitchen of the Sergeants' Mess. My efforts seemed to please the Sergeant in Charge for he rewarded me with a large piece of plum-duff which was a most welcome treat. Although I was fed well, I was always hungry. He went even further by permitting me to glance into the Sergeants' Mess itself. To my eyes it was sumptuous with its draped tables, Mess silver and its uniformed Mess waiters. On the walls were large faded photographs in frames. The men in them, all senior NCOs, were stern, moustachioed and wore pillbox hats. Their muscles bulged under their badges of rank. Later I had an opportunity to take a peep at the interior of the Officers' Mess. That took my breath away with its splendour.

We had three substantial meals a day and there was always a thick slice or two of bread and marge and a spoonful of jam or cheese and pickles with a pint of cocoa for supper. At intervals we were weighed. Most of us had put on a few pounds by the time we went on our first leave, in spite of the strenuous life we led. No expense was spared in attending to our health. Dentists saw to our teeth and there were frequent medical inspections. We were given several inoculations at intervals. Whether these inoculations had anything to do with it I never knew, but I caught a very bad cold which settled on my chest, which was a new experience for me. I had been accustomed to working outside in all weathers, so I had not pampered myself before my enlistment. Anyway, this cold lasted for two or three weeks and although I never went on the Sick Parade or had any time off, I felt like staying in bed sometimes. My only reason for mentioning this is its sequel. For the whole of my service, come rain or come shine, come frost, come snow and sleeping rough in it, I never had another cold which displayed the same virulence.

CHAPTER III

It is no accident that I have left the most significant aspect of our tuition in field gunnery to this point in my narrative. Our main purpose was to support the infantry and our weapon in 1939 was the eighteen-pounder field gun, which was so named of course, because it fired an eighteen pound shell. The 18pr. had given valiant service in the Great War.

Very soon after we had arrived at the Depot we had doubled to the Gun-park, where we had been introduced to the Gun. It lived in a great shed on the edge of the Gun-park and It had several mates to keep It company. Each gun had an attendant known as a limber-gunner, whose duty was to keep it oiled, greased and polished to perfection. The Gun was pampered, sleek and smooth like a hunting cheetah, and in its own way was just as vicious.

Each time we pounced down on It for gun-drill, It had been run out and ready for us, attached to Its limber. The limber was a narrow, high trailer (later called a trailer) which housed the shells.

The Gun was the result of much research by many experts. Its purpose was to harass and to kill the enemies of the King. We had elected to become the servants of the Gun and we followed scrupulously the rules laid down in the Gun Drill Handbook in order that the Gun could achieve its full potential.

Well over the horizon, in the outside world, from which at the moment we were detached, the war-clouds were gathering most ominously once again. Did Sergeant Hardy and our other instructors, as they took us through our paces look upon us with compassion?

> We are the Dead. Short days ago
> We lived, felt dawn, saw sunset glow,

We were the youngsters who were soon to bear the brunt of the fighting which was looming over us, and which was so soon to come. Did we ourselves, with our young fresh faces, jubilant in our spring-time, give it much thought as we aimed, loaded and fired our dummy rounds in the safe confines of the Gun-park at Woolwich? Hardly at all.

But you see, we were so young, and the young of a certain kind give scant regard to danger, even when it is all around them.

Initially, we ran the Gun and limber round the Gun-park just to get the feel of it. Then we were shown how to manhandle them by holding and heaving and grasping in the right places.

"Without drag-ropes — prepare to — advance."

We stooped and heaved, but it was not hard work for the Gun-park was level.

"Halt — action front — action rear — action left — action right."

The Gun was brought into one imaginary action after the other, and the limber was unhooked and run into position alongside.

Then we began to manipulate the traversing and elevating gears, to set the sights correctly and to go through the procedure for loading and firing. There were usually four men to work the Gun and ideally, two more to keep the ammunition moving.

Each of us took a turn at the different numbers. No. 1 was in charge. He was the one who saw that the instruments were operated according to the 'Fire Orders' passed on to him. In the Gun Drill Manual there was a formidable list of duties which were his sole responsibility. He it was who gave the orders to load and to fire. No. 2 worked the breech mechanism and No. 4 loaded the shell into the breech. After the No. 1, who could perform every skill should he have to, and who normally held the rank of Sergeant, the No. 3 was the gunner who needed the most training, for he was the gun-layer. He occupied a seat on the left of the piece (or barrel) and put the angles on the dial-sight and the sight clinometer, which was a kind of spirit level with gradations in degrees and minutes.

We were shown how to use the new No. 7 Dial-sight which was only just beginning to be distributed to service units. It is significant that I was able to master its intricacies before I left the Depot, as I will relate in a subsequent chapter.

I have included these few technical details merely to accentuate what may seem obvious. To achieve the highest degree of efficiency, which is to be aimed at in working a cannon, when the fate of a detachment may lie in the expertise or lack of it in one of its number, rigorous and constant drill must be undertaken.

The ammunition of the 18pr. was fixed, which meant that the cartridge was attached to the base of the shell, like a rifle bullet. The whole projectile was slammed into the breech. For training purposes we used dummy rounds, but they still weighed eighteen pounds.

Gunners who were slow to react or made a false move found themselves doubling round the perimeter of the Gun-park with a shell on each shoulder. If the whole detachment was slow on the up-take we limbered up and the Gun and limber went round and round the Gun-park. We provided the motivation, at the double of course. It was strenuous work, but we learned not to make so many mistakes. If anyone bore a grudge, it was never displayed openly.

Sergeant Hardy, for some reason never disclosed for we did not share his confidences, was absent for a day. In his place came a bull-like Sergeant with a 'china-shop' fixation. He addressed us in a way which matched his appearance.

"My name is Sergeant X" (I cannot recall his real name) "but call me 'Bastard'," he roared. "What is it?"

"Bastard, Sergeant," we responded in chorus, standing rigidly to attention.

We had our rifles with us and we had just come off the Gun-park. There was a very steep grassy bank near by, and with our rifles held at arms' length above our heads we doubled up and down it until towards the end we were panting and very sweaty. He thought he had made a very favourable impression on us, in that he had proved his maturity and reinforced his supremacy. As a matter of fact we were very unimpressed and the only real harm he had done was to himself. He was the only objectionable and boorish NCO that ever crossed my path in the RA. He would never realize that facing him there just might have been in that very squad several people whose intelligence and potential ability were far more superior than his own.

I recorded the experience mentally and filed it away in my subconscious.

I have just remembered that one of us had some advanced qualification in Science. Another chap, whose bed-space was next to mine was an ex-public school boy who had enlisted as a ranker presumably to savour the different social climate before he went to gain a commission. He was doing it the hard way, for his father was at least a Colonel or Brigadier.

I considered that he had strange habits. He would take a cold shower every morning, and at night he would strip stark naked before he plunged into bed. 'Christ,' I thought, tucked up in my woollen vest and long-johns, 'this guy really punishes himself.'

Later, when I read about such things, I realized that Woolwich must have been a rest cure after the rigours of public school. This masochist was also reticent, but he did once confess that the food at the Depot was superior to his previous fare.

The most famous character to patrol in the vicinity of the Gun-park was Gun-park Annie. She was a lady of the easiest virtue imaginable, who, in the cool of the evening when darkness was falling, dispensed her favours to lusty gunners for a reasonable fee. For gunners she was willing to perform in the natural way. This lady, as well as being on the plump side, must have had a kindly, understanding disposition, for she reserved a wrinkle in her knee especially for the gratification of 'Badgies', presumably at a reduced rate.

I fell asleep wondering whether I would be treated as worthy of her full delights, for I was nearly a gunner, or would I have to make do with the relief afforded by a portion of her lower limb? I never came face to face with Gun-park Annie, never even caught sight of her in the distance. I wonder now whether her progeny or successors continue to pursue what must have been an exacting and arduous job; whether a Gun-park Annie still walks by the Gun-park at dusk?

'Bumming one's load' seemed to me a very curious expression at first, until I came to use it as a matter of course. "Stop bumming your load," we would say as a kind of mild reproach if a person was boasting, particularly when it was about his sexual prowess on his last leave. In these last paragraphs which recount the few events which formed the climax and also the end of my three months or so at the Depot, I give due warning that I shall 'bum my load', and may therefore deserve to be reproved.

I was chosen with about half a dozen others from the squad to form the Main Guard. We had now reached the stage when not only were we fit to be seen in public; we also were fit to perform before the public. On the Front Parade, outside the Main Guardroom by the Main Entrance, we formed up in our best uniforms and with our rifles. We had taken all afternoon to prepare and it was now early in the evening. A member of our squad followed us with a duster which we used to give a final polish to our belt and boots before the Orderly Officer marched up to inspect us, with the Sergeant in Charge following closely.

I was chosen as 'stick man', another expression meaningless to the layman. It meant that I was the smartest and best turned out man on parade. I was excused from marching up and down for two hours at a time, 'two on and four off', with only brief intervals at the 'Stand-at-Ease' position allowed for a rest. With a bit of luck I might get a full night in bed.

The appointment of 'stick man' carried two responsibilities along with its prestige. I had to return to the barrack room and change from my ceremonial gear into my boiler suit. The Guard's blankets were there waiting and I had to take them to the Guardroom. After this, I collected the Guard's supper from the cookhouse. Then, hopefully, I could get my head down.

I was very pleased to have been chosen for my bearing and neatness, but in one way I would rather have done my guard duty. My wish was soon granted, after I had done the donkey work, for one of my comrades fell ill and I had to take his place. Back I went, changed again, picked up my rifle and went on guard. My first tour was on the Front Parade; my second was more eerie for it took place in the middle of the night, inside the Main Entrance, by the cells.

In one of these cells were five unfortunates who were being held for desertion. Under a dim light which cast shadows round these old buildings I stood entirely on my own. Occasionally I took a look inside the austere cell and could just make out a huddled figure lying on a low wooden trestle. This place went back to early Victorian times and as far as I could see, nothing had changed. I half expected the ghost of some malevolent gunner who had passed this way a century ago, to materialize out of the shadows.

It was in 1651 that the Government was first associated with Woolwich. The Navy Commissioners were to supply timber to make three butts for the testing of ordnance at the Warren at Woolwich. It remained in use as a proving ground and the place grew.

Two Companies of Royal Artillery were authorized to be established by Royal Warrant on 26th May, 1716, and were based in barracks in the Warren, later known as Woolwich Arsenal. The Regiment expanded rapidly and new barracks were erected on the Common in 1739. This had been our home then, since the Regiment was formed.

No phantom artillerymen appeared for me and I survived to take the dirty crockery and containers back to the cookhouse in the morning. I had done 'one for the King,' and got the best of both worlds, all the work, and very little sleep.

Guards and Fire Picquets became a part of my life.

We drilled on the Front Parade more and more and took part in the Ceremonials associated with the Depot. Attendance at Church Parade was obligatory on some Sundays for the Garrison Church was close to the main buildings. Two of us were selected to take the collection on what must have been an important day in the church's calendar. The church was filled with officers, NCOs and men and their families. Again, it was quite an occasion for us. We had rehearsed beforehand, and were aware of the many critical eyes that were upon us as we moved up to the altar together in step, gave up the plates simultaneously, about-turned, paused and then moved back down separate aisles to our seats.

The Garrison Church of St. George was a memorial in itself, for its walls were covered with plaques and monuments recording the fates and deeds of its Gunners. I wish now that I had visited it more often on my own to savour its atmosphere. But in 1939 I thought that its presence was permanent and could always be revisited.

After Church Parade we would fall in in long ranks to the beat of a single drum. We took our dressing whilst the drum rolled on. It faded away and ended in a single tap, when we would be standing to attention, our ranks straight, ready to march off. We marched the whole length of the Parade, first in slow, then in quick time, with the Regimental Band leading us and playing our own marches. The spectators lined the square.

Events were moving to a climax. During the first three weeks in May we underwent tests in all aspects of our work — in the gym, in the Gun-park and on the square. To be fully fledged Gunners we had to 'Pass Out' in every skill. Throughout the course we had been monitored and our individual progress recorded.

There was a Ceremonial Parade on 12th May when the three batteries of 1st Training Regiment, RA, were drawn up on the Front Parade. The Artillery Band was present in full strength.

We were on parade from 08.00 hrs to 11.00 hrs. I could not see much really, except what was in front of me and what I could catch out of the corner of my eye, but it looked splendid enough and I was glad to be part of it. It was a very hot day and we stood to attention for long periods. We had been warned not to rest the weight of our bodies on our heels, so I eased forward on the balls of my feet now and then. What I had not been told was that my cap should not be placed too tightly on my head. The sun beat down and my hat band bit deeper and deeper into my forehead. Had it not been for the strains of the Regimental Band I might have followed the example of others, and fallen flat on my face in the ranks.

We had a full bed-down inspection on Saturday 20th May. The time had come for us to 'Pass Out' as a squad, to demonstrate our ability as a team. For the last time we went through our paces with canes and rifles and were 'Passed Out' as trained Gunners. We could now put on our collar badges to denote this achievement, which distinguished us from the recruits which we still were on the previous day. We called this procedure 'putting our bombs up'. The term is self-explanatory for anyone familiar with an artilleryman's badges. It was a sad as well as a happy occasion for us when we left the Front Parade at Woolwich to pack our kit and go on leave.

With my head held high under my peaked cap, in my tailored uniform showing off its distinctive badge and gun buttons I bore myself with pride up the village to our cottage. I was fit and alert and had acquired, miraculously, a confidence which I had never had before. With my mates I had survived a strict preliminary training without too much difficulty and I had enjoyed it. I was to remember the last few months as one of the most enjoyable periods of my life.

In my left breast pocket was my Pay-book which stated my identification and my branch of service. I felt pride in this also. In my waist-belt under my tunic was a zip pocket which contained two whole pounds.

Briefly I had returned to this Arcadian colony in the northern lands. It was as if I were stepping into a fairy-tale where the inhabitants were lulled into a state of somnolence. Gently, languidly, life went on, but only just. The soporific effect was insidious, soothing to the aged but not conducive to great activity and achievement in younger folk. I was caught for a second time in this seemingly innocuous mesh for a period after the war. Fortunately I escaped, with some difficulty it is true, for it is so easy to become complacent, and the complacency of the Arcadians is hard to resist, to a place where I could stretch my talents and utilize my abilities in a much livelier and challenging atmosphere.

CHAPTER IV

On my return from leave I only stayed one night at the Depot. Next morning, 7th June, I was on the train to Folkestone in the company of three or four of my former squad, now split up and distributed to several units. A truck picked us up and we were taken to Ross Barracks, Shorncliffe, a mile or two along the coast from Folkestone.

It was at Shorncliffe that Lieutenant-General Sir John Moore had trained the Light Brigade, part of the reformed Army which fought in the Peninsular War at the beginning of the nineteenth century.

I was now a gunner in 22nd Field Regiment RA, which in 1939 had two batteries each containing three gun troops and twelve guns. The Regiment was commanded by a Lieutenant-Colonel (the CO), with a Major, (the OC), in charge of each battery.

My battery was 32/33rd Field Battery RA, later to revert to 32nd Field Battery RA. A battery is described by Shelford Bidwell as 'a formidable fighting force in its own right'. Its complement was ten officers and some hundred and fifty men.

In addition to the Major there were the commissioned officers ultimately responsible for the wellbeing and efficiency of the battery. The Battery Sergeant-Major, the highest ranking non-commissioned officer, was at the pivotal point of control between officers and men, and he was assisted by the NCOs, senior and junior. The private soldier, always a gunner in the RA, might not be a gunner in the strict sense of the word.

A whole range of skills were employed and deployed before the detachments of gunners were eventually called upon to fire the guns. There were drivers, signallers, surveyors or Command Post Staff, clerks, cooks, artificers, mechanics, and storemen.

Ours was a relatively small, self-contained, close-knit family carrying a lot of punch, which could function either independently or as part of a much greater force.

The standard equipment until quite recently had been the 18pr. gun and the 4.5 howitzer, both familiar to field gunners of the First World

War. Now they were being replaced by the 18/25pr. gun howitzer, a modification of the 18pr., which was more versatile and which carried a heavier shell to a greater distance.

The Major was not much in evidence to me at Shorncliffe for he was a god-like figure who lived in his own Olympus. The Colonel was so elevated that he lived beyond Olympus even, and rarely descended to the level occupied by mortal gunners.

I did, however, cross paths constantly with Second Lieutenants and even with a Captain or two.

At Woolwich, commissioned officers were rarely to be seen. I had viewed them from a distance, strolling to the Mess in their splendid Mess dress, but the only common factor was that we belonged to the same Regiment.

Now, almost daily, I observed Mr Lucas or Mr Gethin and a little later, Mr Babington, and began to make silent observations of this different breed who supervised my work, my progress or lack of it, and my welfare.

The officers, being all Regulars were products of 'the Shop', the Royal Military Academy, which was also at Woolwich. This establishment had been founded in 1741 for the training of artillery officers but courses for potential officers in the engineers were introduced later. It was the counterpart of the Royal Military College at Sandhurst which admitted cadets for all other arms of the Service.

Brigadier Bidwell has this to say of 'the Shop'.

'The curriculum was a strange mixture of drill, applied mathematics, riding, military engineering and, later in the inter-war years Commonwealth affairs, military history, science, a little constitutional history, tactics and economics. Discipline was severe; applied today in a military prison it would probably cause a mutiny; original thinking was discouraged, and there was barely time to read. Nevertheless, it was not at all a bad preparation for military life and it produced for both World Wars a breed of competent and warlike officers with a strong sense of their identity and solidarity as gunners.' (I might add that the ones I knew displayed a considerable degree of originality and were very articulate.)

Most of the cadets, if not all, were drawn from public schools before the Second World War. It was easy to criticize and ridicule a class which one did not understand; easy to denigrate a section of society considered to be privileged, and because of some curious misconception, incapable of proving itself in commerce or industry.

It is no idle or facetious comment that the Battle of Waterloo was won on the playing fields of Eton. One has only to walk round the cloisters of that great College to realize how much we as a nation owe to it in terms of dedication, loyalty and sacrifice. This example is doubtless reproduced and reflected in the Rolls of Honours of all public schools in the country. Granted, there were one or two incidents when the intrinsic spirit transmitted through the institutions I have mentioned became distorted and overdone, and in my opinion errors were made, but by and large one came to respect and to admire the judgement of these men, and to follow their orders unquestioningly.

Furthermore, the relationship between officers and NCOs was complementary, for each realized the role of the other, both pursued for a common aim.

The Battery, no doubt the Regiment, was at 'cadre strength', which meant that there was only a skeleton staff. Life was much less hectic than it had been at Woolwich, there was plenty of leisure time, and parades, weapon training and gun-drill did not follow hard on each others' heels.

Not only were the officers a new species to me, but the men were also. Several of them were senior NCOs, which meant they held the rank of Sergeant and above. It might be borne in mind for future reference that it had taken most of them a dozen years, if not more, to gain such a rank.

The ribbon of the Long Service Medal, awarded after twenty-one years of regular service was not uncommon. "Roll on my pontoon" was a favourite remark. The old soldiers would speak of their "twenty-one years of undetected crime." The ribbon for service on the North-West Frontier of India also became familiar to me. It was facetiously referred to as the 'Palm-olive' Medal because of the similarity to the wrapper found on that brand of soap. The seasoned veterans of the tropics 'bummed their load' at times, but far from being averse to their stories, I was captivated by them. They spoke of Jhansi, Hyderabad Sind, Landi-Khotal up near the Frontier, and of the Frontier itself. I began to look forward to my tour of India, for it was more than likely that I should find myself posted there.

I joined Sergeant Prior's detachment. He was tanned and weathered by his long years in India and by his outdoor life. I think that it was only quite recently that he had come home. He was very hard and alert and kept us on our toes. Sergeant Prior wore a spur above his three stripes and a gun, which indicated that he was a Rough-rider. I was informed by others who were in the know that to have earned the right to this rare badge, one had to be an expert horseman. At a later time he was to produce a photograph which showed him on horseback, leaping a great fence. His saddle was held high in one hand as he poised over the jump. Of course, the most of the field artillery in India had been horse-drawn and the vocabulary of many of my new comrades was laden with references to an environment in which the horse took only slightly second place to the Gun, if indeed it did, for there were many, particularly the drivers who put the horse first.

I do not think that Sergeant Prior even adjusted to mechanization, but as he was such a good soldier he managed to keep his true feelings to himself for most of the time. He lived in married quarters at Shorncliffe. Unlike most gunners, he neither smoked nor drank. He was to have a great influence on my future.

Another ex-Indian soldier with several years of service behind him was Sergeant-Artificer Bickle, know as 'the Tiffy' or 'Tiffy Bickle'. He was in charge of, and therefore responsible for keeping the guns in a serviceable condition. I quickly formed the opinion that there was very little that he did not know about their construction and about their repair and maintenance.

As I had been assigned as Sergeant's Prior's trainee limber gunner I was often to be found cleaning and oiling our cannon in the Gun-park. Sergeant-Artificer Bickle, seeing that I showed more than ordinary interest, took me under his wing and began to teach me technicalities which did not enter normally into a gunner's training.

The Sergeant-Artificer was quite small and slender and was of indeterminate age because of his shrivelled features. It seemed as if an excess of heat and sun had dried him up. He had an acute mind, was obviously well-educated, and proved, when I came to know him better, to be very well-read. Like Sergeant Prior he was abstemious in his habits.

One afternoon we were both in the Gun-park. 'Tiffy' Bickle was preparing to test the hydraulic system for we were soon to go on firing camp. He was explaining what he was going to do, speaking in low tones, his thin lips scarcely seeming to move.

Someone whistled. I saw a very young Lieutenant standing a few yards away. He was unknown to me. The Lieutenant whistled again and I sprang smartly to attention in a most regimental way and 'threw him one up'. Sergeant-Artificer Bickle had taken not the slightest notice the first time, but on the second summons he stopped what he was doing only long enough to make one remark. "Is Thy servant a dog that Thou addresseth him thus?" he queried, very quietly. At the very end, after the slightest of pauses he added "Sir."

It was obvious that our visitor was taken completely aback, for he retired without making any further reply.

I never heard of Sergeant-Artificer Bickle being brought before the Major for insolence; I never saw him on a parade or even dressed in a neat and soldierly manner. His khaki uniform, when he deigned to wear it was in a very disreputable state, but most of the time he wore brown overalls which were considerably worse. Always when I met him he seemed to be carrying some large, strange looking tool or other.

He operated outside all routine military duties and he had long since relinquished the daily task of polishing buttons and badges. I never met him outside Barracks, never saw him in 'civvies' and I had no idea where his quarters were.

Make no mistake about it Sergeant-Artificer Bickle was a very able and much respected member of 32/33rd Field Battery RA. I was to discover, before many months had passed, that he possessed courage and a fighting spirit which had never previously manifested itself.

There were senior NCOs at Shorncliffe who had fallen victims to the bottle. Boredom and loneliness had taken their toll. Later in the evenings and at weekends they could be seen coming out of their Mess, their faces flushed and their speech only slightly slurred, swaying only a little, for these boys could really hold their liquor.

Up to now I had only had half a pint of beer or so at a time and had scarcely had a drop to drink whilst I was at Woolwich. Whilst at Shorncliffe I graduated to pints and happily, I have stuck to them ever since. Once or twice a week two or three of us walked along The Leas to Folkestone and had a couple of pints. To have taken more would have strained my finances, for although I was getting a little more money I had still nothing to throw about.

Our barrack room was very large and typical of the style which prevailed in the nineteenth century. There were very few of us in it.

The Trumpeter, who had a bed in the far corner, would rise very early every morning to blow Reveille. On his way back he would collect from the cookhouse a large aluminium bucket filled with tea. The tea was always hot, sweet and well-laced with condensed milk. We called this welcome early morning drink 'Gunfire'. 'Gunfire' was a ritual with us. If we missed it, even when we were in action, there were loud protestations.

The Badgie was frequently pushed for time. After all he had to parade at the Guardroom properly dressed in order to get everyone else out of bed for roll-call. One morning the sound of the trumpet seemed surprisingly near at hand. I looked up across the room and saw a bare backside exposed beneath a diminutive khaki shirt-tail, as the owner bent out of the open window blowing his trumpet.

I forget what correction our Sergeant-Major, 'Teddy' Boyes inflicted, but it would be prompt, for like the artillery he was ubiquitous and knew everything almost before it happened.

Although, as I have said, the routine of the barracks proceeded at a relatively unhurried pace, there was no slackening of discipline. 'Jankers' was always round the corner, leering at us. The culprit was confined to barracks for a short or long period according to the nature of the offence. He might have to report to the Guardroom at hourly intervals in the evenings and at weekends. The NCO i/c Guard would order him to appear in a different turn-out each time he reported. He would attend in a gym-kit, then rush back to change into FSMO (Full Service Marching Order) which meant the lot, including big pack. A kitbag might be included, full of course. It could become very wearing after a time, for there was some distance to travel between these quick changes.

For more serious offences a spell in the Guardroom would mean an endless round of fatigues under strict supervision, with lots of scrubbing, polishing and burnishing. The cookhouse must have had an inexhaustible supply of the dirtiest and most rusty dixies, pans and roasting tins, all made of metal, all capable of being restored to gleaming perfection after much sweat and elbow-grease had been expended on them.

For very awkward non-conformists there was Pack Drill, which will be explained in due course; for the very worst offenders there was the Military Prison, or 'Glasshouse'. Even the most hardened wrongdoers did not lean over backwards to make a return visit to the 'Glasshouse'.

You were all right if you kept your nose clean but punishment was swift and graded in discomfort if you overstepped the mark. The majority kept within the limits, most of the time, but there was always a handful who could not resist kicking the system. They were built that way. Always, without a single exception, they came off the losers. How else could it be?

One of the fellows in my barrack room whose background seemed to include rejection from a razor-gang, for he came from a northern city notorious for that kind of violence, had come in my party from Woolwich. He was an unpleasant specimen who had not got on very well with others. One afternoon I was lying on my bed taking a bit of 'kip' when he decided to stir me up by tipping me off it. If there is one thing that incenses me it is being awakened in that manner. Granted, it does not happen very often, but when it does my hackles rise.

He was not as tall as I was, but he was well made. Over and under beds we went like eels, all the time trying to get in a telling blow. He knew a few tricks, like heading and kneeing, not normally standard tricks in quiet villages in Lancashire, but one soon learns. Eventually he pulled out, but not before we had collected a few bruises between us.

Our set-to had been witnessed by others including a Bombardier, and he knew that I had not been responsible for the brawl. I was not summoned before 'Teddy' Boyes for punishment. My opponent left me alone, but sank more and more into trouble. When we were mobilized and were preparing to go to France he was posted elsewhere. I was glad that I never saw him again.

The new Dial-sight created considerable interest, for no one at Shorncliffe had seen it or knew how to use it. I became an instructor, acting and unpaid of course, to Sergeant Prior and other Nos. 1. Sergeant Prior must have thought that I was proficient enough at laying a gun, for I became his No. 3, or gun-layer when we went to firing-camp at Tilshead and Larkhill on Salisbury Plain.

On 5th July I wrote, 'I am on our Troop Sergeant-Major's gun and he knows his stuff, having been in India for about thirteen or fourteen years. He's a decent bloke if everyone pulls his weight though.' It appears that Sergeant Prior had been promoted to Troop Sergeant-Major of A Troop, my own Troop, but was still taking charge of a gun as a temporary measure, as Nos. 1 were in short supply.

I went with a contingent on the 15th to pick up twelve guns from Lydd, a big Ordnance Depot about seventeen miles from Shorncliffe. It was on this date that the arrival of the first conscripts caused a mild interest and the exchange of a few ribald remarks between ourselves at their expense. In our opinion they were 'treated like little gentlemen' (for how long I wonder?), and had a special area curtained off in the dining hall, presumably so that they would not be coarsened by contact with us rude squaddies. Troop Sergeant-Major Hutchings, another Warrant Officer with long service who was friendly disposed, showed apoplectic symptoms when it was revealed that there was to be a 'reception room for sweethearts'.

CHAPTER V

It was on a summer's morning, the last Thursday in July, just as dawn was breaking that I first caught sight of Stonehenge, viewed from the tractor which was towing our Gun. So impressed was I by this famous relic, just visible in an early morning mist which accentuated its mystery and authority, that I wrote home especially to tell my mother and grandmother.

By 9 a.m. we were out on the ranges at Tilshead. As if in a dream I found myself sitting on the layer's seat of No. 1 Gun (A Subsection) which was the right hand gun of the four. The 18pr. I was about to fire had no dummy round 'up the spout'. It was loaded with a shrapnel shell. The fuse was set to explode at a certain height above the target. The estimated maximum range of this piece of artillery was 6,500 yards, but had probably been extended to approximately 9,000 yards when HE (High Explosive) projectiles were used.

My apprenticeship had advanced considerably since the Gun-park at Woolwich, with its practice projectiles.

Troop Sergeant-Major Prior as No. 1, was kneeling at the right of the trail, fire orders had been given, the gun set and laid. My hand was on the firing lever, my heart was in my mouth, we were waiting for the order to fire and the suspense was almost unbearable for me.

Hovering not far away, constantly vigilant for the slightest error, would be a figure bearing on his lower arm the insignia of a Sergeant-Major, the crown inside laurel leaves with above it the crossed guns. He would have a white cover on his cap and he would carry a clip-board and a stop-watch. This was the A i/G, the Assistant Instructor in Gunnery, and here at the School of Artillery he and his colleagues reigned surpreme. No one, whether non-commissioned or commissioned questioned his word, for he was Lord of the Cannon and knew everything. I had great aspirations to this post, later in my career.

Glancing to the right as I waited, I saw something which brought home very powerfully the full significance of my job. This devil on which I was sitting was no toy. It was not, at any time, to be treated with anything but the greatest respect. As well as being a menace to an enemy it could also turn on its servants and masters if they were careless and indifferent towards it. That is why, in a copse at a discreet distance from the line of guns, an ambulance had slid into position. Soon such ambulances were to become very familiar to me, but whenever or wherever I saw them I was reminded of the arrival of the first one on a sunny summer's day in 1939.

"Fire!" The order came from the Command Post. Troop Sergeant-Major Prior, upright at the trail, signalled that he had heard by raising his right arm above his head. Immediately, he himself gave the order to fire.

I pulled the firing-lever, my seat lifted, the Gun kicked back and I waited for my head, which felt as if it had been ejected ten feet in the air, to reassert itself. There was no respite, however. Another shell had been slammed up the breech and I was already rotating my wheels to readjust the sights. "Hand on firing-lever — report 'Ready'."

The second round did not seem quite as shattering. Of the many shells that I was to fire or that I would order to be fired, that first one on Salisbury Plain was the worst. The 18pr. had a vicious crack, and it took a while to get used to it.

We fired a good many rounds of shrapnel on this exercise. This type of ammunition had been used extensively in the First World War. It was devasting when it was used against troops in the open when it was directed properly. The gunners set the time fuse on the shells, following the orders from the Command Post which had first been relayed from the Observation Post way up forward and not normally in sight of the guns. Hopefully, the shells could be made to burst at the correct height above the enemy and spray him with very hot little metal balls. It was not all that easy to adjust the height of burst to achieve maximum damage. With the advent of the 18/25pr. shrapnel was declared obsolete in the British Army as being 'too complicated to use and relatively ineffective'.

In my youthful enthusiasm (remember I was very much a 'rookie') I wrote home:

'They kick back and a terrific flame spurts out of the bore. I always say or shout something when I fire to prevent the noise from staying in my head. The vibrations flow through the ears and out of the mouth. I never padded my ears and I was quite used to it by Saturday when I fired about 60 rounds of shrapnel.'

We had two of the 18/25prs. with us on this shoot.

My exuberant letter continues:

'The new 25prs. (I meant 18/25prs., of course) made us sweat and they make a hell of a row but they are lovely guns. There were only two detachments from the Regiment who fired the 25prs. and ours was one of the detachments.'

A week later on 7th August the Regiment had been equipped with our new cannon and I was again layer in one of the two detachments who were sent to the School of Artillery, Larkhill to calibrate them.

Calibration was a highly technical procedure supervised by the Lords of the Cannon at the School of Artillery. Omnipresent, omnipotent, omniscient, their orders had to be followed with servile deference.

The purpose of the operation extending over a period of four days, was to find the muzzle velocity, or exact speed in feet per second at which the projectile left the muzzle. All other things being equal, if it went faster it travelled a bit further and if it was slower it fell that little bit short. The MV varied from gun to gun, giving each an individuality of its own. Uniformity had to be established in order that accurate fire could be achieved with a combination of guns from two (a section) to possibly a whole Division of seventy-two.

The computations, using Range Tables which contained mathematical data, carefully calculated, and also such details as accurate weight of projectile, charge temperature and variants in meteorological conditions, were applied to the fall of shot from one gun, using more than one type of charge. From each group of ten rounds the Mean Point of Impact was discovered and the MV was eventually established. This process was known as Absolute Calibration and the gun used was called the Standard Gun. Normally only one gun was used in a Regiment (sometimes in a Division) but for some reason we appeared to have used two.

It was a relatively simple matter to fire the other guns later and in turn alongside the 'Standard', and to set the MV thus deduced on to the range drums so that the deviation was adjusted automatically.

The ammunition was no longer 'fixed', the projectile and the cartridge now being inserted separately. Each shell was loaded and rammed in order to engage the driving band into the rifling. The driving band was the ring of soft metal which encircled the shell towards its base and caused it to rotate in flight. There were three propellant charges, Charge I being the least powerful, Charge III having the greatest thrust. As well as firing with a flat trajectory, that is in a straight line, we could lob shells over hills — hence the term gun-howitzer. The range had been increased by over 2,000 yards and we could, given the right conditions and using Charge III, reach a target almost 12,000 yards away.

Before 1938 Field Regiments were called Field Brigades. 22nd Field Brigade, for instance, had four four-gun Batteries — 32nd, 33rd, 36th and 55th. Three of these Batteries had 18prs., but 36th Battery had 4.5-inch howitzers. This was the standard organization. The howitzer fired a 35 pound shell, but its range was 2,500 yards less than the 18pr. It was most useful in hilly country.

Now we had two twelve gun Batteries, 32/33rd and 36th/55th. Each Battery had three gun troops of four guns. All were 18/25prs. It is worth noting that five months later, in February, 1940 when we were in France, 17th Field Regiment from our Division went to 51st (Highland) Division and 77th (Highland) Field Regiment, a TA Unit, came to us. 77th Field Regiment was still equipped with twelve 18prs., and twelve 4.5-inch howitzers and went into action with them. Though outranged by the modern German artillery such ordnance was still to be used for the next eighteen months.

It was after my expedition to Salisbury Plain that I was promoted to Lance-Bombardier. At first, it was 'Acting-unpaid', but in a little while my pay was increased. I could not get home fast enough to show off my one chevron with the Layer's Badge above it, but I had to wait. One of my first duties in my new rank was that of Battery Orderly, the Sergeant-Major's personal attendant, on whom he bestowed a never-ending round of tasks, such as taking or fetching messages, marching the sick to visit the Medical Officer, rounding up people for Guard Duty or seeing that lights were put out in all barrack rooms. For a week at a time the Battery Orderly had a chequered and hectic life.

On the Monday morning, very early, I called on the barber who never seemed to sleep, to have a very close haircut. I presented myself at the Battery Office at the precise time appointed. The order to enter was given in a most peremptory manner. I came to attention before the Battery Sergeant-Major who was sitting at his desk. My memory projects a person on the short side, well built and immaculately groomed. His face had the healthy glow associated with grouse-moors and port; or with a diet consisting solely of game pies and stout. Quickly but penetratingly he looked me over and issued instructions in rapid succession, like short bursts from a Bren-gun.

"Got it? Dismiss."

"Sir." I turned about smartly and marched towards the door. He pulled me up short.

"And Bombardier," he snapped.

"Sir." I halted, turned about to face him.

"Get a bloody haircut."

"Sir," I responded.

I turned about again, marched out of the door and went straight back to the barber's who registered not the slightest surprise at seeing me back again within a few minutes. He gave me another haircut, or went through the motion, for there were not many trimmings to sweep up when he had finished. I went off to take Sick Parade. My two mates, both called Parker, thought it a great laugh, and so did I. One Parker was a L/Bombardier, and the other one had been a boy soldier in the Gloucesters.

The languid, complacent days of the summer were passing into autumn. A new age was about to begin had we been able to foresee the future. Alas! there were few prophets about and fewer still who listened to them. The Bren-gun training, taken at a leisurely pace, would soon take on a more sinister aspect; the Gun, supercilious and well groomed in the Gun-park would soon be taken out on its leash to sniff out and hopefully, to snuff out its opposite number across the Channel. The mastiffs over there were already preparing to bay at our gates. They had been restless for years but we politically uneducated innocents, misguided by promises of an ineffectual League of Nations which had fallen flat on its face, knew virtually nothing of the terror which stalked abroad under the Nazi regime. A period of darkness was about to descend. War was unavoidable and imminent and we who had suddenly become of prime importance gathered our warriors together.

I am very hazy about this period just before the official commencement of hostilities. The British Army was mobilized at 14.00 hrs on 1st September but two batches of Reservists had already been called back to the Colours for retraining with us at Shorncliffe. They had already served their six years (in some cases, three) as Regulars, and many of them had done a 'Tora buckshee' — that year or so extra served abroad for the King, on the pretext that there was no Trooper available, just then, to carry them home to Blighty.

'Soldiering on for a Tora buckshee,
That's what I call f . . . . g hard lines.'

Thus ran the unexpurgated version of a song soon to become popular.

I found that I had been on a draft for India that autumn but it was cancelled much to my regret, for I would have liked to have soldiered in India. India or no India, I still did my 'Tora buckshee'.

These new intakes which came swarming in were no fledglings. Though very bolshie at the moment, for many of them had only just settled down in Civvy Street, they were hard-bitten and well-trained soldiers.

On the Saturday night, when I was near the end of yet another week as Battery Orderly, or general dog's-body, the lights remained on after 'Lights Out' in a barrack room on the second storey of one of the barrack blocks. I climbed up the spiral staircase, went into the barrack room and told the reservist occupants that the lights must go out. My order was greeted with derision for most of them had been drowning their sorrows. I went to the switch and plunged them into darkness. As I had got about a third of the way down the staircase I realized that something very heavy and cumbersome was following me, was soon to overtake me. I pressed myself into a corner on a landing and a great metal coal bunker passed me, thudding and bumping on the stairs and off the very strong handrails as it went. It must have weighed two or three hundred-weights. There was a great investigation, the barrack room involved was under a cloud, but the high spirited culprits whose idea of a joke might easily have misfired were never singled out. Strangely enough, the newcomers bore me no grudge, neither did they consider me a comic figure for my foolhardy attention to orders.

The Battery was being made up to full war strength and we started to pull ourselves into shape. It was now, surrounded by and working with men quite a lot older than myself that I became known as Badgie. I listened with fascination to the tales told by these experienced fellows who were so different, who possessed such an inner strength and a fatalistic approach to disappointments and discomfort. "F . . . your luck, you shouldn't have joined," they would say if a mate had been delegated to carry out a distasteful task. They would tell me to "get my number dry" or to "get some service in," but it was all in fun.

On 3rd September war was declared. We were busy digging slit trenches on the grassy verges when the first air raid siren was sounded, straight after the news had arrived. It was a false alarm. I looked up from my digging and saw a naval vessel of the Dover patrol putting out into the Channel.

By 5th September we had moved to Etchinghill, a village outside Dover, where some of us were billeted in the Mission Hall. We were issued with battledress and a forage cap and I paid a sad farewell to my tailored uniform, peaked cap and my shining leather belt. More inoculations were given.

At the outbreak of war, much to my surprise and delight, I had been promoted to full Bombardier. We were all given 48 hours leave, but I had little time to parade my two new stripes. My mother fed me well as usual and went with me to Poulton Station on my return. She must have thought sad thoughts as she went back alone on the bus, for the young men, among them her admirers, had set off from this same station when they went to France, only just over twenty years ago. Few of them ever came home again.

Prompted to some extent by the example shown by the old soldiers, I had developed a greater thirst, so my input of pints of beer increased appreciably. The pub at Etchinghill was filled to capacity with jostling, boisterous gunners. They were not unruly and treated with respect the civilian regulars, some of whom were accompanied by their wives. One of the reservists, who had been made up to Sergeant and who was a coal-miner from the North, was in good form. He was rough, tough and well built. Hand clenched round his seventh pint, his great coarse, bronze face glistening with sweat, he bellowed out his favourite ditty.

"With his f . . . . g great kidney-wiper
And his bollocks made of steel
And half a yard of foreskin hanging well below his knee."

Two middle-aged ladies in the corner simpered and tried to look coy and uncomprehending. They were taking it all in though, and loving it.

In a display of animal spirits a very bold fellow urinated on the Sergeant-Major. Lying under his gas cape in an annexe of the village hall, he woke to the sound of water cascading over his covering. He sprang up to face his violator but he was gone. Whether it was some well-wisher who was celebrating the Sergeant-Major's previous promotion in the way that ships are christened, whether it was intended as a protest against his new station, or whether the urinator was desperate and just chose the most convenient corner will never be known. The call to arms affects people in different ways. This brave and foolhardy soul, whoever he was, had responded to a need which almost everyone in the services must have longed to answer at some part in his career.

We paraded at Etchinghill on 13th September as a Division and were inspected by the Fourth Divisional Commander, Major-General Johnson, VC, DSO, MC. We were all Regulars, or had been, and although many were rather rusty there were a great many years of service and considerable experience to be drawn on here on the parade. We all wore the new battledress and equipment.

By the 17th we were at Tournai Barracks, Aldershot. Our 'wheels and trails', our way of describing vehicles, guns and stores, left for Avonmouth on the 27th to be loaded on to the *Lady of Mann*. They sailed for France on the 29th. In the afternoon of the 27th we who remained lined a road in Aldershot (Queen's Avenue) whilst HM the King drove past on an informal farewell visit to the Regiment. I related, for my mother's benefit, that the Queen who was also in attendance, wore a mauve outfit.

On 2nd October we sailed from Southampton on SS *Manxman*, another Isle of Man boat, and disembarked at Cherbourg on the same day. We were quickly reunited with our 'wheels and trails'.

Very little time had been spent in getting us over the Channel, but as is customary at the outset in our major wars, we might have been a lot better prepared.

We were a unit of a Regular Division, the Fourth British Infantry Division, itself part of the British Expeditionary Force or BEF. Field Marshal Slim defined a division as 'the smallest formation that is a complete orchestra of war and the largest in which every man can know you.' I understand that divisional command is considered by senior officers to be the most satisfying of posts. Our Division, when it was brought up to strength, would contain over 10,000 men. There were three Infantry Brigades (subsequently referred to as IB), the 10th, 11th and 12th. Each contained three Infantry Battalions and an Anti-tank Company. These were supported by the Divisional Artillery of three Field Regiments, the 17th, 22nd and 30th, and one Anti-tank Regiment, the 14th. Attendant upon them were three Field Companies of Royal Engineers, a Regiment of the Royal Corps of Signals, three Companies of the Royal Army Service Corps to provide ammunition, petrol and supplies, and three Field Ambulance Units of the Royal Army Medical Corps. To round off the complement there was an Intelligence Section, a Field Hygiene Unit, a Postal Unit, RE, and a Provost Company. I rather fancy that there was also a Machine-gun Battalion which my source does not tabulate with the others.

PART TWO

The BEF, 1939-40

O it's Tommy this, an' Tommy that, an' 'Tommy, go away';
But it's 'Thank you, Mister Atkins,' when the band begins to play.

Tommy, by Rudyard Kipling

CHAPTER VI

From Cherbourg we made what seemed to be a leisurely journey northwards through the mild autumn countryside of Normandy. I was surprised to see peaches still hanging from trees trained against old walls facing southwards.

Our journey to the Belgium frontier, which was where we were heading, took us ten days. On 5th October we bivouacked (splendid verb, redolent of the Crimean or Peninsular Wars — I felt that I really was soldiering) in Le Chateau la Vesusier in Boliere. The part we occupied was derelict and delapidated, but from the peeling tapestries hanging from the wall it was apparent that it had known former glory. I took note sadly that few of my comrades had any knowledge of or imagination for the splendour it must have represented when titled folk strutted on the terraces in peacock fashion.

"Dans les jardins de mon père, les rosiers sont fleuris,
Dans les jardins de mon père, les rosiers sont fleuris,
La caille tou-tou-relle, vient y faire le nid,
Au près de ma blonde, qu'il fait bon, fait bon, fait bon,
Au près de ma blonde, qu'il fait bon dormir."

Using my School Certificate French in 'textbook' fashion, delivered in a strong Lancashire accent, a bizarre enough combination, I regaled the natives with this song with its mildly erotic undertone. It was obviously and surprisingly recognizable to peasants used to conversing rapidly in their own patois with not much regard for grammar, for it never failed to bring cackles of delight and nudges from wrinkled old crones, descendants of those who had sat knitting in the shadow of the guillotine, watching the heads roll.

In markets and bistros I endeavoured to communicate. It was interesting, often amusing and I improved.

Northwards we went to Villette and Bonnevil-Les-Eaux, finally alighting at Sallaumines near Lens, which is a coalmining area not far from Lille. We were billeted in a stadium and there was ample room for Gun-park and parade ground, as well as cookhouse and offices.

In the War Diary for 10th October there is mention of a Guy tractor. These 'Quads' were powerful vehicles with four-wheel drive and were replacing the old six-wheel Morris tractor. I am told that on mobilization we had been equipped with Quads as ammunition wagons towing two limbers.

(Since this was written I have been fortunate enought to meet 'Tich' Greenhill, one of A Troop's drivers. He confirms that it was he who was placed in charge of our first Quad at Sallaumines, and that it was indeed used for the purpose stated.)

Whilst at Sallaumines we worked on constructing gun positions.

A strange unaccustomed situation had arisen. From always having lived on the edge of penury I now found myself enfolded in the soft bosom of riches. Such was the favourable rate of exchange that I could draw one hundred francs each week, the equivalent of twelve shillings (sixty pence now). On it I could wine and dine sumptuously at least by my standards. Instead of having a 'char and a wad' at the NAAFI for our morning break we now had café au lait *avec du rhum*. The inhabitants of the towns and villages were poised, waiting for us, ever ready to make a fast buck. They had been well trained, for their forebears had done the same thing not so very long ago in the Great War. Horse steaks and chips and eggs and chips were cheap and frequent additions to our rations.

In the bistros or bars, and these were numerous wherever we went, a wide and varied collection of bottles was displayed on the shelves behind the bar, just as they are today. They contained either spirits or liqueurs and there were many colours from which to choose. Almost each one was in itself potent but when mixed into a gargantuan internal cocktail the effect was like taking a very fast trip into outer space.

At first, when it was still a novelty, and later for special celebrations, we would choose an inviting looking shelf and drink our way along it, or as far as we could get before our vision became clouded and we groped our way back to our groundsheets and blankets on the hard wooden floor. When we had settled down most of us drank beer, which although different from the English brands, was still very palatable and in plentiful supply.

I have always maintained that had such conditions continued for a couple of years the BEF would have staggered back home *en masse* for immediate hospitalization for terminal cirrhosis of the liver.

Brothels were still recognized officially. The fear of 'getting a packet' as we called it overrode my sexual desire, which was not heightened by the appearance of the sad, coarsened, often raddled women who were offering their goods for sale.

Time was always found to maintain our smug menacing Master; time always found to engage in gun-drill. I was layer in A Subsection, or No. 1 gun of A Troop, normally the right-hand gun of the line of the whole Battery. My No. 1 was a reservist recently promoted to Sergeant, and was new to the job.

All round the interminable maintenance and training went on in other skills. Signallers, drivers, surveyors, artificers all busied themselves with never-ending tasks. But I was where I wanted to be, at the sharp end, on the Gun.

I could dismantle and assemble a breech mechanism blindfolded, check all the sights, even attend to the hydraulic system, thanks to the instruction of Sergeant-Artificer Bickle who clucked about the Gun-park like a mother hen. If a spectre of a Sergeant-Artificer materializes in the illustrious Gun-parks of the Royal School of Artillery you can be sure that it will be Sergeant-Artificer Bickle.

The Gun Drill Manual was my bedside reading. I continued to learn my craft. I was a keen young soldier.

It was at Lens that I had a fierce argument with a miner who had just come off shift. He had slipped into the bistro for a drink and was still begrimed and in his working gear. I also formed the opinion that there was an illicit sexual liasion between himself and *'la patronne'* for he was obviously set to create a favourable impression with her. It was also clear that he was no Anglophile.

He started the ball rolling by saying that French miners could work in a seam which was about three feet high. I knew nothing whatsoever about this and cared not at all, but I retaliated in defence of 'les anglais' by saying that English miners could work quite easily at about two feet.

"Mineurs francais — comme ça." His hand dropped a bit lower towards the floor.

"Mineurs anglais — comme ça," I replied going lower still.

This interchange went on until finally I indicated a height about six inches from the floor. I had gathered that he was not very bright, but even he got the message that I was sending him up.

With a cry of rage he grabbed his dirty battered hat, spat, *"Merde"* in my direction, covering me in absinthe-tinged saliva, and threw himself out of the door, which he banged with such force that the multicoloured bottles rattled on their shelves.

I was lucky that Gunner Earle, possibly L/Bombardier by now for he was on the way up the ladder, was with me or my roguish humour might have ended in violence.

Earle, who had transferred from the Guards, was over six feet tall and must have weighed between fifteen and sixteen stones, trimmed down. He was very powerful and would have given even Anstee, whom I will introduce when the time is right, a run for his money. I was not small and could hold my own when it came to man-handling cannon or throwing ammunition about, but Earle could toss me about like a ninepin. Usually he was a benevolent giant and was, and continued to be, one of my staunchest friends. I called him 'Grease', for when we indulged in horseplay as young men will, I could never get a hold on him. He was a few years older than I was and it was uncanny that he was always there when I needed him most.

Was it whilst we were still at Lens that I was i/c Guard of the Vehicle Park? The vehicles were assembled in a farmyard which was enclosed and had great double doors which were shut at night. It was raining as I posted the sentries, as it had been for days. The farmyard was not kept as well as it might have been and there was a quagmire of mud and manure intermingled.

Our guardroom was a barn which was lit by a single storm lamp. The weather had turned cold and we wore Balaclava helmets. Knitting needles were forever clicking back home, pouring out Comforts for the Troops, and this unattractive but most welcome headgear was to be seen everywhere.

I loosened the laces of my stinking boots which were impregnated and soaked through and through. This act was contrary to King's Rules and Regulations but such things were done. I settled down alongside members of my Guard who were not on duty, pulled my blanket over me and settled down for a spot of kip. We were lying in the lee of a mound of straw which had been stacked in the barn. The light was dim. The rain beat down on the tiled roof. As I was dropping off to sleep something tugged at the top of my knitted helmet. 'Christ! what kind of a guy indulges in schoolboy pranks in conditions like this?' I thought.

"Pack it in," I said to my neighbour and gave him a sharp nudge. He grunted and pretended to be asleep.

The scratching at the top of my head started again. Now I was prepared to be very irritable. I opened my eyes and saw a tail drooping over my forehead. Unmistakably it was the tail of a rat and a big one at that. I could tell by the rings. I hate rats. If there is one animal I cannot stand it is a rat. A great shiver of revulsion ran through me and I leapt up, causing much commotion and waking everyone in the process. We all got well away from that rick and I settled down, perched uncomfortably on a very old mowing machine near the door.

It seemed that only a second or two had passed before a sentry cried, “Turn out the Guard.”

We all piled out, grabbing our rifles as we went and fell in in the farmyard. I had no time to lace my boots. Within a few steps I lost one, held firmly into the mud. It made a sucking sound as I tried to grip it with my toes. If I had been an ape I might have succeeded but I had no prehensile toes so I failed. At the next step the other one went.

I marched up to the Officer on Duty as best I could and tried to imitate the metallic sound of studded boots with my stockinged feet. Those who have tried will agree that it is far from convincing. I came to attention, slapped the butt of my rifle in a smart salute and reported that the Guard was turned out and that all was present and correct. The officer inspected the sentries and took a look at the vehicles whilst I followed in his wake, slurping through mud and manure with as much noise as possible.

Nothing untoward was noticed but it took me a while in much discomfort to salvage my submerged footwear, and a lot longer to get them clean and dry. Some of my Balaclava helmet had been unravelled and was now part of a rat’s nest.

By November air-raid alarms were becoming monotonous in their regularity, but as far as I know, nothing dropped round about, certainly not near me. They occurred in the middle of our working day and disrupted our routine for we had to get under cover.

Our working day. Much of the time — most of it — was devoted to the construction of gun-pits placed at strategic points. We became adept as well as utterly fed-up at filling, placing and patting sandbags into position, sometimes using fillings quite unsuitable, which I fear might have caused as much damage as shell-splinters if there was a direct hit.

There must have been a scare on in the middle of the month. On 13th November the Diary reads: ‘Message received last night that no work was to be carried on outside billets. Gun platforms were brought in.’

This last sentence raises the vexed question of gun platforms. These sturdy metal structures on which the guns rotated were attached by rods fitted to the trails. The wheels rested on them, thus making traversing much, much easier. ‘Running-up’, an ancient ritual and necessity for all field gunners, was the laborious task of reasserting the Gun in its former position after successive thrusts of the recoil had pushed it back. It was particularly necessary when the muzzle had to be pointed quickly in another direction, and the 'spade' at the end of the trail had dug in.

One authority states categorically that though we had box-trails (as opposed to split-trails) on to which platforms could be fitted, and I vouch for this, we did not receive platforms until the middle of 1940, with the new 25pr. gun howitzer, when we were back in England. The Royal School of Artillery says that each Regiment must tell its own story, for some had and some had not. I myself am inclined to react favourably to another of my correspondents who says: 'I seem to remember that 18/25prs. had platforms which were carried on top of the limbers. When the proper 25prs. arrived they had platforms slung under their trails.'

Somewhere or other I have supervised the lifting of a platform from a limber, or helped in placing it. Where else could it have been but with the BEF?

Whether with platforms or not, on 22nd November, the weather being cold, clear and frosty, we went out near Vimy Ridge, to perform an exercise which we called a Drill Order.

CHAPTER VII

On 2nd December, coming up to Christmas and still very cold, the order came for us to move. Everything was packed ready for the journey and the guns were limbered up to the tractors. The seating in the tractor or gun-towing vehicle was arranged like that of a bus, with a passage up the middle. There was a canvas covering to protect us from the weather but there were places which let in draughts. The Quads which were more comfortable and more well-protected against the weather were still to be released for general use.

We were to travel in convoy at night without lights. Previously, we had not been called upon to undertake this manoeuvre. Of course, I was a very insignificant part of the complex organization of the BEF and knew very little, if anything, of what was happening a few miles away. Had I been an officer I should no doubt have known that the Third Division, stationed not far away under the command of Major General Bernard Montgomery, had already engaged in full scale exercises in mobility and battle manoeuvres which included 'motorised movement by night'. Here was one man who considered mobility to be an essential, if not the most essential factor in modern warfare.

'*La Ligne Maginot*' presided like a protective deity, providing an example in 'positional' or static tactics for all to follow save this restless and enlightened genius who had foreseen what others had failed to see, or taking the easiest way out, had declined to see. Between the end of October, 1939 and the beginning of May, 1940 the Third Division undertook five exercises. The result was not hard to predict. In mobility it excelled any other division in the British Army. Alas, it was not so with us. There is no mention of night exercises, or indeed any large scale exercises in the War Diary, except one Divisional exercise not long before the invasion.

A decision was made by our overseers which was to aggravate the hazards of the journey even further. Everyone not on duty was allowed out of billets for a couple of hours before the evening parade. When we fell in for Roll Call in the building where we had lived and slept, the scene might have been taken from a Hogarth print. The rank and file held each other up in the ranks. No section of the Battery could be isolated for its abstinence though I hasten to add that some of our number did not drink at all. Those who did had made up for the rest and it was especially apparent on this occasion. There was much subdued banter and swaying to and fro, and hard to believe but true, one fellow was dangling a dead goose by the neck, thus introducing a bizarre suggestion of Dickens's *Christmas Carol*.

I could view it all with a clear head, for I had been on guard duty and had only been able to slip out for a few minutes when I was relieved.

It was hard to assess how the officer or officers reacted to this boisterous assembly, on the brink of our night march. It was not the least difficult to gauge the effort shown by the senior NCOs, prompted further by the manifest outrage of the Battery Sergeant-Major. Everyone knew that there must be a backlash. No one was disappointed.

The Roll Call was hurried along and we were soon rolling, keeping close when really we should have been well spread out. Our detachment suffered no mishap for our driver was a steady enough chap, but we swerved to pass vehicles and guns which had slid off the road and ended up in the ditch.

'No vehicles were left on the road,' says the entry for this move, 'although two lorries had minor accidents owing to the rain which started to fall heavily about 23.30 hrs.'

That same night we pulled into a big sports complex or stadium called the Establishment Fresnoy in Roubaix. The place was big, sterile and uncomfortable to live in, with its great expanses of staircases, indoor pitches for various games, and its gymnasium. It was very cold. The Battery was under a cloud and we were made to work hard to retrieve our good name. Some there were who felt the rough end of justice.

There were many more night drives to follow, both tricky and dangerous. But the message had been received by most, from high to lowly for we had a corporate pride in our professionalism. There was never again the remotest suggestion of a repetition.

It is on record that Christmas Day dawned foggy and cold. There was a thin film of ice on the roads which made driving very hazardous. To say that there was a thin film was in my experience, a gross understatement.

The Chaplain could not reach us, so there was no Church Parade and for this we were truly thankful.

The uncharacteristic episode before the start of our journey did not stop us celebrating Christmas with a traditional Christmas dinner, with the sergeants waiting upon us at table and the officers visiting us to mingle with us for a while and to wish us a Merry Christmas. It was my first Christmas away from home; my first Christmas in the Army.

Outside the stadium there was music in the cafés and bistros. The familiar sound of accordions could be heard as well as *'J'attendrai'*, a popular song, sung in a plaintive way.

"J'attendrai, le jour et la nuit j'attendrai toujours, ton retourne, j'attendrai." (I will wait for you to return, night and day, always I will wait for you.)

Many of those being awaited were spending their Christmas in the Maginot Line, themselves waiting for the Germans to fling themselves at it and annihilate themselves.

I found Driver Harvey the worse for drink. Poor fellow, he was unaccustomed to it and had sampled a rogue bottle or two to ease his loneliness, and had been knocked sideways. There were many lonely men in France, especially the married ones, and Christmas twisted their heartstrings a bit harder than at other times.

In normal conditions I could have carried Driver Harvey for he was not very big, but the ground was thick with ice. I dragged him like a wheelbarrow, pulling him by the heels, whilst he grasped the tail of my greatcoat. In place of the wheel was his backside. Partly through his contact with the ice, partly through intoxication, he seemed insensitive to feeling. Next day he discovered that his battledress slacks had worn right through and he had a large, raw place on his bottom.

On 6th January, 1940 'an officer and ten ORs (other ranks) proceeded to Sissone twenty miles south-east of Laon as an advance party for a one day's practice camp.'

'Grease' Earle and I were in this group. Happily for us, we only stayed one night. I find it hard to understand and harder to believe that the exercise was cancelled owing to a THAW.

We were installed in a French barracks in a little rectangular room like a cell at the end of a gloomy corridor. Against the far wall was a bundle of straw which looked reasonably fresh. The walls were bare plaster and there was no door. There was, however, a big wooden grid leaning against one wall which we thought we could use should we need some security. It seemed likely, for we were surrounded by foreign troops from North Africa. These Algerian Tirailleurs were a furtive, sly looking lot who moved past our cell like weasels and cast darting sidelong glances with their cold, glittering eyes. I did not care much for their knives which most of them seemed to flaunt.

The lavatory was of the continental type, over which one crouches instead of sits. It was indescribably, unbelievably filthy. The stench made one's eyes water and caused immediate inflammation of the bronchial tubes. The walls could not be used for support for they were daubed in excrement to shoulder height. Of all the French lavatories I have been driven in desperation to use, including an encrusted one at St. Malo out of which I reeled into the strong sunlight and which left a lasting impression on me, that one at Sissone gets the *'Ruban Bleu'* as the ultimate in filthiness.

There was a cookhouse in a large, open shed like a porch. A French cook, repugnantly obese and outstandingly ugly, was stirring the contents of a huge black cooking-pot with an enormous ladle. His assistant was in the act of dipping in a great knuckle bone on which rested an encampment of blowflies. The bubbly scum on the surface and the odour which was given off made me heave as I passed by.

What fascinated me most, however, was the cook's apron. It glistened all over from the superimposition of layer upon layer of rancid fat which had accumulated over the years. I met its rival years later in Ballinamore in Southern Ireland. It was worn by a stout, elderly lady who had an intimate relationship with an enormous grease-caked frying pan which she clasped to her pendulous bosom.

The prize still goes to the French cook.

In complete contrast, we, *'les soldats anglais'* were invited to the NCOs' Mess where we were entertained with Gallic charm and courtesy. Our meal was presented on a snow-white cloth. There was rabbit stew with white sauce and, of course, wine was served.

Earle and I found a bar that evening. It was full of Algerian troops and it didn't take us long to realize that we were in a brothel. Mascaraed women, half-dressed, brazen, several of them near the end of their working lives, were constantly on the move. There was a steady traffic up and down the stairs. Earle and I thought that if temptation had overcome us we could have been guaranteed the biggest doses of syph. ever handed out to men in the history of the world.

In a thoughtless and misguided moment I pulled out a one hundred franc note to pay for the drinks. By comparison British troops were paid far more generously than were the French *poilus*, but the French Colonial troops were really on the breadline. What I had displayed amounted to about a year's pay.

Quick as a flash the light over the bar was knocked out. Grease was just as quick, for being much more experienced in the wicked ways of the world, he had assessed what was happening.

"Down," he said. Still with the note in my hand I shot down on to my hands and knees and scrambled about between legs and furniture until I reached the door, which was not far away. Once outside, still together, we ran as fast as we could down the road to the barracks.

It was dark, so it was hard to judge how far we ran, but for much of the way we could hear that two or three people were following us. The footsteps fell behind though and had stopped well before we reached the barracks.

When we arrived at our cell the couple with whom we were sharing were relieved to see us. They had barricaded themselves in with the gridded structure which they had wedged firmly in the doorway with stout props.

We slept fitfully with one of us always on guard, for from time to time throughout the hours of darkness lithe figures flitted past, there were shadows, and we had that eerie feeling which comes through being watched.

In spite of the friendly treatment we had received from the French NCOs we were more than happy to leave Sissone the next day.

Where were the cannon during all these comings and goings? Surely they must have been somewhere, or why were we here? The cannon were aligned in their fours in one improvised Gun-park or other. She who I helped to tend was among them. There She was, all oiled and greased, gleaming rifling hidden by breech and muzzle covers, and cloaked in a great canvas gun-cover which was strapped securely round Her.

At such times the Gun, which to me was becoming animate and bisexual, or inanimate, could change readily from He to She or to It according to role and environment. Now the gender was feminine, for She was curled up like a great dangerous cat sleeping, with claws indrawn.

When the Gun slid about over ice, or slewed about in snow, or turned awkward and became top heavy on hillsides so that the trail flew up in the air, I used the indeterminate 'It' for I was not all that keen on being maimed by a big gun wheel or chopped in half by the trail. When He was bogged down to the axle in mud and the under-side of the shield acted as an excavator to impede further progress and we were sweating and straining and cursing to get Him on His platform; or when later He was pumping out shells, jerking mightily with every recoil, His ruthless outline showing momentarily against the night sky with every muzzle blast, then it was that He was supreme in His masculinity.

Now She was reclining in feline comfort, whilst we, Her servants were out and about at all hours of day and night in the worst of winter weather in what was said to be the severest winter on record. Muffled against the freezing cold, wearing our Balaclava helmets so that only our eyes and noses were exposed, (mine still rat-chewed with its hole in the top) we were sent out to guard the huge ammunition dumps and supply dumps, growing daily in the countryside.

Four officers and 238 ORs, presumably from the Regiment, went on ammunition guard to Aubigny from the 25th to the 30th January. The War Diary for 30th January states:

> 'The month has been exceptionally cold. The average night temperature has been about 20° below zero.'

It was no great joy to stand out in the open in the middle of a winter's night with only the silent frost for company; it was marginally worse to set off in a 15cwt truck on roads like skating rinks to take out new sentries to relieve the old. The truck flew round and round until if we were lucky we managed to get it moving in the right direction. Every journey was an adventure, full of breath-taking surprises.

Still, on such missions we usually worked in small groups, lodged in empty houses and cooked for ourselves. There was, unless we happened to be so unfortunate as to be completely isolated, some smoke-filled bistro reeking of gauloises in which we could find warmth and café au lait *avec rhum*.

In the vehicle park the engines were started up regularly and run for a few minutes at a time to stop them from freezing up. It was indeed a very hard winter.

I mounted the guard on the cobbles in front of a great church. By this time we had moved to billets in the square at Roubaix, and if I remember correctly this impressive edifice overlooked us as we went about our daily duties. Gunner L —, a signaller by trade, came on parade when he was obviously the worse for drink. The wine had got such a grip on him that he was rarely completely sober, but he kept it in control well enough to do his job efficiently and to avoid detection. On this occasion he did not manage his rifle with the proficiency he had shown at the depot. He swayed very gently as he stood to attention and grinned slightly as if he were enjoying some private joke as I paused briefly in front of him on my round of inspection. I did not 'shop him', however, for I knew he would soon pull round and do his duty as well as the next man.

This was the period of the 'phoney war'. Very few shots had been fired, and none by us. There was a confident feeling among the French that the Maginot Line, manned, overmanned even by hordes of French soldiers, would stop the Germans in their tracks.

Everywhere large posters boasted '*On ne passe pas*' — 'They shall not pass'.

A favourite song in England gave promise of hanging out the washing on the Siegfried Line. We favoured South of the Border, Ramona, and Roll Out the Barrel, when we weren't singing our own bawdy versions of Bless 'em All and the Quartermaster's Stores.

When the weather improved we turned our hands to making gun-pits again. We continued with our shovelling, filling, placing and patting, applying ourselves with a diligence which fell short of being enthusiastic. Presumably these emplacements were chosen, so that if one site became unsuitable we could move to another in either advance or retreat. I wondered afterwards whether anyone had had a chance to use them when France was overrun. One thing is certain, I never saw them again.

In our Battery was a particularly recalcitrant individual who followed his own rules. One order after another was ignored and he was always in trouble. He was a reservist, so he must have caused other people a lot of problems in the past. I was i/c Guard and found him in an improvised cell, undergoing detention and under my supervision. On the night before I took over he had tried to escape, but did not get far before he was apprehended. The Sergeant i/c Guard was now himself on a charge for negligence. As Gunner C- settled down for the night, having finished scouring his consignment of dixies, I sat down where he could see me load my rifle. I made this act very apparent by closing the breech very forcibly before applying the safety catch. I informed him very forcefully that should he attempt to get away again, I should have no qualms about shooting him. All night I sat up with my loaded rifle across my knees and kept a close watch on him, but the message must have got through to him that I was sincere in my intentions, for he made no false move.

Next day I took him out on Pack Drill. He paraded, dressed up like a Christmas tree in FSMO, (Full Service Marching Order) with webbing blancoed and brasses polished. He carried his small pack and big pack, his gas mask and gas cape. His kitbag was under one arm. All his kit was on him, including groundsheet and blankets.

At the end of every few paces I gave the order to change direction.

"Quick — march, — right turn, — about turn, — left turn." This went on for the allotted time, as laid down in KRRs. At statutory intervals he was given a short break. It was all experience. Gunner C- soon had greater trials to face but they were of his own making. He was sent to the Glasshouse, the legendary Military Prison, the threat of which made even hardened 'bolshies' think twice.

In March I went on leave. I took with me Gunner Cyrus Bell, better known as Tex, who was with me in 'A' Sub. Tex had served his six tomato seasons in India, *and* a 'Tora buckshee'. He was stationed in Jhansi for a good part of his service when all Field Batteries were still horse-drawn. He was an orphan, and having nowhere to go, gladly took up my offer. My mother and grandmother made him very welcome and my mother, who had quite a few good contacts, saw that we had eggs, a chicken and a few slices of home cured bacon to go at.

The Shovels Inn and the Wardleys Hotel were not unfamiliar to us. We amazed my Uncle Ben with our capacity. Where was that innocent nephew of yester-year he might well have asked, as pint after pint slid down with no apparent effort or effect. My Uncle Ben performed a peculiar rite when he was under the influence. He displayed the flexibility of his joints by putting one leg or the other behind his neck. Once, years later, when he was past his best, he got carried away and put both legs in this position, and was discovered, inextricably locked under of all places, the billiard table. I fear that sometimes he was on the receiving end of some withering fire from his wife when he fell into the wardrobe after he had been carousing with us. He had to turn out at an unmentionable hour to work on a threshing machine. One hoped that the pure country air did much to clear his head.

Quite a group of rustic well-wishers went with us to Poulton to see us on our way back to France. The table was still full of pints when we left hastily to catch the train. With great cries of goodwill, willing hands helped us as we bundled ourselves and our kit into the carriage. Then it was post-haste to Preston, London, Dover and Boulogne. "Roll on Death and let's have a bang at the Angels," was the expression coined by some irreverent fellow back in the Battery, or had it been recalled from previous wars? Although nothing of note had happened so far it was obvious that the balloon was going up soon. We with the still young but now weathered faces, we the agile and strong and irresponsible at times were going back to face it.

Sitting by the farmhouse fireside, snoozing in its glow and warmth on a winter evening was all right for some, for they had a whole long lifetime to savour gently and without haste.

But how long had we? Do not be too hasty to judge us for having snatched our pleasure wildly when we could. You only saw us in our playtime mood, never when we were working. How could you? Had you done so, some of you might have come to understand us better.

CHAPTER VIII

'When first under fire an' you're wishful
to duck,
Don't look, or take 'eed at the man
that is struck,
Be thankful you're livin', an' trust to
your luck
And march to your front like a soldier.'

The Young British Soldier
Rudyard Kipling

The more I discover about the BEF in the campaign of 1940, the more bewildered and limited I feel in writing about it. It would take a military historian of no mean stature to unravel the mesh of very complicated texture which was woven during the next three weeks, from 10th May to the first day or two of June. Whilst restricting myself mainly to my own part and to that of my immediate comrades, I must perforce include from time to time such general details as I consider relevant to the understanding of the interplay of strengths and weaknesses, strategies and deployments which brought about the dangerous predicament in which we were to be placed, and miraculously, from which so many of us managed to escape.

As in all armies, the terms of employment dictated that we were to be jerked about hither and thither like puppets, at the beck and call of generals, competent and less competent, themselves manipulated by statesmen, not all as wise and firm as the occasion required. These remote Olympians, though moulding our fates were to us, operating up forward, of less consequence than the officers to whom we were directly responsible. We relied utterly on them to do the best for us, and we for our part strove to reciprocate. For instance, it has recently been pointed out to me by one of our officers that Lieutenant Colonel H. A. Young, RA, CO of 22nd Field Regiment, was very able and 'that it was largely due to him that we gave the service we did and suffered so little in doing so.' When it was all happening I took such competence for granted. Alas! it was not always so. There were less able commanders who made incorrect and bad decisions, chose positions unwisely, made excessive demands on their men and left decisions to escape from tight corners until too late. Even Montgomery himself is not entirely free from criticism for ordering an operation to be mounted by his 8th Infantry Brigade on 24th May on the Escaut, which most thought was unwarranted, which proved costly in lives and which caused bad feeling.

It must have been extremely taxing even for the most skilled, let alone the ones who were limited. For the Divisional, Brigade and Regimental Commanders it was as if they had been projected on to a very slippery dance floor. There they were forced to execute what was for many an unfamiliar dance routine in syncopated rhythm at a fast tempo, accelerated, to the accompaniment of a basically competent orchestra. This was augmented on the edges by unreliable and inattentive amateurs who did more harm than good. They were prone to slip a few beats, causing anxiety and confusion, or even to stop playing altogether, and to get up and walk out in the middle of the performance. This Gilbertian situation our commanders met, by and large, with amazing terpsichorean dexterity.

I went through a phase when I thought that Britain had again managed to enter a major war quite unprepared. Accounts of successful performances in certain clashes with the enemy made me change my mind. We often gave blow for blow, and sometimes more. If some elements of our Allies crouched in terror or fled at the name 'German', we didn't. There seems to be good evidence that had we been sole adversaries of a German army of reasonably comparable size we would have held, even though the air-strikes and paratroops were revolutionary.

I suppose my initial assessment was based on the state of my own Regiment at Shorncliffe which, it will be remembered, was very considerably reduced in numbers when I first joined it. On mobilization the ratio of young serving regulars was about half and half in the infantry, but in the gunners the balance was very different. There was a great expansion in the artillery at the outbreak of war, so that there were far more reservists than regulars. I, of course, was one of the minority waiting to join units overseas. The reservists had three or six years colour service, and the majority were in the latter category. Eight months had now elapsed which gave the trained men of the Regular Divisions time to settle into a very capable fighting force. In January,

1940, Lord Gort, the BEF Commander, strengthened the Territorial Divisions which had just joined the BEF, by exchanging units with Regular Divisions.

The enemy had been busy long before the bullets started to fly. A skilful 'softening up' process had been going on, with infiltrators whispering seditious rumours to the civilian population in the bistros, so that when it was known that the Germans had invaded, confusion and panic reigned, and did so for the entire campaign. We ourselves did not witness this at first, for when we were waiting to move off from Roubaix on the first day, the population was 'quite calm'. It was soon to become otherwise.

As the day appointed for the start of the 'blitzkrieg' drew nearer, we, unaware of its imminence, sensed a tense, sinister atmosphere. There was increased talk of Fifth Columnists and saboteurs, who, as we were soon to learn, had been previously briefed and positioned.

At 04.30 hrs on 10th May, 1940, the Germans attacked Holland, Belgium and Luxembourg. On the following night I was i/c Guard over 'A' Troop vehicles lodged in a large old warehouse in Roubaix. We had packed during the day, ready to move, and our personal kit had been dumped in the grandstand of the racecourse at La Madelaine. Troops, presumably of 3rd Division had passed through Roubaix all day, on their way to Brussels and Louvain.

The grimy, bleak warehouse, its great doors firmly closed with a strong bar across, seemed vast when the darkness closed in, with we few sealed inside, with only a storm lamp or two to light up the immediate surroundings. The roof, stretching way, way above us was lost in the blackness. Up there was an upper storey, a great barren meandering place, partitioned off into compartments by low brick walls. We were alert to every slight sound and were by no means as comfortable and composed as we might have been. There are some places that one would rather not be placed in, and this was one. It would have been all too easy to drop a grenade or two on to us, for the whole Battery would have been needed to guard this place properly.

There were mysterious noises from above. I and one other ascended the Jacob's ladder which ran vertically up the wall. We took our rifles and a storm lamp with us. I was reminded very vividly of the picture I had seen of valiant attackers climbing upwards to embrasures in castle walls. They were very fortunate indeed if they were not thrust off as they put their heads over the top. It was small comfort that the risk of boiling oil was negligible.

No one was waiting at the top, so we moved cautiously from bay to bay round corners in the ancient brickwork thick with cobwebs, the storm lamp throwing ominous shadows. We were all too alive to the fact that in these dark corners could be a person or persons, ready to pounce with most villainous intent.

The event may seem to be over-dramatized as nothing was seen, but whether justified or not, we were beginning to look over our shoulders. It is interesting for me to note that in the War Diary for the next day, 11th May, there appears this entry.

> 'Suspected attempted sabotage in 'A' and 'C' Troop garages — no damage but rope and ladder found.'

Three days later a Henschel aircraft directed accurate shell fire on to 9th Brigade Headquarters at Louvain. Marks pointing to the HQ were being cut in the grass by a civilian. He was arrested and shot. The 2nd Grenadier Guards at the Escaut on 20th May executed 17 snipers of the Fifth Column who were operating in their rear. More evidence of this widespread aggression from within will appear later.

Why was it that when the Battery passed the Starting Point at 11.00 hrs on 14th May, in Battery Column, I was sitting in the No. 1's place in the tractor? Still only a Bombardier, I had been given charge of 'D' Subsection of 'A' Troop and the Gun which it served. If it was a temporary measure until a Sergeant could be found it lasted a long time. I took the Gun right through the campaign to the bitter end, and was rarely without one after that. My driver, Driver Burbanks, technically 'Gunner', and 'Fishy' to his chums, barely concealed his disdain at first for this boy of just turned twenty who was setting himself up in a man's clothing. Driver Burbanks, being an 'India-wallah' with, as he was never tired of telling, 'long service in bad stations' had, unlike say Sergeant-Major Prior or Sergeant-Artificer Bickles, little time for 'rookies' whose numbers were not dry, particularly if they had managed to pull a tape or two. Driver Burbanks's India was populated by birds called kite-hawks, which he called 'shite-hawks'. The skies became alive with these greedy predatory fowls every time 'Fishy' walked across the sun drenched *maidan* on his way from the cookhouse. As far as I could gather from his reminiscences he must have been inept in defensive measures or indifferent to eating, for he was always having his food snatched off his plate into the heavens. Coupled with his gradual debilitating state of malnutrition, his constant companion was prickly heat. His atrabilious appearance may have been the result of these dual burdens. His guarded manner meant very little to me, for I knew, and he knew that if he tried the 'old soldier' act, I could and would retaliate very smartly to his disadvantage. Actually, we pulled pretty well together. Deep down he was proud of his skills, as he had every right to be, and taught me a trick or two.

He was to get us very adroitly out of a tight spot at least once. Being rather deaf he never got into a flap as others might have done when missiles went off quite close to us.

I had one thing at least in common with these old soldiers. A few may have been in action against tribesmen on the North-West Frontier of India, one or two may even have had First World War medals, though I cannot remember any, but most of us, older or younger were about to come under fire for the first time. The gun-drills, the exercises, the practice shoots with live ammunition were now to be tested against the enemy. In the limber were live rounds of HE and Smoke. There were also a few rounds of AP (Armour Piercing) shot in case we met a tank or two. It was only twelve months since I had been about to 'pass out' at Woolwich. I had learnt a lot since then, met some unusual and intriguing characters and matured considerably. By the end of the next few weeks I would be quite a few more years older still. To be in charge of a powerful weapon, firing to kill quickly and efficiently, carried a certain responsibility, but it went further than that. For much of the time our task would be to give covering fire for our infantry when they attacked or to help them when they were harassed. Although it was not unknown for a round to go astray and to fall among our own troops, it was considered to be very bad form indeed.

Montgomery's 3rd Division led 2 Corps through Belgium from 10th May. The BEF was left deliberately free from air attack for the moment, though the dive bombers were very heavily committed in places on the perimeters. The Germans, already briefed on our plan to enter Belgium, wanted us as far forward as possible, so that we would not interfere with their Ardennes breakthrough to the south of us. They must also have had a good idea that the defences of the Belgians to the north, and those of the Dutch might not be so hard to crack. 3rd Division were at the moment very actively at grips with attacking forces at Louvain, beyond Brussels.

Our own route took us through Wattrelos, Espierre, Rossuyt, Bercher, Audenarde, Eename, Hemelghem, Suitegem, Aalst then southward to Aasche, Brussels and on to Laeken. At 16.00 hrs it was reported that Aalst, which we had come through only a short time before had been bombed. We fired wildly with small arms at a hostile aircraft and wasted ammunition. Few refugees were encountered by us as yet, as they had been diverted to other roads. We were interested to observe our first Belgian soldiers pedalling smartly southwards from Aalst onwards. They must have been the Chausseurs, cycle troops just mobilized who had been so determined to defend the ancient city of Louvain. When the first German shells arrived they found they had little stomach for the fight, so with much whistle blowing they up and went, bending over the handlebars and treading heavily on the pedals.

It was the Dutch who had the dubious distinction of being the first to experience an airborne attack on a large scale. They were bewildered, totally surprised and quite unprepared for such a sudden and venomous onslaught by paratroops and air transport. It is easy to be critical of their lack of resistance, as we were when we heard about it on our way to the line. But they did resist for five days to such effect that the Third Reich had to bomb Rotterdam heavily and to send reinforcements from the Air Force from the Belgian front 'to facilitate the rapid conquest of Fortress Holland.'

On the 14th May German radio announced:

'Under the tremendous impression of the attacks of German dive bombers and the imminent attack of German tanks, the City of Rotterdam has capitulated and thus saved itself from destruction.'

The Dutch had surrendered. Queen Wilhelmina and members of her government fled to London for the duration on two British destroyers.

On the evening of the 14th the Battery went into hides on the west bank on the canal north of Brussels, in a factory near an aerodrome and gasometers. We were warned that we should prepare for a tank attack at dawn. I remember looking out towards Louvain, from whence came alarming war-like sounds and a myriad of flashing lights. I smoked a cigarette, cupping it in my hand and putting it in my greatcoat pocket between puffs to keep the glow hidden. I felt for all the world like the solitary figure in a picture of the Great War entitled 'Before Arras'. The soldier, an officer I think, was awaiting his dawn, just as I was anticipating mine. It was not a happy night.

We went into action at Wezembeke, near Vilvorde at 04.00 hrs on the 15th. The OP (Observation Post) was north of the Brussels-Louvain road. My image is of a large open piece of land, possibly parkland, on to which our tractors had taken us. For some reason, we had to manhandle our guns forward when we had dropped into action. An unexpected episode took place. A young officer, whose identity I cannot recollect but who must have been one of ours, took out his revolver and flourished it as if he were a principal character out of *Boys' Own*. We heaved on the drag-ropes and bent our backs to the wheels, keeping our heads down.

The crackle of small arms fire and ominous thumps and thuds, only previously heard on ranges or at the cinema, seemed nearer. Enemy paratroops were dropping a couple of miles away. Very unsporting chaps, some of ours, were making determined efforts to shoot them down.

Someone passed the word that the figures swaying to and fro, drifting groundwards might be dressed as priests or nuns. Authentic Servants of God would be well advised to creep into crypts and stay there whilst there were so many trigger-happy guys around. The revolver continued to flourish until we were in position. To be charitable, the display may have been for our defence, but generally the act was interpreted as a threat lest any of us should falter, in this our hour of trial. It went down very badly and there was a spontaneous growl of disapproval or resentment which was a very rare, if not unique reaction. What we considered, rightly or wrongly, to be a reflection on our own courage, professionalism or loyalty, did not pass without discussion among ourselves and it was never really forgotten.

Let it not be forgotten that many of this bunch with whom I was so happy and so proud to soldier, were rough, tough and hard-bitten and would have won few awards for high moral values as subscribed by conventional society of the time; but they could have given a few valuable lessons in comradeship, courage and sense of duty.

The tanks did not come, but we stayed in support of the 10th Infantry Brigade.

> '06.00 hrs. One hostile aircraft brought down near Battery position. Much air activity. SAA (Small Arms Ammunition) wasted on parachutists.'

This aircraft traversed the sky from right to left. It carried German markings and looked like a transport plane. Smoke was coming from its rear and it was losing height. As we watched, the interior was lit by flames and we could see quite clearly the frenzied movements of the figures silhouetted at the windows. They did not have a chance. The plane plummeted into a copse two or three hundred yards away and blew up. In the midst of Life we are in Death, one minute sitting in comfort, Lords of the Third Reich, the next scattered to the four winds, or charred like pieces of burnt cork. For them it had been a very short war. A Messerschmitt or two came over low and gave us a few bursts in protest but no bombers were called in.

A day or two previously on the 13th, the battle for Sedan had begun in the Ardennes to the south of us.

On the left flank of the Maginot Line, the 1st Panzer Division of General Guderian's XIX Corps had led the attack, but the brunt of the fighting had been done by artillery and dive bombers working together. They concentrated on selected gun positions and strong points, whilst the heavy bombers put down a carpet of bombs. Guderian ordered Anti-aircraft Regiment 102 to cover the crossing of the Meuse, firing to pin-point ground targets. The 8.8cm Flugabwehrkanone (18 or 36) anti-aircraft guns were probably the best known weapons of the war, largely because of their use as field and anti-tank guns. Any loud bang was likely to be heralded as an '88' by Allied troops. An idea of its all-pervading mental image may be gained from a cartoon in the *Stars and Stripes* showing a US intelligence officer interrogating prisoners and reassuring a nearby GI, "Don't worry; if I find the one wot invented the 88 I'll let you know." The Royal School of Artillery, from whose documents this quotation is taken, goes on to say that although there was no doubt about them being effective weapons they did not excel the comparable British 3.7 MK 3s or later in the war, the US 90mm MIs in the role for which they were originally intended. Where they did gain was that the Germans had a lot of 88s to use as anti-tank guns when the Allies had little or nothing to compete with them. They were given much effective publicity as 'all conquering super weapons'. To attack ground targets like us, which they were doing more and more, as in the Ardennes with Guderian, the HE shells were fitted with either percussion fuses which detonated on impact, or with time fuses which were set to explode above the target in the manner of shrapnel shells. It was the latter use which bothered us most, for the 'air bursts' were demoralizing as well as dangerous. As regards the use of 88s for anti-tank work, our 18/25prs. were entering the arena as competitors in this field. Our new 25pr. gun-howitzers, soon to appear, were to prove highly effective against tanks and were to get better as time went on.

So Guderian slammed away with aircraft deployed in co-ordination with ground forces, especially artillery, against French troops who were spread over a wide front, and who were quite unprepared for the new ruthlessly efficient, elaborately planned type of warfare.

The Third Reich hurled bits of metal at them, manufactured by Krupps of Essen, aiming wherever and whenever they could at weak oppostion.

French tanks and British bombers tried desperately to destroy a pontoon bridge over the Meuse which had been hurriedly built during the night. Forty RAF planes out of seventy-one were shot down, most of them by flak in a single attack. Seventy French tanks were destroyed in the attempt but they could not stop the Germans from using the bridge.

The contest was very unequal. There were other pockets of valiant resistance, one example being that of the French XXI Corps at Stonne, but the weight of the German forces and the pace at which they moved overcame the French armoured divisions, half of which had been eliminated in a few days.

The 15th was, considering the environment, uneventful for us. We were in action still, and when not called upon, continued to dig in gun positions and at OPs. The intense bombardment in the direction of Louvain went on all day and all night.

On the 16th we had orders to move. The Recce Party went off under the Battery Commander to seek out yet another position before it got too hot for us where we were.

Doubts were displayed about 'getting the guns across the canal'. We moved at 17.00 hrs, via Savemthem-Laeken and Steembek-Bever, successfully tackling the problem of the canal, for there is no comment to the contrary.

Although there is sometimes an element of doubt when relating an event to its precise locality, there was one point early on in the withdrawal, where we crossed a bridge, edging our guns precariously round rubble and debris, with the sappers ready to blow it very soon after we had passed. This bridge blowing became a way of life for the Engineers and it is mentioned constantly throughout the campaign. I did not envy these fellows, whose task it was to wait until the very last moment in order to let stragglers across. The Grenadier Guards were withdrawing and were still spread along the canal bank, still engaging the enemy. The crackle of small arms fire was very close and all round us.

As 3rd Division was in the process of leap-frogging through us on this evening of the 16th, whilst we were to hold on for the time being, and as 2nd Grenadier Guards were in 7th Infantry Brigade of that Division, it is reasonable to assume that this was the occasion.

The Belgians had been unable to resist further pressure to the left and 3rd Division, though reluctant to draw back because of its successful defence and spirited counter-attacks, was ordered to withdrew westwards to a line along the River Escaut for fear of being overrun. The alarming breakthrough at Sedan and the insistent impetus of the Panzers, intent on performing their part of the encircling manoeuvre, added greater urgency to the decisions. Until now the Allied operations in which the BEF were involved had gone quite well. Between Antwerp along the River Dyle through Louvain and down to Namur, a front of sixty miles, there were thirty-six divisions opposing only twenty of Reichenau's Sixth Army.

The Prime Minister had come from England to Paris to find out what was happening and to try to enforce a combined attack on the flanks of the armoured spearhead, still moving westwards. He asked General Gamelin the whereabouts of the strategic reserve. There was none, said Gamelin. To hear that a great army had no reserve was on Churchill's own admission, one of the biggest surprises of his life.

Only rumours filtered through to us. Having crossed the canal we went on to take up prepared positions from 32nd Field Regiment RA. We had been bombed on the way but came through unscathed. Our tasks were the same, by which I understand that we were still in support of 10th Infantry Brigade. The next day refugees became more numerous on the roads. At 02.00 hrs they were still digging at the OP when good christian folk in England had been long abed. At 09.00 hrs the last units of 10th Infantry Brigade withdrew across the canal and we fired on targets called for by 11 Infantry Brigade. Bridge blowing went on all day. No. 4 Gun of 'C' Troop fired at an enemy patrol in the afternoon. At 17.00 hrs there came a request from the Brigadier of 12 Infantry Brigade to shoot at bridging parties and armoured cars on Vilvorde Ford. Over the last twenty-four hours we had been called to assist all three Infantry Brigades in the Division which does more than suggest there was considerable reshuffling going on.

At 21.00 hrs on the 17th came the warning order to move. The German armour was still rolling on to the south-west of us and was opposite Laon, half-way between Brussels and Paris aiming for the Channel ports. The claws to north and south were extending, ready to crush us when the time was ripe.

CHAPTER IX

Now it was our turn to trek westwards. At a quarter to midnight on the 17th, the witching hour almost upon us, we moved off in record time through Brussels. The War Diary states laconically, 'Column divided in Brussels.' It left a lasting impression, not least on two of our officers. "Back through Brussels on the darkest night I'd ever known, with use of light forbidden," says a Troop Commander. "We became hopelessly lost," exclaims another, "and were scattered over several roads."

Several factors conspired to make this momentous journey stick in people's memories long after the event. We were less practised than we might have been in movement by night, and driving with no lights at all was still new to most of us. The Army had not long been mechanized and we were unaccustomed to large-scale assignments such as this, using motor transport. Soon our units would be supervised very adeptly by DRs, (Despatch Riders) riding up and down the columns on motor cycles and guarding us at crossroads. The Royal Military Police were still learning with the rest of us, techniques involved in this new mobile warfare. They were very quickly to become remarkably efficient. Not least was the lack of orders *en route*. I assume, studying the complex troop movements and the numbers involved, that there had been the minimum of time to prepare even the most basic of plans for this withdrawal.

Floundering along in a strange war-torn city in the middle of a pitch black night with unexpected obstacles to circumvent, with persistent representatives of the Third Reich hard at one's heels was scarcely a joyride.

We were earning our pay the hard way, instead of frittering it away in riotous living in village pubs. Civilians, wagging fingers and tut-tutting over high spirits indulged in at closing time, would never see us as we were now, tense and straining into the blackness. How could they? This was our very own world, and we were welcome to it.

Our route was Brussels — Asshe — Aalst (again, we never seemed to get away from this place!) A detour round Audenarde was made, to hides one and three-quarter miles west of Anseghem. What roads we actually took will never be known, but by some mysterious means, by the use of some unconscious homing device which some of our members preserved to an amazing degree, most of us collected together in one place by the morning of the 18th. We must have laid low all day. '2/Lt. Tallents and party arrived at 21.00 hrs completing the Battery.' Mr Tallents was our Troop Commander.

The infantry had marched twenty miles from Brussels to Resseghem and were worn out. Always, always, the PBI, the Poor Bloody Infantry, were taking the really hard knocks. They stood their ground, fought bitterly, incurred heavy casualties. The survivors pulled out of action, quite often having over-stayed their welcome and already stretched to the limit, and found the reserve of strength necessary to get themselves back to the next position, on their own two feet.

It was 'wagons roll' for us at 09.00 hrs on the 19th, setting out on one of the few journeys we were to make in the daylight, which made it all the more dangerous.

The weather was glorious, as it was for almost the whole month, and this did much to ameliorate the hazards and discomforts attendant upon our assignments. In appearance 'well trimmed, a crowd of shepherds with as sunburnt looks as may be read of in Arcadian books'; we drew out on to the open road, at first well spaced between vehicles in case of air attacks. Soon we met and mingled unwillingly with the refugees. The scenes are familiar enough, having been re-created often since in films and books.

There were prams, home-made carts, some of primitive design and construction, wheelbarrows, and motor cars of vintage appearance, together with horse-drawn vehicles. All were bearing as many possessions as could be crammed and lashed on to them. Mattresses were much in evidence and I was attracted to them. I was becoming increasingly tired. We always seemed to be on the move. One action followed hard on the heels of another and the distance between was relatively short. There was never an occasion when we could undress, rarely a chance to take off our boots to relieve our hot, sweaty feet. What sleep we had was taken in catnaps. As one day merged into the next what I wanted most was a long, long, uninterrupted sleep.

The refugees moved slowly onwards in their nightmare migration with here and there a cow for good measure. Bent old folk, both men and women stooped over burdens far beyond them, rubbing shoulders with the young and the strong. Babies were being suckled by the roadside; unfortunates who had succumbed to the heat or who had been wounded were being tended hastily by the few more kindly-disposed than the rest. There were those who would never rise again. At first I thought that these recumbent forms, lying on their backs with the upper parts of their bodies protected by bits of clothing, were taking a rest by the wayside. I soon learnt to recognize, by the lifelessness and unnatural position of the sprawling feet and the flatness under the covering that these people, civilians and soldiers alike, were dead. Another sign was the swarms of flies which collected. As the heat of the day intensified the living mass of people grew more dishevelled, hunger and thirst intruded and tempers became frayed.

Struggle as we might to keep our formation of twelve guns, or even our Troop of four with its attendant vehicles, it was at times impossible to move for the heterogeneous mob, crowding and seething round us. By sheer weight of tractor and gun we forced our way as best we could. When we should have been breaking up clusters of enemy troops, or helping our infantry, or blowing up bridging parties we were stuck defenceless against the German fighters which zoomed in low. These roaring, spitting things injected their venom and were gone. Our only way of retaliation was with our Brens, mounted on trucks, and with our rifles, but these latter usually proved ineffective. If there was time, which was rare, we might fling ourselves in the lee of the tractor or gun or as far off the road as we could get. More often than not there was no warning and we were sitting ducks.

We passed files of infantry, footsore and so weary that they looked ready to drop in their tracks. They kept to the verges as was their custom and there was usually a steady stream of transport. Our guns threw up dust on these poor foot-sloggers, causing them more discomfort. Unlike us they carried weapons, equipment, ammunition, even rations on their backs. Some of them piled on to our limbers. A couple of them perched precariously across the trail of the Gun and fell asleep.

Hidden in the hedgerows waiting and pointing in the opposite direction to which we were travelling were the guns of the 14th Anti-tank Regiment, RA. I did not envy them, for they would wait for the German advance column when we had gone, if indeed we *had* gone by the time they appeared.

More and more I became obsessed with sleep. I wanted to find a lair in which I could sleep on and on, undisturbed. Had I, by some supernatural intervention found myself in bed with a beautiful nubile young woman and a supper tray on which reposed fish and chips and a pint of mild or bitter, I should have proved neither attentive nor gastronomic. Promptly I should have fallen fast asleep on the scented bosom of my companion without even sampling a chip, without even reaching for a swallow of the ale.

On a side road devoid of refugees, French field artillery had been attacked in column just before we appeared on the scene. The guns and limbers, lately taken from a museum specializing in ancient ordnance by all appearances, had been blown off the road and the horses were lying dead, their entrails showing. The artillerymen who had survived had managed to hurl themselves into slit-trenches which, conveniently for them, had been dug by a unit which had occupied the area previously. The artillerymen were not to know that the slit-trenches were really latrines. And then we witnessed a farcical situation. Several Frenchmen peered over the edge of the trench, half-dazed, half-bemused and covered from head to foot in human excrement. However would they manage to cleanse themselves and get rid of the stench? It wouldn't be very healthy to take a bath in the open as things stood. Nor come to think of it, would it be very healthy to stay in those clothes for long either.

They had been 'stonked', which was our term for being at the receiving end of a concentration of shells or bombs, delivered without warning. I thought that if I could choose between the 'stonk' and the latrine trench I might decide on the 'stonk' if it were a lightish one and not quite on top of us. Poor bastards. They had got both, all at once. I felt sorry for them and sorry that they were so poorly equipped.

By now we had begun to develop a much keener awareness to sounds. There were the short burst of the Spandaus, like typewriters run amok, and their British counterparts, the Brens so stiff upper-lip but nevertheless effective.

Low flying aircraft came in fast and their machine-guns strafed us, or others dropped their bombs. The Stukas we had not experienced but we had heard all about them. The German artillery would try to knock us out when they could spot the chance, whether we were on wheels on the road, or sitting still in action. We were lucky in France and Belgium and usually escaped from the really big fellows. Maybe it was because we were never static enough for them to get themselves into position and to range on us in time.

It was a new world we had entered with no place or time to lay our heads, with constant upheaval and an acquaintance with injury and death.

Bird-song in the warm spring countryside had been superceded by the harsh conversation of war, always present. Sometimes it was intermittent and diminuendo, sometimes it was constant and crescendo but always it was with us in one degree or another.

Puffs of smoke appeared in the distance like those exhaled through the canvas of the mock countryside of the miniature ranges we gunners practised on in barracks. When these puffs became nearer they became more noisy; when they grew even closer they threw out harmful bits of metal and went off with a hell of a bang.

Ears became attached to new alarms, eyes became more watchful, heads began to turn this way and that. We were ready to throw ourselves for cover, but not I hoped, into trenches which had been used as lavatories.

Yet I was not really afraid. Apprehensive yes, and with an animal instinct for self-preservation and for smelling danger emerging. But I was too wet round the ears, too young to feel fear as I was to know it later, for I still believed that what happened to others could not happen to me. So the mature part of me carried on a man's duties, whilst that which had not yet quite grown up observed with childlike curiosity.

We began to see animals roaming about wildly, frantic for food. Cows were lying on their backs in the fields with their four legs pointing at the sky, their bodies blown up with gases. Living cows never adopted this position. Those still alive were mooing loudly, desperate to be milked, their udders swollen so much that they seemed on the point of bursting.

We pulled into action in the Hoogstraat area, behind the River Escaut, alongside a canal near to Heestent. One of the Command Post officers reports that the Command Post was in a well stocked farm, and goes on to add, with what I take to be a gleeful recollection of mouth-watering indulgence — 'chicken soup for supper.'

On this day, somewhere else, it was considered by the French General Gamelin that there was just a chance that an immediate turn to southwards by the Belgian, British and French armies, and a push through the German armour, would result in a link up with the French forces coming up from the south. It was never to be discovered whether the plan was feasible or not, for as soon as the order to proceed was given it was cancelled by General Weygand who had taken over. Such was the unpredictable fluid state of High Office. Weygand wanted time to confer, not seeming to be disturbed by the fact that time was just not on his side. Three days later, having conferred he came up with Gamelin's idea and authorized it. Too late. Further disintegration had taken place, and anyway, no troops appeared from the south. How could our own commanders hope to cope with such vacillation? There must have been some bad language and a temporary relaxation of the renowned 'stiff upper lip'.

"Bloody hell," we protested, "surely not bloody-well limbering up again?" Under the orders of our officers we got out quite often when we had only just dug in, or even before we had had a chance to start digging. No doubt there was always a very good reason, though for us it was not apparent. Sometimes it was because our infantry were in trouble and we had to get to a convenient spot in order to support them, and quickly; sometimes it was because it was getting too warm or would soon get too warm for us where we were and it was expedient to take a deft step backwards or forwards or sideways out of the way. There were 'rover' troops of four guns, or sections of two, or even one gun which was placed for a special duty. Back went the 'ammo' into the limber and the tractor and we belted hell for leather to drop our trail, slot our dial-sight and clinometer into their brackets and receive yet another aiming point from which to take our bearing.

On the Escaut the fighting became more determined on both sides. 3rd Division had side-stepped across the front of the 4th to occupy positions on the right. Our FDLs (Forward Defence Lines) of infantry, which meant the battalions of 10 Infantry Brigade, were on the banks of the River Escaut itself.

Our OP was at Avelghem. Registration of targets was carried out by shooting, and a church in Escanaffles was hit, presumably by us. We seemed to have gone pretty wild round here. We fired at bridging parties and, at the personal request of the 2nd DCLI (Duke of Cornwall's Light Infantry), on hostile infantry, horsed transport and trench mortars. Our OP was shelled. On the 20th we supported a counter-attack by the 2nd Beds. and Herts. (Bedfordshire and Hertfordshire Regiment) on the bridge-head at Escanaffles. This was a Battery target, so all twelve guns were engaged. The unfortunate occupants of the OP caught it again. 'OP in factory shelled and hit — No grief,' is the terse but adequate comment. 'A' Troop moved a section. 'B' Troop moved position forward. The OP found a house from which they could operate.

It was in a farmyard that the episode with the cow took place. We had dropped into action on the edge of darkness but we could make out buildings and trees in the vicinity. One great danger in night firing is the possibility of hitting a nearby obstacle which happens to be in the line of fire. A small tree or a post a few yards from the muzzle would be enough to do the trick. Here we had a whole haystack. It was a small one, but as we couldn't shoot through it and as it was impracticable to run in front of it, we set about to take it down. We found pitchforks and flattened it, strewing all the hay round about it on the ground.

From the Command Post the orders came thick and heavy. It was very dark now and I checked every reading with my torch.

Troop Target
H. E. 117 Charge II
Zero 125° 15
Angle of Sight 1° 25 Elevation — 4,500
No. 4 Gun
One round gun-fire
Report when ready.

I reported, "No. 4 Gun ready."

"Fire," came from the Command Post.

I knelt on the right of the trail and shouted "Fire."

The layer pulled the firing-lever. To our amazement the flash from the muzzle was enough to outline a large black object right up against the barrel, on the right-hand side. The most startled cow in the whole of France shook its head, its ears ringing and doubtless with one eardrum pierced, and took off into the night. It must have gained solid ground for we could hear it clop-clopping unceasingly until the sound of its hoofs were lost in the distance. It may have been attracted to the hay. It may have been hoping for a quiet rub against the smooth, hard surface of the Gun. We kept a sharp look-out for cows after that; from that moment the Gun was allergic to cows.

The night was still, apart from our single ranging shots. But it was not still for long. We had a habit of stirring people into activity. First the Spandaus, then the Brens opened up. The horizon began to flash and glow. The mortars joined in, then the guns. A lot of hot metal was being exchanged. It was like an orchestral composition which begins with a light instrumental texture and builds up gradually to 'Tutti'. Rockets went up. The signal 'Red over Green over Red' which sticks in my memory, may well have been a call to put down Defensive Fire (DF) which had been previously arranged with our Infantry as a surprise to help them out of a tight spot. In contrast was the HF (Harassing Fire) programme which was fixed and recorded previously and for which no light signal was required.

We got a misfire. The detonator in the cartridge had failed to work. Normally I should have carried out the procedure laid down in the Gun

Drill Manual but I couldn't wait. I dropped the breech block, with everyone out of the way, and flung the cartridge back over the trail. Then I threw it clear, hoping the thing would not go off.

A lot of guns seemed to be at work on this particular night. The sky was alive with flashes; the air was filled with whines and detonations. Just as it had brewed up so it subsided. Before dawn there was only the occasional short stutter, the final stubborn word at the end of the argument.

He who had snorted most fearfully and flung Himself about on His carriage was now still. His barrel was hot to the touch. When He had cooled down we poured boiling water down His muzzle and pulled Him through. You may wonder where we got this hot water from. Ah! ah! we could usually spare someone to make the fire and brew the 'char'. Used cartridge cases were lying all round Him. His lackeys were also tired and retired to the farmhouse which had been evacuated in a hurry. The remnants of a meal were on the table.

I went outside, found another cow, restless and swollen with milk, and took one or two of my detachment by surprise when I relieved its suffering by milking it. It was a complacent beast and I who had some rapport with cows, felt sorry for it, for it would die. Swede-bashing, a derisory term given by city dwellers to rustics, was now added to my eccentricities. We knocked up a dish of scrambled eggs and washed it down with very fresh milk (a drink which normally I never touch) before we retired. A roster of sentries was arranged, which was standard procedure.

In the bedroom was a great feather mattress. Little did we know that it was infested when two or three of us sampled its comfort. That mattress should really have evacuated itself for it must have been capable of walking out on its own. It was not long before the 'crabs' we had caught began to make their presence felt. For the unenlightened the crab-louse or *pediculus pubis* is a tiny parasite which is attracted to the area of skin which lies beneath the pubic hairs. It can spread to the armpits and even as high as the eyebrows, but it simply loves digging in to the pubic area. It operates not singly but in huge droves. The number packed into one pubic area must be astronomical. Its tiny claws cause constant irritation. A young doctor, to whom I mentioned my affliction, was of the opinion that 'crabs' could only be transmitted through sexual intercourse. If this is so, I must have been violated by some tainted and over-heated female during this campaign, whilst I was asleep. I suppose that it is not beyond the bounds of possibility, but if so, it must have been a very swift mating, of which I was completely oblivious. I was never asleep for so long.

From that night, until my arrival in England I scratched my genitals with relentless fervour. Had I been in a civilized community I should have been censored for indecent behaviour. A new order was incorporated into the Gun Drill Manual especially for me. It was "Load" — scratch — scratch — "Fire".
(Since writing this, I have come to suspect that the mattress was innocent. The crabs may have migrated to me from one of my bed-fellows whilst we slept.)

I gained a look of gratitude from another cow when I milked it, and admiration and satisfaction from my gun detachment who drank the fresh warm milk.

Down a side road was a row of ambulances, not one as at Larkhill, but a whole line of them. They were being loaded with a continuous stream of wounded men. As we passed them, moving out once more, with enemy shells bursting on the ridge close by, screams arose from these vehicles and the more imaginative of us suffered inwardly for the occupants and felt qualms for ourselves. The ambulance at Larkhill had conveyed a tiny message of warning. Needless to say, this being the real thing it was far more disturbing.

3rd Division was complaining of a shortage of shells, owing to obstructions in lines of communication.

Guderian's XIX Corps had now reached the vicinity of Abbeville, having travelled the record distance of fifty-six miles in one day. Lord Gort, Commander of the BEF, assembled reserve TA Divisions between St. Omer and Douai. The next day, the 21st, a British counter-attack was made at Arras, causing heavy losses to the 7th Panzer Division, but there was insufficient weight for it to be effective. The Germans were not alarmed at this abortive attack, for it helped to deplete British forces.

In the early morning of the 21st, the divisional front on the Escaut was attacked. Our artillery dispersed another assault at Escanaffles. The Germans retaliated with heavy and accurate fire from guns and mortars. More attention was given to brigade headquarters and to British gun positions. 77th Field Regiment, well forward and exposed, lost several of its guns.

We gunners, thumping away with our cannon at whatever there was to offer, might as well have been in a sealed bottle for all the news we got. Momentous decisions were being made whilst we held the Escaut. The

British Government received news that Lord Gort was already making preparations for the BEF to retire to the coast. The CIGS, Lord Ironside, was sent out with instructions for Lord Gort to make an attack southwards towards Amiens, but he was persuaded that this was out of the question as the divisions were fully engaged. This decision, a wise one under the circumstances one would have thought, terminated whatever co-ordination still remained with France, and saved the bulk of the BEF.

'An astonishing number of guns began to fire at Kerkhove, the fire being directed by an observation balloon.' (History of 4th Division.) Kerkhove is five or six miles north-west of Escanaffles. There may be no connection with the above statement and my experience which follows. Only one mention of an observation balloon appears in the War Diary, and that is towards the end of our journey. As there were no other guns round us, we may have been detached in a 'rover' position. One thing is certain. I did not dream the incident.

My Gun was placed in a deserted farmyard very near to a pigsty. It was clean, which was a wonder and did not seem to have been used recently. I sank down on the bare floor and promptly went to sleep. A second or two later I was on my feet, shaken into action. An observation balloon, spotting for the enemy artillery had appeared just over a mile away and was looking straight at us. We could see the basket in which were the two observers. Major G. McL. Bartlett, our Battery Commander, was standing by my Gun, carrying his map board with a pencil fastened with a short string. It was said that he was of the old school and could work wonders with a map and a bit of pencil to measure with. I threw the trail over and pointed the Gun on to the target. We were firing over open sights so the layer trained the wires of the telescopic sight on to the centre of the balloon. The Major took a look through his binoculars, consulted his map and related it to countryside, measured the distance with his pencil and gave the fire orders — the angle of sight to adjust the elevation, for we were firing uphill, and the range which I think was about 2,000 yards.

The response to the first round was immediate and dramatic. Within seconds of its arrival the ground crew who operated the cable had reacted, for the balloon dropped with such a mighty jerk that we could almost hear the rattle of the observers' teeth. The Major made slight adjustments as we continued, to use his own expression, to 'poop off' at the target which was being plucked downwards, not steadily but several yards at a time. When it was nearing the ground two figures shot out of the basket in a desperate attempt to escape, as the balloon burst into flames. They lived dangerously, those boys, and were not much loved. They were better out of the way for they would surely have got us, had they remained and had we opened up on another target.

The Major nodded, gave what I assumed to be a grunt of satisfaction, for he seemed to be a man of few words, and disappeared into his billet in the farmhouse. I went back to my pigsty — but not for long.

By the 22nd the defence of the River Escaut had to be discontinued. Amiens, seventy miles to the south had fallen and the German tanks were at Boulogne, threatening the Channel ports. The effort to outflank us from the north went on relentlessly, with more concentrated attacks on the Belgians.

The BEF was placed on half rations, but it did not seem to make much difference. It wasn't all that unusual to see a squeaking piglet or two being hoisted into the cooks' wagon. The cooks were admirable providers, assiduous for our well-being, and worked better under pressure.

There was hostile shelling at Avelghem and Escanaffles and once more we put down fire on the bridge. Hostile air-burst ranging is reported for the first time, possibly, probably, by 88mm guns.

At about three o'clock in the afternoon the main German attack had developed and the 6th Black Watch of 12 Infantry Brigade had been pushed back on Castor Bridge. Two of the companies had to fight their way out.

We manhandled the Gun into a private garden, up the narrow drive, over the tiny lawn at the back and forward into a flower-bed with the summer flowers just forming. There was no sign of life. The occupants had either fled or were hiding. If they were at home they got a big shock when the first round went off, for the blast cracked a few windows. One bright, new, yellow shell followed another, rammed into the rifling and then up and away over the garden fence. The rest of the Troop were belting away in other gardens up the road and the air was filled with the sound of rotating projectiles, whirring away in their trajectories.

We pulled out, very hastily, just as it was getting dark. It was very lively, there were shell-bursts quite near and the small arms were rattling away too close for my liking. We sped away after the others, the fourth gun in the Troop, so it was harder for us to keep up and particularly difficult to catch up. We took a wrong turning. In a narrow road at the bottom of a hill with steep banks on either side we ran into the Black Watch who were withdrawing and dragging their wounded with them.

They were slipping and sliding down the steep slope. I was half out of the tractor, about to give the order to unlimber in order to turn round, when Driver Burbanks, shouting for me to stay, did an impossible about turn, mounting a yard up each bank as he did so and saving us a valuable two or three minutes. Again, it was little short of a miracle that we found the right road and joined the Troop, for we had gone a few miles out of our way.

By 02.30 hrs on the 23rd the whole Division was across the Courtrai Canal. The infantry had marched another twenty-three miles. We were now north-west of Roncq in support of 12 Infantry Brigade, on a defence line erected during the winter by the BEF. I am as certain as I can be that no gun positions, previously prepared by us, were ever occupied by our Battery. On this day there was no firing. The enemy were busy catching up with us. In the afternoon of the 24th they arrived and shelled Lauwe and Haluin. Our own ammunition was now restricted.

This was the day when news finally got to us that we were in a very tight spot indeed and that we were edging our way to the coast. It was a good thing that we had no crystal ball in which to peer; and that the gauntlet that we would have to run when we got to the sea was hidden from us.

The day before, leading units of 1st Panzer had passed Calais. Now they were only fifteen miles from Dunkirk. The British assessment was that Dunkirk would fall the next day, the 25th. Then a curious decision was made, the reasons for which have been speculated upon and discussed ever since. Herr Hitler decreed that the determined columns threatening Dunkirk should halt. Everyone sat back in amazement, wondering what the next trick was to be pulled out of the bag. None came. We, unknowing, had been reprieved for a vital few more days. It was still far from a happy situation, however, for Dunkirk was overlooked by enemy guns from vantage points on high ground.

To the north the German infantry and guns were concentrating on the Belgians whose morale was deteriorating steadily. It would appear that they had given up.

From now on the adrenalin flowed faster. An atmosphere charged with anxiety and foreboding had crept in. Our primitive instincts of stealth and cunning became more pronounced in our struggle for survival.

Our Troop went to a 'rover' position at Werwicq on the 25th, with the wagon lines north of the river at Comines. The refugees were appearing in droves on the north side of the river, struggling to keep ahead of the fighting. They were not allowed across the bridge. What was left of a medium battery stayed with us for the night, but drew out next morning to join 4th Medium Battery RA. By the evening the BEF was almost enclosed, with eight French divisions.

On the morning of the 26th we came back to rejoin the Battery and pointed our guns northward. Massed columns of German troops of all arms, with a lot of horse-drawn transport could be seen moving along the Weleghem-Menin road. I wondered at the time why we did not blow them off it. Now I know that our ammunition was in short supply. The OP was shelled by an enemy field battery.

From this point decisions changed almost hourly. Recce parties went out to find positions, only to find that they were already occupied by the 'mediums'. Other places were found for us west of Ploegsteerte. There was an OP at Messines, an FOP (Forward Observation Post) at Warneton. Some trucks were abandoned (by orders from above I presume) but some left by other units but still in working order were commandeered. They should have been destroyed. From now onwards, wrecked vehicles were to be seen wherever we travelled.

Now it was revealed that King Leopold of the Belgians had surrendered and his army with him. To say that 3rd Division was in ever graver danger of being outflanked would be to understate the crisis. The Belgians had left bridges intact, just walked away from them as it were. They were blown by 3rd Division's sappers, just as the German recce patrols appeared.

Our own recce parties were reconnoitring positions and laying wire near Elverdinghe, north-west of Ypres. The OP was to have been at Brielen, a little over to the east. The wire was ordered to be cut, the recce party redirected to join the Regimental Column at Woesten, north of Elverdinghe on the Furnes road. In the late afternoon or early evening of the 28th, we were rolling our way northwards on the main road to Furnes.

The 3rd Division and the 50th were to hold the line of the Yser Canal, and were to fall back to an intricate plan, once the 2nd, 4th and 44th Divisions had withdrawn to what was to become known as the Dunkirk perimeter. Obviously the whole front was becoming compressed and the roads more and more congested.

The Colonel of the 12th Lancers of 3rd Division had the foresight to realize that the bridges over the Yser at Dixmude and at Nieuport would not only be undefended but would still be whole. He sent parties of his regiment to these places, accompanied by sappers of the Royal

Monmouthshire RE, who blew the bridges. Had it not been for forethought such as this, and there must have been many such examples, we should never have got out.

The whole of the route from Louvain must have been spattered with wrecked bridges.

There was this village in which we hesitated and halted, running into the Hun, under shell fire and pointing the wrong way. Our infantry were busily engaged kicking open doors, lobbing grenades through windows and protecting each other as they darted from cover to cover. It must have been the village of Woesten, an intermediate point to which the 2nd Battalion, Royal Ulster Rifles of 3rd Division had just withdrawn. I understand that their Regimental History records that the events of the following day were to be one of their most disagreeable experiences.

This was no place for us so we did not waste much time unhooking Gun and limber, turning the tractor (with great difficulty — there was congestion), and hooking up again. Through debris, past sagging walls and burning interiors we edged along, as if on a conducted tour. Through a broken window I glimpsed a body hanging by the neck, swaying from a low beam. Summary justice was meted out in these parts. We crept along, up a corridor with enemy troops very close on one side, and not very far away on the other. Through Dickebusch and Vlamegtinghe, which is about half-way between Ypres and Poperinghe, with Passchendaele some ten miles over to the east, we made our slow journey. Veterans of the First World War were familiar with these names and so was my mother, for these were Flanders' fields where the poppies blew 'between the crosses, row on row'. More had come to join them, a new generation. It was a blessing that my mother could not see us, but she and many another would be aware of our dilemma and would be sorely troubled on this night and on a few more nights to come.

At 02.00 hrs on the 29th, the column halted at Furnes. Enemy patrols arrived at Dixmude a few hours later. Lord Gort had been told to evacuate as many as possible and about seven thousand troops had got away.

Not far from our final position we were in hiding under trees which lined the road. Sgt. Artificer Bickle was resting under a hedge, manipulating his primus stove, brewing up as casually as if he were on some Victorian picnic. He invited me to take tea with him, whilst overhead, flying low, contemptuous of our presence, wave after wave of heavy enemy bombers throbbed onwards, intent on spreading more suffering and devastation.

It was here that he gave me his book of Kipling's *Barrack Room Ballards*, signed H. V. Bickle, Jubbulpore 1935. Of all my books, with the exception of those given me by my family over the years, it is the one I treasure most. He must have foreseen the grim struggle for survival which lay ahead for us, but he remained non-committal.

2nd corps, consisting of 3rd and 4th Divisions were assigned to hold the left or eastern flank of the Dunkirk perimeter. This they were to do until the night of 31st May/1st June.

We were in action early in the morning in our last position north of Oost-Dunkerque, on either side of the road to Nieuport. It became very lively. The OP was on a bridge at Nieuport until heavy hostile shelling forced the occupants to move to a house on the front at Nieuport-Bains. Under the direction of these persistent, harassed people at the OP, the Battery shelled Nieuport. The Belgians had failed to blow two more bridges. One Troop of 18prs. of 60th Field Regiment RA, joined us.

When the Battery had taken up position in a large clearing, surrounded by trees which gave us some air cover but did not interfere with our field of fire, I still did not know where I was. The English Channel was over there beyond the dunes and there was this place called Dunkirk further up the road which was becoming something of a talking point.

We dug slit-trenches and gun-pits in the soft, sandy soil. At least here was one place where we could dig in, for not only was the ground suitable but we stayed here two or three days, which was quite a change for us.

We recorded and fired on targets and dropped into our routine. Very few civilians showed themselves, none if they were wise, and there was a rumour here that Fifth Columnists were lurking about. Bullets were certainly being fired, for single rounds could be heard swishing through foliage, sometimes fraying branches. The sharp-shooters must have been banging away haphazardly or have been very bad shots, for as far as I know, no one was hit by their missiles. Gunner L —, his courageous spirit made even better with wine, took an anti-tank rifle with him into the lower branches of a tree, mouthing a string of indecipherable Gaelic curses with the word 'bastard' frequently interpolated. The anti-tank rifle was a big cumbersome weapon on the lines of an elephant gun. No one ever discovered what L —'s target had been. Had it been real or was it some wild Scottish wraith summoned by his wine-fevered brain?

At his one and only shot, L — was propelled from the tree by the powerful recoil and was brought hastily to the ground, shaken but with no limbs broken. We laughed a lot as we dusted him down. I was glad to have been at Woolwich with him.

The Command Post had its troubles. Heavy shelling caused it to be moved. The one hostile observation balloon was reported, but there is no evidence to suggest that we did anything about it. Signal wires were being cut by shell fire and also by saboteurs, for those lines laid along the roadside suffered most. 'A' and 'C' Troops took two guns each from 'B' Troop. I remember them coming in on the left of my Gun.

We were not short of ammunition now. On the 30th two guns from each Troop were destroyed by their own gunners. More rounds were distributed to us, the ones who were left.

A sergeant of one of the guns which had joined us was sitting on the trail having a bite to eat when he dropped over dead. A small shell splinter from a shell exploding at what was thought to be a safe distance had pierced a vital part and killed him immediately.

By this date 100,000 French and British troops had already been evacuated. At night two officers and sixty ORs 'left for home'. I have always been under the impression that the married men and those under a certain age were chosen. There must have been few who were younger than I, yet I remained. As for being married, I must confess that I wouldn't have shied away from the matrimonial knot just then, provided that I could have obtained a lightning divorce. Nor would consummation have been insisted on in my *mariage de convenance*. I was too worn out.

It appears that embarkation points had been set up. I am told by one of the officers in charge of the party which had just left that the Regiment's column was split up at Bray Dunes, between La Panne and Dunkirk, not far from where I was, by an air attack just after dawn. People had to make their own way in groups or individually.

Here was I still, however, on this night of 30/31st May, with Sergeant-Major Prior and one or two others, including Driver Dodds.

Round the Gun the shells and cartridges were stacked. I was not unmindful of the fact that if they were hit we would be distributed over a wide area.

The Sergeant-Major, back at his former role as No. 1, took over as No. 2 as well and rammed the shells and also operated the breech. I brought up the ammunition, loaded, layed and fired the Gun. Doubtless the lean and nimble Sergeant-Major brought up a few rounds between whiles. We had quite a time of it, the Sergeant-Major and I, for although the firing was by no means continuous we indulged in short, hectic bursts of energy. Our frenetic movements, had anyone been there to see, must have appeared like an old film which had been speeded up.

Appropriate tunes should have been played on the honky-tonk piano, but we had our own accompaniment.

Deeply engaged in one of our lonely, vociferous escapades, with the Sergeant-Major and I throwing ourselves about in slavish fashion and the Gun rearing back and belching, we both registered a very short whistle followed by an ominious dull thud which seemed to come from under the Gun. We exchanged quick looks of alarm.

Of course, this happened in the small hours when the body's resistance is said to be at a low ebb. We, the unwashed and smoke blackened, were still very much awake, in our begrimed uniforms which we had worn night and day for three weeks.

There was just one redeeming feature. It had seldom rained.

Between times I sprawled on the mound of shells, regardless of the danger, and pulled on a cigarette, concealing the glow of its tip as only soldiers can. I could have sunk a pint or two, but no alcohol had passed my lips during the campaign. We got a long break for two or three hours before dawn, so I settled down in a slit-trench and ate two tins of bacon, which was rolled in greaseproof paper. They were delicious — an outstanding gourmet's delight. There was no shortage. I could have had a hundred such tins, for who was left to eat them? Afterwards I chain-smoked my way into a cylindrical tin of Players Export.

My eardrums were still buzzing, but then, I was accustomed to it. It went with the job.

At dawn the Sergeant-Major and I looked under the Gun. In the centre, between the wheels was a hole in the ground, clearly visible. We could only conclude that a large projectile had burrowed its way in and failed to go off.

On the 31st the shelling and air attacks continued, and intensified as the day wore on.

It was a strange atmosphere, for although we were not 'stonked' in the strictest sense it was as well to be watchful, for things flew about with no set pattern and at no set time. Sometimes simultaneous explosions accompanied great clouds of dust and smoke which flew up in a line a hundred yards or so in front of the Gun. I did not investigate, but there seemed to be nothing just there to shoot at. This thunderous group of giant hammer strokes would occur periodically. One of my mates did have a look, but all he got was a severe wound in the back. The last I saw of him was when I helped to lift him into a 15 cwt truck which was brought into use as an ambulance. He arrived home safely and made a good recovery.

Others were not so fortunate. A cook walking through the clearing to collect wood for his fire caught a piece of metal in his chest. The fragment spun his woollen vest into the cavity it made. A young officer was machine-gunned from the air and was found wounded in his truck.

We fired off more ammunition from our great pile, but there was still some left when, towards evening, we were ordered to destroy the guns.

There must be few gunners who have had to undertake this drastic task. It is a shameful thing and is only done when all else has failed. Little did I know that mass destruction was taking place everywhere. Vehicles, weapons, equipment and stores were being smashed and wrecked so that they would be useless to the enemy, who was now right on top of us.

Sergeant-Major Prior and I went to each gun in turn.

The Sergeant-Major says that 'Tiffy' Bickle was present, and there is every reason to believe that he was, for he was the obvious person most qualified to supervise such drastic action, even though he would resent it most strongly. I personally cannot recollect his being there, but the occasion was, to say the least, tense, and I have discovered from other researchers that the mind tends to distort or to bypass some details.

The procedure is set out in the 'Gun Drill for Q.F. 25pr.', in Appendix IV under 'Disablement'. 'The extent of disablement ordered will depend on the time available and the probability of recapture. To destroy the gun. Place an HE shell in the muzzle. Load with HE. Fire the gun from under cover by means of a length of rope or telephone wire attached to the firing lever.'

The defiant death-cry of the Gun was in keeping with His arrogant nature. He went out with a very big bang. His last round had been fired and I, His Personal Bodyguard, had destroyed Him.

Neither I nor the Sergeant-Major looked back or spoke as we climbed into the remaining vehicle which was to take us to the beach; nor did we talk much about it afterwards. There was firing all round us. Shell bursts, mortar fire and bullets from light weapons were closing in. It really was time to go.

I had removed the Dial-sight and Telescopic Sight. These I took with me. I placed the stiff leather cover of the Dial-sight between my legs, tucked well into the lower part of my body as I sat in the tractor. My intention was to save not only the valuable instrument but to protect those parts which were to me even more valuable.

It appears that we were not quite the last of our Battery to leave. Almost the final entry in the War Diary reads:

> May 31 1900hrs. Destroyed most transport and all guns exc. I see, under 2/Lt. Babington, which remained in action until 2400 hrs.

CHAPTER X

Everyone who was at Dunkirk will have his own personal story. There are as many tales as there were people. This is mine. It cannot be verified, nor can it be queried except by those who question its truthfulness, for I travelled alone for much of the time.

On alighting from the Quad, it was just getting dark. We walked down a narrow street, presumably leaving the driver to wreck this, our last tractor.

Three things happened to me in very rapid succession, convincing me that I had been dumped in a very unhealthy spot indeed. I had been given no indication at all of what to expect, but in all fairness, I don't think many in authority would have anticipated such a violent greeting either.

With no warning at all there was a brilliant flame and a tremendous crash. It took me a few seconds to collect myself and even then it was difficult to assess what I saw. I was sprawled out alongside what looked like a naked woman. There had been no preliminary love-play. Here it was, laid out on a plate. The earth had really moved for me.

On further inspection, more figures were revealed, some with fragments of flimsy clothing attached. The figures were not made of flesh or bone. I had been blown through the glass window of a shop specializing in ladies' underwear. I stood up and dusted myself, stumbled over a dummy, said "F . . . " and found the Dial-sight.

Launched once more on my journey, I followed other cautious wayfarers until I came to what I took to be the edge of a beach.

The earth moved again, but this time I was very, very conscious of it. I seemed to be part of and surrounded by a kaleidoscope of coloured lights. There were green, yellow, many colours, but purple predominated. I was deafened temporarily by the explosion. I think it must have been a big shell which had burst almost on top of me for there was no sound of aircraft. It had buried itself deep in the sand before it burst.

My ears hurt, my eyes had gone out of focus but I could still walk, even if I did stagger about at first.

As I walked over the sand I could see the light reflected on what I took to be the sea. Now that I was more orientated and my eyes had readusted themselves, I observed a great glow over to the left which was Dunkirk. There were flashes all round, even out to sea, the unmistakable flashes of guns. Over the horizon, way out to sea, these glows came and went. Express trains passed high overhead and there were great 'crumps' inland. I assumed that the Navy's battle-wagons were sitting way out to sea, firing their big stuff at Jerry.

By the water's edge was a long queue of men waiting patiently. There was some sort of pier or pontoon stretching out into the sea but I could not see any boats. No one spoke. We just stood and waited on that night of 31st May, staring silently out to sea, each one of us aware of the menace which surrounded us, each one intent on his own preservation.

It is only recently that I have discovered that this structure, seen only by me in the darkness, was indeed a causeway which the sappers had constructed on two columns of lorries which they had driven into the sea. The idea was to run a shuttle service of small boats to and from this pier to the destroyers and whatever other vessels had collected a mile or so out to sea. At the start of the evacuation from this point there were only fifteen small boats and the journey out took over an hour. Three squadrons of bombers had attacked at dusk, before I got there, or did I catch the tail-end of it, and the 'Fourth Division' account states that a medium gun had ranged on the area. It concludes: 'The embarkation began at nine at night; four hours later not more than four hundred men of the Division had been embarked.'

To my mind, there was not just one medium gun. Quite a few cannons had their muzzles pointing in our direction, and there were plenty of free samples being distributed, courtesy of Krupps ammunition works in Essen, to show for it.

Nothing was fair in these encounters. Out of the blue there came a salvo of high velocity shells firing air-bursts. I thought they were 88 mm. The fragments whistled and screamed down on us, clearly visible like fire-flies in the darkness. The shells burst above our heads with ear-splitting force. I knew at once that this 'stonk' was prerecorded. Jerry was putting down harassing fire on a target on which he had ranged accurately during the daylight. We had done the same thing to the Hun many times in the past weeks. I was getting some of my own medicine, and it was not nice. As a fellow artilleryman I could not help but admit his accuracy, but I did not stay to appreciate it.

I turned and ran as fast as I could, ducking instinctively as I went.

Of course, others had the same idea. A soldier running in a crazy uncontrolled fashion in front of me, let something fall. I caught it as it fell and shouted, “Hey mate, you’ve dropped something.” Indeed he had, but he never returned to retrieve it. It was his arm, severed at the shoulder. I got rid of it. It was no use to either of us.

“Bloody hell,” I said to myself, “let’s get out of here.” It was not a very articulate statement, but it had a great feeling behind it.

On the edge of the dunes was a beach hut, still undamaged, from which came signs of activity. I looked inside and wonder of wonders, on all that beach, in all that turmoil here were a few of our chaps brewing up. Among them was Bombardier Anstee, huge and brawny, possibly more formidable than Bombardier Earle, and the ubiquitous Sergeant-Artificer Bickle. Anstee had left the Battery the evening before, but had only got this far.

“What are you on, you little bleeder?” quoth Anstee. He didn’t get up to give me a characteristic nudge, the nearest he ever came to affectionate greeting. I was glad, for it would have knocked me over. Instead he proffered a mug of char. Like Sergeant-Artificer Bickle, wherever Anstee was there was a pint of hot, sweet tea with plenty of tinned milk.

I kipped down with them for the night. If the events of the last hour or so could be considered as a sort of hors-d’oeuvre, an introduction to the main course, I was not very keen on sampling the rest of the menu.

But it had to be sampled. Either we went on and faced what there was to face or we would be taken prisoner, possibly shot in the process. I did not relish the thought of being stuck away in a prisoner-of-war camp for the duration. If we stayed where we were and waited for Jerry we would be shot at anyway. Our backs were really up against the wall. England was only a few miles across the Channel, but apparently it was inaccessible.

Sergeant-Artificer Bickle had me up and about just after dawn.

“Bombardier Bowman,” he said, “come down to the beach with me ek dum. There is an anti-aircraft gun which, with a little repair, we can turn on the Hun.”

My heart sank right down to the soles of my boots. I was not very happy as it was, and being a night owl I was even less happy when I was expected to peck about on dangerous beaches just after sunrise.

‘Christ,’ I thought, ‘this Kiplingesque gesture is going a bit too far.’

I obeyed his order and went out with him to inspect his bloody cannon, hoping that it had been blown away. My attitude may not have been in the best tradition of the Regiment, but he had caught me at a bad time.

We arrived at our objective, a strange looking, small anti-aircraft gun of foreign extraction. It was smaller than a Bofors and stood out in splendid isolation. 'This is where you hand in your dinner-pail, Bombardier Bowman. Open up with this bloody thing and we'll be stonked by the whole f . . . . g German Air Force.'

I was reminded of Lord Cardigan's comment before the Charge of the Light Brigade.

'Lord Cardigan saluted once more, wheeled his horse and rode over to his second-in-command, Lord George Paget, remarking aloud to himself as he did so, "Well here goes the last of the Brudenells." '

He survived, against tremendous odds but I didn't think that there was much chance for us.

The expert artificer cast his professional eye over his discovery. Everything seemed to be in order. There was ammunition. But on closer examination the firing pin was missing. Without tools and material there was no way of making or even improvising such a fundamental part.

My cold perspiration subsided. The opportunity of earning a posthumous VC was gone and I was reprieved. My friend walked disconsolately back to the dunes. I never saw him again. By that one act alone, unrewarding though it had proved, he had earned his place in Valhalla.

It was a beautiful morning, with the sunlight reflecting on the water, but there were few I think who would appreciate it. All along the water's edge were ragged lines of khaki-clad figures, stretching out into the sea. One or two groups were struggling with rowing boats. Apart from these I could see no other vessels of any kind, apart from one intrepid naval vessel standing at a distance offshore. It was either a frigate or a destroyer. As I looked an explosion seemed to take place and the ship sank with no fuss whatsoever. The bows tilted right up out of the water, then the hull went down vertically until it disappeared. Only a few seconds seemed to have elapsed from beginning to end. I saw no survivors, no wreckage. Where that brave ship had been there was only the smooth glistening surface of the sea.

As I was still blinking in disbelief at what I had seen, or thought I had seen, the Messerschmitts came in flying low, one following the other at a safe distance and firing their machine-guns as they came. Everyone in sight flung himself to the ground like a puppet jerked on a string. The heart raced and the adrenalin really flowed. Lying stretched out in the sand and trying to burrow into it, I tilted my head a little and saw the sardonic leer of the pilot, his head encased in a black flying helmet.

The bullets spat into the sand in straight lines. One hit the ground between my body and my left arm with a great smack, just below the armpit. I watched the line of bullets spit along. One hit the water-bottle of the man two or three yards in front of me and another hit him in the shoulder. The fellow further along was not so lucky for he looked as if he had been stitched by a giant sewing machine. Bullets had gone up the middle of his back and the last one had taken off the top of his head. Blood spewed out of the stitches. Discarded equipment littered the beach and all along there were rifles sticking up in the sand with tin hats on top to show where the owner had been hastily buried.

I saw no future at all in staying in this area, so on to the road I went, by the beach huts and bungalows. Fortuitously, I met Driver Dodds, the same who had driven us to the beach. He was at the wheel of a 15 cwt truck now. Where he had acquired it or where he had got the petrol from were twin mysteries. Driver Dodds had unrevealed properties. One of them was a cheerful optimism in a very tight corner, the other was resourcefulness of a very high quality. Dodds considered it would be a good idea to take a gentle morning drive into Dunkirk, for he thought we should have a better chance of getting a lift home. There was a lot of sense in what he said so I climbed aboard, with a couple of others. The driver leant back in his seat as he drove, passing the time of day and making pleasant small-talk about the scenery, seemingly oblivious to the fact that there were shells, bombs and hostile aircraft all conspiring to kill us. Furthermore, as we drew near to Dunkirk there were increasing signs of destruction, unpleasant sounds and much smoke and fire.

It goes without saying that I was tired. I was also so dirty that no self-respecting tramp would have come within sniffing distance. My socks felt as if they had been soaked in treacle. No longer was I a milk-faced boy, for three weeks the sun had shone and for the whole time I had been exposed to it. I took off my steel-helmet and wiped the sweat off my face and brow. There was a great dent in the helmet where something very solid had tried to penetrate.

I still had the Dial-sight. Having brought it so far I was absolutely adamant about hanging on to it.

Driver Dodds, he with the compass grafted into his brain, did not think it prudent to drive any further when bits of masonry started to fall on the bonnet of his truck. Nor did I. We decided to ditch it and put it out of action. Very warily we made our way through empty streets where walls were bulging dangerously and threatening to fall on us and where fires burnt unattended. The only movement was from hunted folk such as ourselves. Once we stopped for cover in a big cellar which was filled mainly with civilians. They made us welcome but we could not stay. Time was running out for us. Eventually, having threaded our way over mounds of rubble and round wrecked and burnt out trucks, taking whatever shelter we could get when the whistle of a bomb told us it was close, we came to the Mole at Dunkirk. It was getting on for late afternoon on 1st June.

At the approach to the pier, on the left-hand side were sitting two brass-hats eating their haversack rations. I could tell by the red tabs on their collars and by the elaborate braided insignia on their hats that they were military men of high rank.

I went on to the pier unheeded, walking cautiously over planks which had been laid over great gaping holes caused by explosions. Drifts of smoke hung about and there was the stink of cordite. A guarded, watchful atmosphere surrounded the pier, common to places which are under surveillance by an enemy.

Bodies were lying to one side, motionless under greatcoats or groundsheets. Round them flies buzzed and hovered, attracted to the blood.

A boat was moored to the pier, making steam. Wounded men were being taken aboard and some of them were in a sorry state. Faces were hidden in blood-stained bandages, legs which had been hastily tended with field dressings showed savage, raw gashes from which blood oozed. Men with abdominal wounds groaned and writhed, or just lay back, their faces drawn and waxen.

I became devious. Here was a ship and given the slightest chance I would sail in her. I mingled with the troops, a motley lot representing several regiments, who were carrying the stretchers on board. As I helped with one stretcher after another my own clothing became blood-stained.

The vessel was almost full and I could see that she was preparing to cast off. When my last burden had been put down I promptly got lost in the crowd. As we slid away from the jetty Jerry had one final go at us. We suffered a near miss from a bomb, but there was no apparent damage and we slipped out of the harbour and into the gathering darkness.

In a cubby-hole below decks a sailor in a blue jersey and trousers was curled up asleep. There was room for one more so I edged in quietly beside him with my few possessions and fell into a deep sleep.

I must have awakened when the engine stopped throbbing. There were signs of movement on board and the ship was stationary. Nudging my companion who had not moved an inch I said, "Hey mate, we must be in Blighty."

There was no response so I examined him more closely. I found that he was ice-cold and rigid, but there was no outward sign of injury. Afterwards, when I thought about it, for my reaction at the time was vague, I considered that there must be few people who had crossed the Channel, unaware that they had a corpse for a bedfellow.

There is always a certain type of chap who can come up with the answer. Up on the deck, leaning on the rail I asked the bloke next to me where we were and what was holding us up. We were standing off Dover Harbour, he said, waiting for the boom to be lowered so that we could enter and dock. I understood that the boom was a chain which was raised underwater to stop submarines from getting in, but I never checked the authenticity of his information.

The white cliffs were there all right and just down the road was Shorncliffe Barracks where it had all started nine months before. It seemed a lot longer than that and I felt a lot older.

As we disembarked we were directed straight on to a train which was in the station waiting. It was early in the morning of 2nd June but the WVS, bless them, were on duty with hot drinks and snacks.

The customary exchange of pleasantries, characteristic of troops in transit, was absent. A tremendous feeling of gratitude went out to those ladies. We all felt overwhelming relief at being back home, but we were too weary and numbed by recent stresses to take it all in. Slowly, as if sedated we put what little luggage we had on the racks and took our seats.

We were taken to Aldershot and from there almost straight away we were sent to the Divisional Collecting Point at Yeovil in Somerset. My belongings did not need much attention. Apart from what I stood up in, my torn, dirty, stained battledress and my battered tin hat, I had my haversack or small pack which I called my 'war bag'. In it was my shaving kit, soap and a very dirty towel, none of which I had used for days, a few cigarettes, the telescopic sight for the Gun and my book of *Barrack Room Ballads*. The Dial-sight was still with me, but I handed it in at Yeovil and received no acknowledgement or thanks whatsoever. I do not think that anyone in that camp knew what it was. It is probably still there with the dust of forty-five years on its leather case. I was a bit 'cheesed off' when I heard that some Quartermaster Sergeant or other had been awarded a medal for saving the cigarette ration at Dunkirk. This was probably just one more unfounded rumour.

We were under canvas in a field not far from a tree-lined road. The weather was fine and warm, there were no parades and there was enough food. There was even a pub down the road but we were rationed to a couple of pints each. This rationing of beer was a new, grim, and worrying aspect which was creeping into social life in wartime England. We might be off duty, all bliffed up with our boots blackened and with a pound or two in our pockets. What would happen? We would turn up at a pub and the beer was off.

Just now, however, I was very content save for one irritating problem. My crabs, now that my mind was not on other things seemed to attack with concentrated vigour. I reported sick, along with another member of my Troop, who turned out to be none other than 'Tich' Greenhill. We did not even see the MO. The cure was simple. An orderly instructed us what to do and gave us some ointment. We stripped down at the entrance to the tent in broad daylight if I remember rightly. Standing on newspaper, we shaved off first our pubic hair, then our armpits. The little creatures could be seen dropping on to the newspaper as we went about our toilet. Where the tiny claws had gripped the skin was raw, but after a right good wash from head to foot and after applying the 'blue unction' which had been given us we felt soothed and at peace. *Pediculus pubis* had gone for good.

Our next move was to the village of Litton Cheney in Dorset which was the new Battery area. Here I met most of my old mates. A few faces had disappeared but I was surprised that the majority had survived unscathed.

Telegrams had been sent home soon after we had arrived in England so my mother knew that I was safe. Now from Litton Cheney we were sent on 48 hours leave. I travelled from Preston to Poulton on the milk train which got in very early in the morning.

After walking towards Hambleton for a couple of miles or more I kipped down under a tree just inside a field gate near Shard Bridge. I caught the Ribble bus which put me down at Ryecroft Corner at eight o'clock. My mother, I knew, would be sorting the letters at the Post Office prior to going on her round. I cannot remember what was said but there would be no clutching and kissing for we were not openly demonstrative. I only knew that she would be just as glad to see me as I was to see her.

For a while I went and sat on the ground by a tree at Ryecroft Corner, watching people going to work and passing a brief time of day with them. I was still in my battle-stained gear, still in my tin hat and still with only my haversack.

I watched the children on their way to school. Their fresh, young faces turned in my direction for they knew me well enough, even knew from hearsay where I had been.

I thought of the rifles upright in the sand, on which the steel helmets hung; the unknown soldier whose back had spurted blood; the line of sack-like things under greatcoats on Dunkirk Mole.

'We are the Dead. Short days ago
We lived, felt dawn, saw sunset glow,
Loved and were loved, and now we lie
In Flanders fields.'

Flanders is not far from Dunkirk. The poem was written not long before I was born. My mother, in one of her bouts of sad nostalgia, which I never understood until I was much older, had quoted these lines quite often. It was a sobering thought for me to reflect that she might have had a greater cause to recall them at this very moment had things gone differently.

Up the village I went home to Ingol Cottage and lifted my grandmother above my head by way of greeting. Laughing, but with tears on her cheeks, she begged me to put her down. She was a frail old lady and I thought the world of her. I know now that I should have been more careful, but I did not understand old age and ill health.

I washed and shaved and put on my 'blues', my navy blue serge walking out uniform which I had bought at Shorncliffe and which had been specially made by the Regimental tailor. The red and blue side hat never did get a 'bomb' put in it, so I wore the Artillery badge instead as a wartime measure.

I picked up my little cousin, my Uncle Ben's little girl Shirley who was only a toddler, and took her for a walk round the village. A kind lady gave her a boiled sweet which got stuck in her throat. She went purple so I turned her upside down, held her by her chubby little legs with one hand and gave her what I thought was a gentle tap. The sweet shot out of her mouth like a high velocity shell and bounced off the floor.

That night Ronnie Critchley came round and took me for a pint. When I arrived home, slightly intoxicated, the kitchen appeared to be filled with people. A voice from a corner chair asked "What was it like Edwin?" Without pausing to think I said, "F . . . . . g rough."

There was a strained silence for a moment or two. I realized what I had said and apologized immediately, for we never swore in front of ladies in those days. I expected my mother to blow my head off afterwards, but she never said a word. As for my grandmother, she took it in her stride. I suspected that she had heard the word before, but I couldn't think where.

A day later, back in my old gear, I returned to Litton Cheney. There was a strong rumour that we were going back to France.

The collation of facts after Dunkirk revealed a disheartening situation. 3rd June was the last day on which men left France by way of Dunkirk. Of the 338,226 men evacuated 139,097 were French. British casualties totalled 68,111.

The RAF lost 477 aircraft, the RN six destroyers and a further nineteen damaged. Vessels of the Merchant Navy and those privately owned suffered badly. All guns, tanks, vehicles, equipment and supplies had been abandoned and destroyed, most of it with our own hands.

PART THREE

Home 1940 — Early 1943

An' if sometimes our conduck isn't all your fancy paints,
Why, single men in barricks don't grow into plaster saints.
Tommy, by Rudyard Kipling

CHAPTER XI

At Litton Cheney there was nothing much to do except rest, eat our meals regularly and collect our new kit and assemble it. My Troop was billeted in the comfortable second storey of a farm building. Its purpose was most likely a granary or storage place for fodder, but now it had been swept out and bunk beds had been installed. There were no sounds of battle here. For me Litton Cheney is remembered as a sunlit, restful village from which narrow lanes led into the adjoining countryside. The hedgerows and verges were fresh with grasses and wild flowers of early summer, among which insects hummed and droned, inviting one to lie down and sleep.

Yet, during the warm nights I would awaken suddenly from a deep sleep and sit up straight, thinking that I had to take cover. My body would be drenched with perspiration. I was not the only one. There were others in that billet who cried out in the night and sat up in alarm during those few weeks after Dunkirk.

There was a farmer who lived just down the road, whose bluff I called when I milked one of his cows. I was always milking cows, wherever I went. This time the udder was not swollen abnormally, nor was there other background music save the swishing of the milk in the pail. We discovered the potency of scrumpy, the local cider which had bits of apple floating in it. 'Busty' Cox, a most powerful man with enormous biceps, who had been a farrier in the horse-drawn days, felt so uplifted by this witches' brew that he took hold of some poor peasant's bicycle which was leaning against the pub, and crying out like Tarzan, bounced it hard on the ground. The wheels buckled so much that each one became a straight line. Shameful to relate, we young men reeled away full of laughter and scrumpy and no one thought about reporting him to the OC. Once the Passion Wagon took us into Weymouth, but for most of us no passion was to be found.

Our idyll with Litton Cheney did not last long. Our next move was to the New Forest near Lyndhurst where we set up camp. 'A' Troop had a large marquee with the floor dug out to a depth of two or three feet and the earth thrown up round its perimeter for extra protection.

There was no more talk of going back to France. That great country was totally under the dominance of the Germans and would be for another four years. For the time being we were infantrymen, ready to assist in repelling seaborne or airborne landings, or both.

It was more than likely that there were enemy agents about, ready to spread panic and sedition as they had done on the Continent, should the Germans attempt an invasion. Our only weapons were rifles and a few Brens. Huge quantities of arms, vehicles and stores had been destroyed in France and Belgium and we had lost a disturbing number of the best trained men in the Army.

From 20th June the Division, which had suffered heavily particularly in the infantry and was short of half its fighting men, was assigned to defend the coastal areas of Southampton, Portsmouth and Gosport to a depth of twenty miles inland. The Isle of Wight was included. Reinforcements arrived who had recently been called up. They were the conscripts who had for the most part been drawn most reluctantly away from civilian jobs and the cushioned domesticity provided by mother or wife. They must have thought us a strange species, as of course by comparison we were. For a start they would not understand our language, that pastiche of words and phrases from different continents together with technical terms which had become integrated into our own tongue. Most of these new arrivals put on a brave if resigned front and one or two who served in my detachment were later to display what I considered to be outstanding fortitude under harsh conditions. There was of course, a great difference in attitude. Just over a year ago I had been a recruit just as they were now. But whilst I wanted to be in no other place, they would almost have given their right arms to be somewhere else. Another thing I noticed. Some of these newcomers were much older than I was, older than the reservists, but the age gap no longer mattered. Like the old sweats, I had acquired a cynical attitude to orders but responded, I hoped, with the speed and efficiency of the professional.

It was whilst at Lyndhurst that I went up the ladder quite a step, for with effect from 1st July, 1940 I was promoted to Lance-Sergeant and my pay went up to 5s.3d. per day. As a Senior NCO I was entitled to more privileges and could now take my place in the Sergeants' Mess. There must always be a price to pay for 'life at the top', however, so to even things up a bit, more duties and greater responsibility came my way.

From Lyndhurst each Troop was sent in turn to patrol and to guard a chosen stretch of coastline. On the beach near Keyhaven two of us were on duty manning a Bren-gun from a slit trench when a Messerschmitt shot over at wave-top height and gave us a short burst or two. He was gone before we could retaliate. No holiday-makers would come to sprawl out, basking near the water's edge with such intruders about. They couldn't anyway, for Britain had become a fortress. The shores were fenced with barbed wire and planted with mines.

On August 3rd I wrote home: 'I am down on the beach again doing a guard every night with my six merry men. You know, the sort of stuff that in the papers is billed "Silent Vigil" or "Watchers of the Night".'

As far as I could see, if the Jerries did come they would be met by smocked country-folk brandishing pitchforks and scythes as they dropped from the skies in droves, ruthless and heavily armed; met by our uncoordinated small arms fire as they thrust inland with flame-throwers and mortars, from beaches already softened up a bit by the Stukas. It would be Sedgemoor re-enacted, only this time the hanging judge would be none other than Adolf Hitler.

We did a stint at Hurst Castle where we bedded down on groundsheets and blankets in the great bays or emplacements which in former days had held coastal guns. As i/c Guard I inspected sentries in the castle itself. They were staring out into the darkness, for it was particularly important to be alert during the night-time. I associate this memory with wind and rain, and as I went from one post to another, up stone stairways on to the battlements I thought it was on such a night as this that Banquo's Ghost should have made his presence felt.

It was at Lyndhurst that the Gun came into my life again. New guns started to trickle in, brand new ones at that. This new Mark II model, the 25pr. proper, looked as if He meant business. He looked less sleek, more aloof and arrogant as He stood on His metal platform.

Much foul language, heaving and sweating was removed with the introduction of the platform. There would be times when it slid or became tilted, or the spade, even with the box on, would get stuck. But there was no doubt at all that the platform was a great advantage.

Brigadier Bidwell has this to say of the new 25pr. field gun:

'The Mark II, taken all in all, was one of the best field guns ever made, and had in its final form a range of 13,400 yards, weighed 1¾ tons and was extremely well engineered.'

When I asked one of my colleagues, Sergeant Stoker, on the rate of fire, he thought that the average was about six rounds per minute, "providing we had not been drinking 'Jungle Juice' (rough vino with a drop or two of whisky added to liven it up) the night before."

It speaks highly for the technical efficiency which accompanied the planning, construction and testing of this gun, for the only significant change which took place in the whole of its service was the attachment of the Muzzle Brake, that curious but most effective device which was fitted to the end of the muzzle.

Charge 111 had previously been used with the 20lb Armour Piercing Shot, but as armour on German tanks increased in thickness it was proposed to use a more powerful propellant charge called Super Charge. Because of instability due to high recoil stresses, the Chief Superintendent of Armament Design suggested the employment of Muzzle Brakes. These first came into use in 1942.

As it took some time to manufacture and to distribute them for general use, they were fitted first on guns in areas where it was anticipated there would be armour to face. Muzzle Brakes were rarely seen in the Far East, and were never put on 25prs. of the Australian and New Zealand armies. I think ours came in 1942 and were almost certainly standard fittings when we went overseas.

Incidentally, guns suffered from a malady known as 'muzzle droop'. The test for 'muzzle droop' involved placing an instrument called a Field Clinometer on the muzzle and taking a reading. It needs little imagination to relate this imperfection in ordnance to human imperfection.

Later in the war, Sgt. Anstee, first mentioned at Dunkirk, was not above roaring out from afar as I was performing my natural function up against a tree, "Put the f . . . . g Field Clino on it Badge."

The Gun over which I had assumed guardianship, fourth in line from the right in the Gun-park, was so versatile that He could be used as a gun, howitzer or anti-tank weapon, with equal effectiveness in each role. He was entitled to even greater arrogance and aloofness.

Guns and limbers were towed by four-wheel drive artillery tractors or 'Quads', and were fitted with winches. Four manufacturers produced them, but the ones familiar to me were either Guy or Morris.

In July Lieutenant-General Montgomery, he who had commanded 3rd Division so ably in the BEF, became our Corps Commander. He was now in charge of two Divisions, the 4th and the 50th. By inimitable manipulation he had exchanged the 50th for his old 3rd Division by November. 3rd and 4th Divisions were now in one Corps as they had been in the BEF.

From July, 1940 to the end of April, 1941 we were dominated by this illustrious Commander. When he took over 12 Corps in Kent he was to write soon after his arrival there:

'I rather fancy I burst in Kent like a 15-inch shell and it was needed.'

He had the same effect on us. Never to be satisfied until he had beaten the Germans utterly, thus redressing the humiliation of Dunkirk, he devoted himself to training men in accordance with his own almost unattainable ruthless standards of efficiency. Motorized mobility at night was joined by several other innovations. But the means by which the pinnacle of achievement was to be reached was through fitness of the individual soldier.

"Military fit — mentally fit — physically fit," was what he preached and practised continually.

Runs before breakfast for all ranks became compulsory. Strange creatures such as storemen, clerks and cooks, blinking in the unaccustomed light and clad in gym kit which had lain dormant since the day of issue, shivered and protested in the chill of early morning. A greater complement of officers than ever before now obliged us with their presence. They also had no option but to obey the great man on high.

For the likes of me it didn't matter. We who were gunners in the strict sense always attended 'Roll Call'; were accustomed to physical training or a run before breakfast. I was a cross-country runner anyway. What I did not much care for was when we were required to wear gas masks on our morning airings. I hated this cumbersome apparatus which seemed to be fascinated by me and which gave the impression that it was following me about.

No matter how I treated the goggles with a special preparation they always steamed up. I could always get round this visionary problem by slipping my fingers surreptitiously under the mask and letting some air in, but it wouldn't be an action to recommend in a gas attack.

There was 'belly-aching' about the emphasis on fitness and a lot more on the introduction of gas masks. It was a paradox really for that which he had introduced he had also forbidden.

"Cannot be full of 'binge' if you are always 'belly-aching'. Too much of it in the Army. Stop it.

Must have 100% binge — No belly-aching."

We continued to keep watch over vulnerable installations such as power stations in case of sabotage, before we moved from the Southampton area to the village of Hambledon in Hampshire, a few miles inland from Portsmouth. The suspense which prevailed over the land of the southern counties where landings were awaited was now transferred to the air. In that late summer and early autumn of 1940, we in our encampment in restful pasture or parkland, watched dogfights taking place between the fighters of the Luftwaffe and the RAF, when the Battle of Britain was at its height.

Distant bursts of machine-gun fire were heard high above. The planes manoeuvred and dived, their engines roaring. When, as sometimes happened, an aircraft dived uncontrollably, smoke pouring from its tail, we strained to see whether it was one of ours or one of theirs.

I recall vividly that the Sergeants' Mess at Hambledon was in a marquee, hidden from the air by great trees, and there was a bar of sorts where beer was served. This was privilege and luxury indeed. Not only did Senior NCOs dine in privacy with waiters in attendance; they also indulged in a social life among themselves without needing to go elsewhere to find it. In this holiday setting, in the balmy evenings with nights already drawing in, I drank beer and played 'Pokey-Die' with Sergeant Jordan and others, whilst other young men of my age were failing to return from their missions in the skies above us. My close school friend was such a one, but I did not find out about it until two or three years later.

Sergeant Jordan, cynical and jaded by his years of service in unkind stations, was kindly disposed and introduced me to 'Pokey-Die' — Poker Dice, I suppose. Three dice were used, and the game followed certain simple rules. Sergeant Jordan was particularly pleased when he threw three Jacks. "Three Early Mornings," he would proclaim and his lethargic eyelids would rise in a gesture of enthusiasm which he never showed for anything else. We might have played for money or for beer, but whatever the stakes it was very pleasant and my pay had risen again so I could meet the cost. I liked Sergeant Jordan. He could very easily have resented my arrival in the Sergeants' Mess, for it must have taken him years in peacetime to reach the rank which I had just gained, but he greeted me and treated me like an equal. On my arrival or induction, so to speak, I had been required to buy drinks all round as was the custom, but I had been more than pleased to 'fork out'.

I was taught to drive. As well as taking instructions on a 15 cwt and a 'Quad', I was placed on a motor cycle and went chugging round a circuit, until I revved up too quickly and sped through tented areas placed in a wood. Avoiding tent-pegs, stays and even trees in my headlong flight, causing startled gunners to leap for safety, I came to rest in the latrines amidst a collection of large latrine buckets which had just been emptied. There was no damage to the machine and no physical damage to the rider, but there was much repartee from the troops.

Undeterred by my escapade, Authority turned me loose on the roads soon afterwards. We were now in training as gunners, and instead of going out with my detachment as No. 1, travelling in the security of the 'Quad', I went out as Acting Sergeant-Major. My duty was to supervise the convoy, see that vehicles kept their correct distance and direct traffic when necessary. I was also to lead the Troop on to its gun position. I was scarcely competent to direct or supervise myself. This unpredictable throbbing mechanism on which I clung, decided to accelerate yet again. I veered off to the left, crossed in front of a Quad, and shooting through an open gate conveniently placed, entered a field which as it happened was a pasture. I circumnavigated the field which was quite small and emerged from where I had entered, now in total control, and rejoined the convoy three guns lower down. I chugged past each gun to the derisory cheers of each detachment. It was better after that, although I always treated motor cycles with respect. If there was an accident whilst we were on the line of march it was more often than not a DR who was flattened against the bonnet of an oncoming vehicle, or flung headlong into the ditch. I lost a good friend like this, when he was shepherding the convoy at night.

Before winter we went into quarters at Purbrook not far from Waterlooville and nearer to Portsmouth. The situation had improved so much that we went on leave in batches, and my turn came before we moved. The Battery must have sent a telegram, for I was redirected, got off the train at the wrong station and found I had to make a forced march through the night. I humped my big pack along deserted country roads, which, by the faint light of a waning moon, looked to have wide level verges with woods beyond. I had only owls and woodland creatures for company, or so I hoped, for there was still talk of lurking enemy spies who were ready to attack the lone traveller. I felt very exposed, marching briskly along in my studded boots which rang on the metalled roads, trying to keep a good look-out. The grass verge was no good for walking on in that dim light and I was in a mighty hurry. I arrived in Waterlooville at dawn and was told how to get to Purbrook, a mile or two to the left, by a cook from HQ who was just going on duty. When I reported to the guardroom I was six or seven hours late and had been reported AWOL (Absent Without Leave). After listening to my explanation and after assessing the distance I had travelled Sergeant-Major Prior, our new Battery Sergeant-Major, spoke to the Guard

Commander and the incident was closed.

Field Regiments were reorganized. The lesson learnt during the withdrawal had shown that the three Troop formation had proved too unwieldy to manipulate with maximum efficiency. Now the best plan ever achieved was put into practice and stayed at least for the remainder of the war. 22nd Field Regiment now had three Batteries, 32nd, 33rd and 36/55th. Each Battery had two gun troops of four guns. The new Battery, the 33rd, which had separated from us was given 'C' Troop, whilst 'D' Troop was transferred from 36/55th. Other Battery personnel were provided from the old 32/33rd and from the 36/55th. Sergeant Jordan went with 'C' Troop as its Troop Sergeant-Major.

It was now obviously easier to find a suitable position for two, rather than three Troops controlled from one Battery Command Post. Smaller bodies provided greater flexibility. Not least in importance, as there were three infantry battalions in one infantry brigade, there could be more liaison between each of these and the three batteries of the Field Regiment, RA, which supported them.

Our new billets were very good, for we occupied what had been a private school for boys. Facilities for the other ranks included lines of wash-basins and lavatories. The Senior NCOs had plenty of living space in the main building. My room, which I shared with two or three others, looked on to the road and on to open fields. Some of us organized beds of sorts, but I didn't bother too much for I was young enough to dispense with finesse and sleep on the bare boards, I considered myself lucky to have a solid roof over my head for the winter.

We settled down to training in earnest both in the Gun-park and on exercises. Many a time we took our guns up to Portsdown Hill and practised dropping into action. I took gun-drill frequently and helped to integrate the recruits into our gun detachment. As usual a good deal of time was spent in cleaning and polishing the Gun and its equipment. A rigorous inspection took place once a week, usually on a Saturday morning.

By December we were firing live ammunition again at Okehampton Practice Camp, which I describe in a letter as a 'black expanse of moor', and which is about ten miles from Dartmoor Prison..

It was about this time that a 5 Corps exercise pioneered by Montgomery took place, when 1st Armoured Division temporarily replaced 3rd Infantry Division. Close support aircraft were used, as were paratroops for the first time. Some 30,000 troops were involved. 4th Division was required to travel on a night march of 30 miles across

Salisbury Plain. It got snarled up and came to a halt in the night until matters were sorted out.

Sir Alan Brooke 'had felt sorry for the poor 4th Division who, had had a bad night . . . stuck in the mud on the mock desert ranges.'

At 2 o'clock on a February morning of 1941 we were struggling with the Gun which had decided to slew off the track sideways into a deep ditch, and we had to winch it out. When it was comfortably placed we slept without cover in the chilling rain and our blankets and clothing were soaking wet. On this exercise we were on half rations.

It was also in the month of February, 1941 that Lieutenant-General Montgomery felt able to declare, "I am satisfied the 3rd and 4th Divisions can be classified as 1st Class Divisions and fit in every way to engage in battle with the Germans."

My grandmother, Elizabeth, died towards the end of the month and was laid to rest with her husband John, who had preceded her by a few years. I should have liked to have attended her funeral but it must be apparent that I was otherwise employed.

I came more into the company of Sergeant Anstee, he who had offered me a cup of char in a hut on the edge of the beach at Dunkirk, now L/Sgt. I think, like myself. He had joined the Battery in an intake of reservists at Shorncliffe. Anstee came from Banbury and was called 'Ban' by his buddies, but this became distorted to 'Bam'. His frequent boast was that he had served "three years (or was it six?) with the bastard Pack," for he had been with a Light or Mountain Battery in Egypt. The 3.7 howitzers of Mountain Batteries were carried by mules and were often called Pack Batteries because of the mode of transport. The mountain gunners were big and strong, as they had to lift the parts of the gun off the mules and assemble them in an amazingly short time. They also had to march very long distances at a very fast pace over difficult country.

John Masters in *Bugles and a Tiger* has this to say:

'On manoeuvres in 1939 one mountain battery covered seventy-three miles in twenty-three hours at a steady pounding trot; the men hung on to the mule saddlery or to the stirrups of the few horses.'

Anstee was larger than life, bigger than big, stronger than strong. He looked on with disgust whilst one young gunner was struggling to put back a gun wheel which was jacked up. The poor unfortunate, straight from an office job and small and weedy, tried his best but it was falling back on him. Anstee caught it and with a mighty clunk slammed it back on. The lad had to be transferred to the Signals section, where he could sit in a truck with his headphones on.

The blitz was warming up. There were frequent raids on the ports and Southampton and Portsmouth took a hammering. Parties of us would go down to Portsmouth to help in digging out those who were trapped or buried, and in clearing up the rubble. Someone had hit on the idea of putting up decoy lights in the open country in order to invite the German bombers to unload their bombs where it would hurt least. Whether it was as a result of this plan or whether we got the overspill from Portsmouth is open to speculation, but both bombs and land-mines began to fall round us and almost on top of us. Incendiary bombs were dropped. We turned out and were even known to crash our way into civilian property if it was untenanted at the time and was seen to be on fire.

One morning at Reveille after a prolonged raid on Portsmouth which had also kept us awake, I looked out of the window and saw an unfamiliar object sitting up in the field right opposite. It was a mine which had descended gently on its parachute and chosen that particular spot on which to rest. I gave the alarm and we were all soon astir and preparing to withdraw to a safer place. Should this great container of explosives decide to function there would not be much left of either us or the property. These devices were very sensitive and it was said that the vibrations from the engine of a car or those of an aircraft flying overhead could set them off.

There was a store of ammunition in the yard at the back. I was put in charge of loading a truck. As we were finishing off and I was standing on top of the boxes on the truck, supervising the stacking of the last layer, what should come into view but a light aircraft, flying quite low, proceeding on its amiable way right above the mine. It was as if Providence had chosen this opportunity to lift us to a Better Land. With bated breath I stood on the ammunition, whilst all round became motionless. The plane's engine receded, we finished our task and crept stealthily out of the rear exit with all our impedimenta. Some bold people must have come and removed the mine for we returned in a day or two and it was gone. It was not always so successful. In a churchyard not far from Purbrook are the graves of young men who perished whilst dismantling a bomb.

Another mine dropped on one side of us, about two hundred yards from the Gun-park. Where a copse had been there was only a huge smoking crater. Sgt. Burman, known as 'Swaz' because of his professed admiration for the Nazis which we all found amusing, was walking back from a country pub with me one night, when we saw something swinging in the branches of a tree by the roadside. In a previous age we might have been forgiven for thinking that it was the corpse of a felon, swaying in his chains. As we paused and looked more closely the metal container undulated gently and threatened to break away from the cords by which it was suspended.

The unflappable Swaz turned to me in speculative manner. "Badge," he drawled, "I don't know about you, but I don't like the look of that. I think we will put our skates on, *a tora jildee*."

With quickening footsteps, though not too quickly for Swaz was never known to run, except on one occasion when even he had been forced to take part in physical training before breakfast and had entered into the spirit of it with a marked lack of enthusiasm, we increased the distance between us and it. We thought it also was a mine, but only a little one.

With all these unpleasant things going on, with tales of injury and dying about me, and with what I had seen for myself, I no longer possessed the security and immunity of a year before. What happened to others could very easily happen to me. There were times now when I was frightened, very frightened, not just of being killed but of being maimed in some dreadful way. I began to wonder whether there was much chance of reaching old age, or indeed living much longer. From all appearances the war was going to last for years and it was inevitable that we would not be kept in England for ever.

At Christmas I went on leave again. Quite out of character, I went to a pantomime and was captivated by the Principal Girl. I discovered there was still a good deal of tinsel and glitter left in wartime England, as I edged my way through the crowds in the Tower Buildings. My amazement grew at the number of uniforms which milled all round me.

After relaxing in the comforts which were provided at home and after dropping in for a few jars at the local hostelries, I returned to my quasi-monastic life-style minus the religious trappings, in a totally masculine environment, to do a rough, tough job grappling with the Gun in all it humours.

'The mission bell told me that I mustn't stay,
South of the Border down Mexico Way.'

I needed a steady girl-friend who would write warm, sentimental letters to a poor bastard of a lonely soldier, but so far no one had fallen over backwards to respond to my charms.

Financial security had never been one of my selling points, although

I could claim that it was getting better. Now the uncertainty of my future was ever more pronounced. No prospective mummy-in-law, solicitous for the well-being of her daughter, would entertain one who pursued such a dangerous trade as mine. This was good really, for although I indulged in exquisite fantasies of intimate embraces in scent-laden bowers, these did not extend to the bridal chamber. The thought of a mother-in-law breathing her dragon's breath down my neck gave me cold sweats. I could, I suppose have enticed her to examine the Cannon when no one was about, then tied her over the muzzle and blown her apart with AP shot, as they did with enemies of the Raj in the Indian Mutiny.

The Sergeant-Major told me that my name had been put forward for an A i/G Course. I couldn't believe my luck, for to me the post of Assistant Instructor in Gunnery at the School of Artillery was a very prestigious post, and required considerable technical training. Ever since I had seen those Warrant Officers with the Crossed Guns and the white hat covers at Larkhill I had coveted their positions. After indulging in private dreams of grandeur for a few days I was informed that the application had been withdrawn as the Major had decided that I could not be spared. I suppose that it was nice to be wanted, but at that moment I could have survived without this apparent need for my services.

It may have been in consequence of the first of several 'flaps' or strong rumours that we were preparing for overseas which rippled round us for the next two years, or it may have been routine procedure which sent Bam Anstee and me one Saturday morning to the MI Room at HQ for inoculations.

After our 'jabs' we debated whether we should return to catch the tail-end of the inspection or whether we should drop off for a pint. We were both of the same mind, so we cadged a lift and were dropped off at the White Hart. The atmosphere was so snug, we found each other's company so convivial that Anstee and I, having already sunk several pints each, finished off with a few shorts. There was a good supply as it happened and it was too good to miss. When the doors closed we walked solemnly back to billets, our bearing so soldierly, our side-hats set at such a correct angle that we might have been on our way to mount the Regimental Guard under the scrutiny of the Regimental Sergeant-Major. Oncoming civilians were given the most courteous of wide berths.

On my way to bed, for it was Saturday afternoon and there were no parades, I dropped into the barrack room to mention some matter or other to my limber gunner. A young officer was enquiring whether anyone would care for a game of cricket. I was standing by the door and was just about to come to attention and reply when a great hand gripped my upper arm, (not the one which had been inoculated), a voice said, "Get to bed, you little bleeder," and I was whisked away into the wings like a pantomime fairy who had proved incompetent in the chorus line.

That evening I was sitting shivering over a glowing stove, with a blanket round me. My arm was swollen to such an extent that it threatened to burst open my shirt sleeve. It was blue and throbbing and I had a mighty thirst. Anstee came in dressed to go out and asked me if I was ready for a pint. I gulped at the thought, shivered even more, and in a weak voice declined his offer. I felt afterwards that he was disappointed in me and that he considered me a bit of a weakling.

A few weeks after my grandmother's funeral I went home for a few days and felt her absence keenly. My mother put on a brave front, as always, and managed to lure a chicken out of one of her contacts. She cooked it for me to take back.

There was an air raid when I arrived that night at Portsmouth and the train was kept waiting outside the station. When I did get off the train I went to a big air raid shelter. There were the usual fires and fire engines and the ambulances forcing their way through the debris when I put my head out to see what was going on. It seemed quieter, there was no transport and I had a stiff walk ahead. I thought I would chance it even though a few bombers droned overhead. The searchlights criss-crossed in the sky, trying to intersect on single aircraft, the flashes from the anti-aircraft guns coincided with their fire, and more to the point, bombs were still dropping on the city.

As I walked and ran alternately in an effort to get away as fast as I could, I heard that shrill, terrifying whine which heralded the approach of a missile. This one was very close, almost on top. I flung myself headlong. The bomb burst and a great weight fell on me. There was a dreadful sound of breaking bones in my back and I knew that this was 'curtains'. I lay still and waited for the end. The weight moved off my back and a stranger helped me to my feet, apologizing for having introduced himself in such an unconventional and abrupt manner.

I sped out of Portsmouth, my legs still functioning well, my arms working normally, my lungs seemingly unrestricted. How did one explain the breaking of brittle bones? It was not till I took the chicken out of my big pack which I had carried slung on my back that the mystery was explained. That fowl was already dismembered to such an extent that we sat round at midnight and picked out succulent slivers with our fingers. We finished off with a fruit cake, no less delicious because it had been reduced to crumbs.

Gunner Bowman on first leave from RA Depot Woolwich, May 1939

Gunner Bowman with the two Parkers, walking along the Leas, Folkestone, July 1939

Kit laid out for inspection, Larkhill 1939

Six-wheeled Morris tractor, drawing limber and 18-pounder Gun, Okehampton 1939

With my little cousin Shirley, immediately after Dunkirk, 1940

'Dearest love from Mother', June 1943

Bid in the dress she wore on Boxing Night 1942, the night we became engaged

The author, taken towards the end of 1942

With all my love, Bid, February 1944

A gun of 22nd Field Regiment RA, moving up through Tegoletta, Italy 1944 (Photo: Imp. War Museum)

A 25-pounder gun on training exercise, Libya, 8 March, 1942 (Photo: Imp.War Museum)

Troop in action, Adriatic sector, Italy, 18 April, 1945 — note long straight rows of pollarded trees, with vines trained between (Photo: Imp. War Museum)

October rains, Po valley, Italy, 1944 — 83/85th Field Battery RA, 11th Field Regiment RA, in action near Scorticata among the vines (Photo: Imp. War Museum)

266 Field Battery, RA, 67th Field Regiment, RA, south of S.Clemente, 2 December, 1944 (Photo: Imp. War Museum)

Author and Bid on their wedding day, 23 October, 1944

CHAPTER XII

In retrospect, a superficial and preliminary appraisal of the years 1941 and 1942, with the exclusion of two or three brief high spots, spell routine and at times boredom. Nothing seemed to happen. A deeper inspection, however, reveals that much did happen. There was such continuous activity that at times it seethed and boiled to such an extent that it was hard to keep pace.

Whether some of it was misdirected is debatable. Steady improvement which progresses towards an ultimate peak of achievement is the aim of all training. There comes a time when the examination must be taken, the race must be run or stagnation and boredom will lead to less successful results. It would appear that we had been ready to go overseas as a fighting division in early 1941. We had overcome most of the tactical drawbacks if not all, and had replaced the losses incurred in 1940. Due to the fluctuations of the battles in the Mediterranean Theatre and the subsequent alterations to plans which affected us, delays took place. By the end of 1942 we were on the borderline between the trained and the over-trained and it was time that we went.

We only moved three times during the two years. The precise date of the departure from one to the arrival at another is not important. To me an analogy from music would seem better to explain this symphonic movement by giving a broad outline, revealing the main sections, phrase structure and such salient features as interesting modulations, characteristic chords and possibly some idioms, rather than attempt a bar by bar analysis.

Before continuing it may be as well to interpolate a brief historical background concerning the unstable and often melancholy state of affairs from mid 1940 to the end of 1942. In August, 1940 Britain was still threatened with invasion of one kind or another. There were less than 100,000 troops in the Middle East. 36,000 of these were in Egypt, which was invaded by the Italians in September. The tension by then showed signs of easing at home and an armoured brigade was sent by the much longer route round the Cape to strengthen Wavell's forces.

British naval aircraft sank three Italian battleships in Taranto Harbour on 11th November. Between December, 1940 and February, 1941 Wavell defeated the Italians, destroying ten of their divisions. The slight hopes which were raised were short lived. The next few months were not good.

German forces entered the Mediterranean Theatre. Squadrons of their planes, operating from Sicily, threatened the Central Mediterranean. The Afrika Korps under Rommel was sent out to Libya. At the end of May there was a British defeat. More followed. In April British units withdrew from Greece almost as soon as they had entered, losing 12,000 men and much of the equipment. Crete fell in May, with 12,000 men taken prisoner. Three cruisers and six destroyers were lost. In another theatre the battleship HMS *Hood* was sunk, but we destroyed the *Bismarck*.

The Germans invaded Russia in June and we became Russia's allies. In the autumn an aircraft carrier and a battleship of ours became casualties. Two more battleships were put out of action by the Italians in Alexandria Harbour.

On 4th December the Russians stopped the Germans in their headlong drive on Moscow. Japanese bombers destroyed nearly all the American Fleet at Pearl Harbor on 7th December. On the 10th the battleships HMS *Prince of Wales* and HMS *Repulse* were sunk by Japanese bombers.

Up to now we had been on our own against Germany and Italy, with some help in equipment and supplies on the side from America. Now the Americans were our allies but we had additional commitments to meet in the Far East.

So far one telling punch had followed another and we were reeling from the blows. There seemed to be no respite, no chance to sink into the corner of the ring for a breather. Two more blows followed. The first one not only reduced our powers further, it also hurt our pride more than we chose to talk about in public.

When Singapore fell in February, 1942, it dealt such a humiliating and shattering blow to our prestige in the Far East that it is debatable whether we have ever recovered from it. 60,000 more men were lost to us. An abortive raid on Dieppe in August, which was a preliminary exploration on the feasibility of a seaborne landing, proved so unsuccessful that fresh decisions had to be taken. The Second Front, in spite of pressure from Russia and America, was delayed by two years, from 1942 to 1944, in favour of an Anglo-American landing in French

North Africa in November. The decision had a great influence on our own destiny, as a Division.

In June, 1941 General Wavell had been replaced by General Auchinlech who was in turn superceded by General Alexander. General Sir Bernard Montgomery went out to command the Eighth Army.

In January, 1942, after some ineffectual cutting and thrusting the British Army in the desert was pretty well where it had been in February, 1941 when General Wavell had defeated the Italians.

Now in August, 1942, Rommel's last attempt to break the British at El Alamein sixty miles from Cairo, had failed. Montgomery had arrived but took his time. When he did strike it was most effective. His conclusive battle against Rommel at El Alamein, begun on the night of 23rd October, lasted until 4th November. Rommel and his army retreated and for the time being escaped. It was, as everyone knows, a great victory for General Montgomery and his advance was to continue westwards through North Africa, through Sicily to Italy.

Three days after the Battle of El Alamein, on 7th November, there was an allied Anglo-American landing in French North Africa. These forces were to drive eastwards to join up with the Eighth Army. There were unexpected delays. For one thing the Germans had managed to establish themselves in Tunis.

The fighting went on until 12th May, 1943.

From Purbrook in November, 1941 we went to Blackwater, adjacent to and on the edge of Camberley in Surrey. 'A' and 'B' Troops were on the edge of Yateley near by. By mid-April of 1942 we were at Selkirk in the Border Country of Scotland. In August of the same year we had travelled to Milkbank near Lockerbie in Dumfrieshire where we stayed. These were our home addresses but we were fickle people, given to depart suddenly to distant places, Had the vicar called for afternoon tea so to speak, he would rarely have found myself and my detachment on the lawn to greet him.

We were wandering far afield, trundling the Gun behind us. Self-contained with all our luggage in our holiday coach for six, we enjoyed great vistas of English and Scottish countryside, from sweeping golden fields of standing corn to sleet lashed mountain peaks, from verdant pastures studded with farmhouses and great trees in full leaf to bleak, barren moorland in the mist. We would have seen a lot more had our superiors not had an obsession for transforming us into nocturnal animals. Monty had certainly caught on. Much of the time, most of it I should say, we journeyed from one place to another with our eyes glued on the vague shape of the Gun in front of us, for we had the minimum of light to help us, or none at all.

Then there was the snowstorm when we practised coming into action on a steep hillside. The trail flew up into the air when we unlimbered and the muzzle bit into the ground. Handbrake on we clung to the up-ended trail, our feet just off the ground, making spasmodic movements to bring it down again. Not content with this skittish behaviour the Gun tried His best to overtake the Quad as the whole equipment slid out of control down a steep incline covered with packed snow on which ice had formed. We all baled out to steady Him but He still tried to crash His master against a stone wall before He came to rest. The Bastard, when He was perverse like this I just could not bring myself to love Him.

There were other bastards who sat comfortably round polished tables, passing the port whilst they invented new games for their unlovely, roguish, coarsened, cynical children to play, to keep them occupied and sheltered from the evil of strong drink and naked women.

As if we had not experienced enough of the darkness, it was ordained at Camberley that night should be turned into day. Parades, training, drill all went on throughout the night and we were allowed to sleep during the day if we were lucky, for there were plenty of extraneous duties. An officer serving with the Battery tells me that the officers "had a pint in the local pub on the way to breakfast in the Mess at 8 p.m." One telling stroke followed another, another jolly jaunt was arranged. When the Nos. 1 heard it there was a loud outburst of foul language; when the gunners got to know it was said that the gods were so impressed by their invective that they responded with applausive flashes of lightning in the night sky.

I might add in passing, that care was taken to avoid bad language in the presence of officers. They, for their part, were consummate artists, skilled in knowing when to hear and when to overlook.

The cannons were dragged out on to a stretch of swamp land on which clumps of coarse grass grew and hid deep hollows. 'A' and 'B' Troop competed against each other over a course about half a mile long. Gunners heaved on the drag-ropes, shoulders were put to the wheels, and I and another, holding tightly on to each side of the trail were swung and snatched hither and thither as first one wheel and then the other hit obstacles or sunk into holes in the uneven ground. At the end of the race it was a matter of indifference as to who had won. We all sank to the ground, sweating, panting and exhausted.

I was already in training for the Regimental cross-country team. A day for two later I ran a gruelling race over a course in general use as a training ground for tanks and in places sank up to my knees in mud. I finished, but gained no place of distinction. In fact, I think the winner was an Oxford Blue. In addition I acted as Troop Sergeant-Major for a spell and attended a Small Arms Training Course at RHQ, when I fired rifle, Bren, anti-tank rifle, tommy-gun and service revolver and threw grenades

During a short period during the previous summer I had found time for sunbathing and swimming at the outdoor baths at Cosham. Now the tempo had increased, although in all fairness outdoor bathing would not have been attractive, for we were at Camberley in winter and there was snow and biting cold. I must not deny that occasional pub crawls or an occasional visit to the cinema in Camberley relieved our curricula. One evening I dropped into a pub for a night cap in an area occupied by troops of a Scottish infantry battalion. There had been some ancient feud between it and the gunners which had lingered on. I looked round and saw that I was a lone gunner amidst strangers. One of them came up and upturned a glass on the counter, a sure sign of trouble. I edged away to get my back against a wall when who should walk briskly in through the door but 'Grease' Earle. He had saved me again. It was uncanny how he always happened to be there when I was in a tight spot or was going to be 'roughed up'. The infantry didn't fancy tackling two of us, or rather three, for 'Grease' Earle counted for at least two ordinary folk, or more, if it came to a rough-house.

Whilst still at Purbrook in August, 1941, we had been again to Okehampton Practice Camp in Devon on the edge of Dartmoor. No doubt we had travelled through the night, arrived tired and hungry and after a snatched meal, gone straight on to the ranges, where it would usually rain. Dartmoor attracted mist and rain and the gun-fire aggravated the low clouds even more.

As well as shooting off some HE we engaged dummy tanks with AP shot. Tex Bell was my gun-layer and we made a good team. We hit a tank with the first round. On another occasion a Sergeant was unfortunate in that he had 'fired off for line', contrary to directions relayed through the Command Post, and the shell had burst in forbidden territory. He was suspended from duty, but I forget what the sequel was.

When we came off the ranges we always 'boiled out'. Our evening meal was usually preceded or succeeded by a meeting of officers and senior NCOs, to iron out the successes and failures of the day's shoot.

I remember the Sergeants' Mess at Okehampton, if only for the arresting photographs of former occupants of the Mess which hung on the walls. Carefully posed in their blue patrol uniforms, they looked grimly and reproachfully down on us as we ate our soya links and powdered egg. They were moustached to a man and their pill-box hats were tilted at just the correct angle of dominance and authority. What impressed me most of all was their size. They were surely giants abroad in those days. Their arms were folded across bulging chests, showing the great broad stripes of their rank. I finished my breakfast and slunk away, feeling small and insignificant in their presence.

At the School of Artillery, Larkhill, two months later in mid-October, 1941 we had taken part in a Divisional Shoot using all 72 guns, and there was a great noise. Was this to practise bringing fire rapidly on an 'Uncle' target, a procedure introduced recently? Quite apart from the reward of being able to fire the Gun instead of pretending, whilst we were acting as Depot Battery, working under the instruction of officer cadets who were giving the fire orders, there was a greater pleasure awaiting me. I had 'pulled my gun'.

On Battery Orders there appeared the following statement:

L/Sgt. Bowman J. E. promoted to Sergeant.

I had gained my 'Three Stripes and a Gun', and was from now onwards a full sergeant, the youngest in the Battery by a few years. I was rewarded in the usual way. That same night saw me in charge of a Guard which consisted of: 1 Sergeant, 1 full Bombardier, 1 L/Bombardier, 12 Gunners. Such is fame.

Towards the end of May, 1942 we were on the ranges at Redesdale Camp in Northumberland. Whilst at Milkbank we frequently visited the temporary ranges at Beattock between Lockerbie and Moffat. In January, 1943 we practised anti-tank shoots on the Solway Firth.

CHAPTER XIII

The Division began to move to Scotland in March, 1942 to join the 1st Army and to prepare for a seaborne landing with an Expeditionary Force. Soon there was another change of plan which was to set us back. The Division was ordered to reorganize as a 'mixed' division. The 21st Army Tank Brigade with its Churchill tanks replaced the 11th Infantry Brigade, which went to 78th Division. The integration of infantry and tanks took longer than was expected and an accepted standard of readiness, reviewed at intervals, took some time to achieve.

The implications and repercussions behind these comings and goings, this casting off and putting on, were not divulged to us. We were aware only that we were being hammered into the ground with training, and rumours of assignments ebbed and flowed so much that we become immune. 'Wolf' had been cried so often that when the time came in early 1943 we were still sceptical. On February, 1943 the Divisional History pronounces:

> 'After a while practice of any kind becomes wearisome,
> and the man in training longs to use his hard won skills.'

This statement only echoes what many of us had been feeling since the beginning of 1941.

Two Gas Courses were included in my curriculum in 1941/42. Why on earth I should have been selected for this non-starter I have no idea, except possibly it was less trouble to send me instead of one of the older ones who had no inclination to settle down to study. Maybe my superiors thought that I had a Pass in School Certificate Chemistry and was therefore an ideal choice for the study of gases. I could have told them that it was in a state of bewilderment that I had taken the exam, and that I had forgotten everything that I must have known immediately afterwards, and forever.

The first course was at Woolacombe, not far from Ilfracombe, and it was in October, 1941. I was billeted in a house which had been commandeered and which overlooked the sea. The resort, as deserted as such places are out of season, was even more desolate because of the war.

I returned to my unit unimpressed. I had crept in and out of confined spaces wearing my gas mask. Sometimes, if the stuff being demonstrated wasn't lethal, I was ordered to take off my mask and inhale some of it. One lot made my eyes stream and ache, another lot got at my chest or my throat and all of them put me off my grub.

It was with considerable chagrin and a lot of curses aimed, *sotto voce*, at my leaders that I went to report to the Army Gas School towards the end of November, 1942. Glenridding is at the southern end of Lake Ullswater. Unlike everyone that I have ever met, the Lake District has a depressing effect on me, mainly I suppose, because it always rains when I go there. I was depressed at the atmosphere of the school itself. The instructors had entrenched themselves and were there for the duration. A contingent of young women called ATS danced attendance upon them. Very compact cliques had been formed so that we birds of passage with the hungry, searching eyes and the ruffled plumage were given only disdainful glances by the groups of doves cooing over their 'chars and wads' in the canteen.

Once more I stooped into chambers, snorting through my mask; once more I sniffed out characteristic odours, suffered the old symptoms, only this time there were more and it was worse. My psychopathic fantasy rose to the surface. It rises more frequently as I get older and see on television the hordes of vicious youths and I yearn to help the police. How I longed to run up my 25pr. and through open sights, blast the whole bloody lot of gas chambers with HE.

We had to prepare and deliver a series of lectures and to instruct on specific topics, following patterns laid down by the school. It was an intensive course and there was little spare time. The Army is very good at such courses and knows how to achieve maximum efficiency in minimum time. You stick at it relentlessly and emerge amazed at your own capabilities. At least I learnt lessons here which I was able to apply to advantage in a different environment a few years later. I would have welcomed a more suitable subject but it was a challenge. No doubt self-conceit and showmanship played their parts when I addressed groups of my fellow students and enjoyed it. Whether they did is another matter. It goes without saying that we were assessed on every phase of the course.

I was awarded an 'A' and was told that I would be welcomed as an Instructor at the Gas School. Now I had a chance to infiltrate the groups of doves and coo with the best of them.

I was not attracted. There was a very special dovecote in Preesall not far from my home, in which lived a turtle-dove with the sleekest feathers and brightest eyes. I had no mind to linger here. Had it been Gunnery instead of Gas it would have been hard to have made up my mind. As it was there was no doubt as to what my answer should be. Anyway, I was pretty sure that if my Regiment were approached the answer would be a terse and final "No". Or did Army establishments have more pull? I never found out.

Without a backward glance I returned to Milkbank. Shortly afterwards I was summoned before the Colonel. He dwelt, aloof and remote, at Regimental HQ and only appeared unexpectedly in a flash of lightning like a pantomime devil, to hurl thunderbolts of invective at his junior officers and senior NCOs.

I bliffed myself up and presented myself at the great house, since demolished I believe. It was with some trepidation that I was shown into his august presence, for I had not been told what this interview was about. There was only time for an impressionistic glance but the Colonel seemed to live in Edwardian splendour surrounded by *objets d'art*, as a super-being should. It contrasted very favourably with the Nissen hut in which I lived with about twenty others, down there in the dampness by the river. I didn't care about that, for he was the Colonel and had earned his position and perks.

I came to attention. He looked up from his papers, gave me the usual short, piercing stare which saw everything, and congratulated me on my success on the Gas Course. The interview was ended. I thought that he might bring up our last meeting, when he had materialized to call me "a bloody ape".

We were out on a stunt, chugging up a hill, ready to pull off the road on to the ranges to come into action. The Quad was boiling over. A fault had developed in the engine, quite suddenly, and we were making steam in a big way. This forbidding figure sprang in front of us about ten yards away, with arms upraised. It was the Colonel. The hatch of the Quad was open and I was standing up, looking out. The Quad stopped when I gestured to the driver with my hand.

The figure beckoned. It was my turn to spring out of the hatch like a golliwog when the catch on the box is released, leap off the bonnet and run towards him. Like a ramrod I stood before him and delivered a salute which would have been the envy of Woolwich. It cut no ice.

The Colonel interrogated me in elementary chemistry. I could not escape from this chemical albatross hanging round my neck.

"You bloody ape," barked the Colonel, "what is that?" He pointed to the Quad which was standing as if ready to charge, with great snorts bursting from its nostrils. I overlooked his unkind reference.

"Steam, Sir," I replied.

"And what causes steam?" he asked, in a controlled voice charged with menace.

"Boiling water, Sir," I answered respectfully, wondering whether there was some catch in this and that I had given the wrong answer.

To my surprise he lost interest immediately and motioned to me to continue. I couldn't see where I was at fault, but ours not to reason why. If there was one discipline that surmounted all others and which was inflexible it was that the Gun must be got into action and firing. It was the sole and ultimate purpose of our existence to get that Gun into position as quickly and as efficiently as was humanly, or superhumanly, possible.

This was what I was doing. We rushed onwards, still snorting, and were soon firing.

Up the line of guns a far more serious misdemeanour took place. A Gun had been fired with the 'stops, running back' still attached. This projection was bolted to the rear of the recoil system, to stop it from sliding back and off its bearings when the hydraulic pressure had been reduced whilst it was inspected or repaired. These cannon were complex machines, designed and manufactured by expert engineers, but parts needed replacing and the hydraulic system kept under surveillance by both artificers and gunners. You didn't just slam a round up the spout and hope for the best or you might find yourself flying through the air with some parts missing.

Someone had blundered. No one was infallible but guns are dangerous things to play about with. This time there were no casualties. I never had the misfortune to fire a gun with a 'stops, running back' in place, but I should have thought there would be a very nasty noise and a terrible jolt especially with Charge III. It would be a job for Field Workshops.

One man's gain is another man's loss. 'F . . . your luck, chum, you shouldn't have joined.' The spotlight was taken off me, on to another. The Sergeant-Major tore me off a strip in private for poor maintenance and my driver got a bigger one torn off by me. The can was passed. Honour was satisfied.

The ears had been tuned, the grapevine had been at work. In the Sergeants' Mess they thought it was a great joke and went on about 'bloody ape' for days.

'In October, 1941 the Division began a long period of intensive training punctuated by equally intensive flaps.' (History of Fourth Division.)

Cadres, or small selected groups, were sent to Inveraray in Argyllshire for training in combined operations. I went with a few others from my Battery. It may well have consisted of senior NCOs and a few officers who were to learn the business of embarking and disembarking to and from landing craft, with a view to acting as unit instructors later. This was in late February and early March of 1942. We went by train and passed through Preston Station at four o'clock in the morning.

At Inverarary we lived on board a ship anchored on Loch Fyne. I have an idea that this vessel was called the 'Ettrick' or the 'Ettrick Shepherd' — or was that the name of a pub? It was bitter weather with frozen snow lying thick on mountains and roads.

One event remains vivid in my memory. We loaded a Quad, limber and gun on to an MLC, a Motor Landing Craft. It was very small in comparison to a TLC, or Tank Landing Craft. The underside and engine of the Quad had been waterproofed. A long pipe was attached to the exhaust. It ran vertically up the back of the vehicle and reached level with the roof. The same treatment had been given to my motor cycle.

I practised loading the equipment, using hand signals specially devised and understood by every driver. As can be imagined, some tricky situations were apt to arise when carrying out such manoeuvres, and accidents happened. Once loaded, the wheels were either blocked or shackled and the Navy took us out on to the loch. Half-way across, in choppy water, enclosed by a mist which cut down visibility to a few yards, one or other of our three wheeled-vehicles slipped and we listed to one side. The angle was not drastic but it was sufficient to give us a few uncomfortable minutes. None of us fancied a dip and there was no rescue craft that we knew of.

We grounded in the shallows and the ramp was lowered. I went off first on my motor bike and dropped into two or three feet of icy water. Using my legs and my throttle I struggled up the slope which was gentle enough but covered with packed snow and ice. We got the Gun off, after the Quad had objected a little, in spite of the power of its four-wheel drive. I led us home round the edge of the loch in a snowstorm. It was not the easiest of rides, partially blinded by the blizzard and slithering all over the insecure uneven surface. I fell off two or three times but the driver of the Quad was careful to keep his distance. We were all glad to get back into the warmth and comfort which the ship provided.

There was one other time, maybe more, when at least one section of us went to Rothesay and Dunoon with our own guns and vehicles to practise loading and unloading on the big TLCs with the great ramps in the bows. I cannot trace exactly when this was.

CHAPTER XIV

Tex Bell continued to come on leave with me, missing once or twice when he had an urge to visit London where a mate lived and there was more going on. We played hard in our own ways to compensate for the spartan privations we normally endured.

My mother looked on, saying very little, but with inward consternation when we unleashed our high spirits. At a dance, for instance, at Hambleton Reading Room (a misnomer if ever there was one for no one read there in my day) Tex and I startled the wallflowers and matrons-cum-chaperones by marching on to the dance floor during a lull in the dancing and coming to attention before the Master of Ceremonies. There was nothing outrageous in this act in itself were it not for the fact that we also clinked a sack of bottles behind us. Had this happened at the Church Sunday-school up the road, the officials there would have unfrocked us and torn off our epaulettes for unseemly behaviour.

An unknown benefactor slipped a half-bottle of rum into the pocket of my greatcoat, as I stood at the bar of the Seven Stars Hotel in Stalmine. Making my way home on foot along the unlit road I discovered this gift of a lifetime and tried it to see if it were indeed real and not an hallucination. One nip led to another. When I arrived home my mother who was ironing, or as she would call it, 'smoothing', noticed that some unidentified trailing plants decorated the bottoms of my slacks and that my shoes were wet.

Next day as she delivered her letters one of her clients or customers had a tale of woe to tell. An unknown animal, presumably a vicious or hungry one, had tried to knock off her goldfish and played hell with her lily pond. She wished she could lay her hands on it.

Once or twice those lads of the neighbourhood and particularly those in outlying villages who were not anxious to show friendliness towards us, would make snide comments. They operated in packs and were I suppose, like other animals, jealous of guarding their territories. One of these rustics emerged temporarily from the cloud which engulfed him to enquire, "What them was on my arm?" I said they weren't bloody banana skins, a standard enough answer, and showed him very quickly that there was a bit of power under them.

All in all though, we had a great time with the favourable lads who were left. Their number was diminishing and some were already abroad fighting and a few were already dead.

On 1st May, 1942 two or three cronies and I cycled to the Bourne Arms Hotel at Knott-End-on-Sea, six of seven miles away. Knott-End sits right on the edge of the River Wyre, opposite Fleetwood. A resident who had spent a lifetime in Knott-End was assured of a simple epitaph on his tombstone, 'He was born, he lived and he died'. The air purified constantly by winds which swept in over the Irish Sea had such health giving properties though that people seldom died. They only appeared to have done so. There was hardly any sign of life. All activities seemed to be carried on strictly behind closed doors.

That night I was in civvies, for there was no one to bother about such little details. I wore my navy blue suit with matching shirt and tie and was, as one might expect, very presentable.

It had been a mild, friendly session. We were making our way back when we saw that there was a dance in progress at the Parochial Hall in Preesall. Inside there were several chaps that I knew and Arthur was playing in the band, the same one in which I had played before I joined up. It was the usual village hop, with no one swinging from the chandeliers, no satyrs with goats' feet, no Bacchanalian characters with vine leaves in their hair.

There was this girl I had my eye on. She was small and well made — what you would call bonny. She was fresh and neatly dressed, had the most beautiful eyes, and her dark hair glowed with vitality. It was her eyes which gripped me and I wasn't normally an 'eye' man. They were warm and inviting, but when they glanced anywhere else, you knew that they took in everything.

I asked this young lady for a dance and behold, she accepted. She was nice and cuddly to hold and furthermore she could dance. As I swung her round I tried to disguise the fact that I had taken a drink or two, and my efforts must have been successful or she chose to ignore it, for we danced again — and again. She would know though, for I was soon to find out that she missed nothing. It was arranged that I should see her home.

After the last waltz I went to pick up my bicycle and waited for her in the drive. Everyone was coming out at once and I thought I had missed her, for she never came. Just as I was moving off I heard her tiny feet tapping on the hard path, and up she came running. It was only afterwards I found out that she was with her aunt and had to ask permission which had never previously been given. It was this concession, and the happy outcome to that confusion in the drive that decided not only our own destinies, but the existence and destinies of several others.

I walked her a few hundred yards to a gateway almost opposite where she lived. She couldn't stay long but there was enough time to write out my address on some scrap of paper or other which I had in my Pay book. There was no chance to continue our acquaintance for I was back at Selkirk the next day, and within three weeks I was at Redesdale Camp on the ranges.

Meanwhile, I was delighted (and possibly surprised) to receive a letter. I now had a pen-friend, a new dimension, an extraneous interest to occupy me. I found that my girl-friend was just about to celebrate her eighteenth birthday, and that she was still only seventeen on the night we had met.

It was in September that I had my next leave, after we had moved to Milkbank. I polished up the buttons on my 'blues' and set out to Preesall on the bus. I had discovered that Miss Joan Nield lived with her aunt and uncle, and that her uncle was Headmaster of the village school and quite a local dignitary. As her aunt was in failing health and could not get about well, Miss Nield kept house and acted as companion. She had a mother and father in Cheshire and no less than six brothers and five sisters. Here was I, who had really wanted an attachment with an orphan with no relatives at all to please, and thought I had found one, surrounded and in danger of being stifled by this formidable retinue. Furthermore, it had not escaped me that if I pursued this course I might end up with not one mother-in-law, but two. Christ!

Still, Joan and I got on well. She had a sense of humour, which was of paramount importance. I took her to Blackpool and Tex and another friend accompanied us for a while. We all had an hilarious ride in a landau along the promenade from the North Shore to the Pleasure Beach. We went on a machine where we were enclosed in a cabin which rotated in all directions. High in the air it went, then down into the depths, spinning all the time. Joan clung on to me and gave what I hoped were cries of delight. The more it spun the more she clung and the happier I was. We had a meal and I took her home. I was with her the next day — and the next. Poor old Tex was left to his own devices on that leave.

On the night before I returned to Milkbank, Joannie and I strolled through woods near Parrox Hall, and beyond into a cornfield, lying golden under the harvest moon. It was a perfect night for lovers' meetings, a silent moon-blanched night in which we alone existed. Remember, I was the expert on moons.

I had lain under harvest moons before; under rising, waning, new, half and gibbous moons, but my companions then had been hard and made of steel, whilst this one was warm and responsive. The stooks of corn were inviting so we dallied awhile in their shelter. The Gun was far from my thoughts. She, sulking up there in the Gun-park at Lockerbie would have to play second fiddle to my affections from now on.

Once or twice in a lifetime there is a fleeting spell which one would like to capture and suspend in Time. This was such a one I should wish to have frozen in Eternity, this precious moment when we lay side by side, moon-kissed, outside the abnormal, artificial conditions imposed by war, as are the figures in Keats' *Ode on a Grecian Urn*. She with her rounded arms snow-white around me, her almond face with the smiling lips and tiny teeth of pearl, she with the gentle considerate ways. I wanted to stay always just like this, and be with her.

'Fair youth, beneath the trees, thou canst not leave
Thy song, nor ever can those trees be bare;
Bold Lover, never, never canst thou kiss,
Though winning near the goal — yet, do not grieve;
She cannot fade, though thou hast not thy bliss,
For ever wilt thou love, and she be fair!'

Next morning I went to say goodbye. It was a difficult parting, and she cried. I felt like crying, but unlike the Elizabethans who are said to have had no inhibitions about showing their feelings in this extrovert way, I refrained. Aunt and Uncle had treated me well. Aunt had some very good qualities and was generous. There were indications, however, that she had a mind of her own and liked a lot of her own way. I had a natural inclination to retaliate with people like that and I foresaw that there might be a clash now and again. If I gave way she would have me for breakfast. I didn't think she would though.

Back I went to Milkbank, to Dryshod, to the Gas Course, the Gun-park, training for myself and training for others. Come Christmas and I was back home again. Joan and I went from one place to another, over-eating (I had some leeway to catch up on) dancing, going to shows and revelling generally. If the truth were told a drink or two came into it as well.

'South of the Border, down Mexico Way,
That's where I fell in love, when stars above,
Came out to play.
And it was fiesta and we were so gay,
South of the Border, down Mexico Way.'

The sands were running out. When I got back to Milkbank on 31st December 1942 people were already preparing to go on embarkation leave. From my diary I see that it was very cold. Sunday 3rd January, (1943) Frost prevails. The guns are frozen. Regimental Orderly Sergeant. Mounted the Guard. Tuesday 5th January. Blasted cold. Probably it will snow. Covered the Gun with several layers. It should not take any harm. Acting BSM today. Wednesday 6th January. Beattock Ranges today — at OP. v. cold. Letter and gloves from Joan waiting when I got back. Mounted Regimental Guard again. Saturday 9th January. Prepared Gun for anti-tank shoot. Trouble with sights. Raining like hell. What a dump. Only ray of sunshine is letter from Joan. Sunday 10th January. Anti-tank shooting on Solway Firth. Quite successful. Nearly blew my ears off, as usual. Battery Orderly Sergeant — mounted guard. Big leave party back. Monday 11th January. Laying drill. PT in gym. Shorts and vest. Took equipment lecture. Took weapon training — Bren. Tuesday 12th January. Took Gun to have trail-eye bracket removed and repaired. Thursday 14th January. Battery route march. Steady 12 miles before noon. 'Pulled Back' (i.e. pulling back the piece to test the recoil system for air and oil — strenuous task, like playing tug-of-war with a Gun). Loaded limbers. Saturday 16th January. Raining. Don't fancy the idea of Beattock Ranges tomorrow. Sunday 17th January. Took Cannon to Beattock Ranges. Fired 52 rounds HE. Quite interesting. Could see fall of shot. Back at 17.30 hrs. Boiled out. Battery Orderly Sergeant at night. Monday 18th January. Maintenance all day. Dismantled whole breech mechanism.

All this time there were frequent letters from Joan, or Bid as I now called her. It had been Biddy at first, but often it became shortened to Bid. My mother, who also wrote regularly had kept me supplied with food parcels and articles of warm clothing right from the start. Now with Bid, and sometimes her aunt, what had been steady, single rounds of gunfire increased to a constant bombardment of goodies. I was pampered.

On Thursday, 21st January, I left camp at 17.00 hrs to go on embarkation leave. Tex was with me, for he had a girl-friend in the village. We marched four miles to Lockerbie, caught the troop train, arrived at Preston at 50 minutes past midnight and got home about 6 in the morning.

I stayed at Joan's place quite often. We did the usual rounds. *Old Chelsea* at the Winter Gardens — danced at the Winter Gardens — had a meal in Blackpool — *Belle of New York* — walked to Knott-End and back along the shore.

We were not always rushing about, however. There were warm, snug evenings when we stayed in and talked about what we would do when the war was over. The salon and the chaise-longue, I thought, matched more the feline charms of little Miss Nield, rather than the sports arena and the hurdles, over which sprang angular women with heavily muscled thighs. There were other good things to discover, more mundane, but satisfactory nevertheless. She was already an expert housekeeper and an excellent cook. Who needed more?

We had our photos taken together. Bid wore a frock with a lace collar which I called her Puritan frock. The mischief in her eyes detracted somewhat from the demure appearance which it gave her.

On the Tuesday I took Bid home and on the Wednesday, the 27th, we became engaged. She was wearing a black velvet dress, and looked very beautiful, for black suited her.

'The mission bells told me that I couldn't stay,
South of the Border, down Mexico Way.'

It was with a heavier heart than I had ever felt that I bade farewell to my mother, aunt and uncle and to my fiancée.

In the background, ever present, whether at table, theatre, bar, or on dance floor, we had known that soon there would be the inevitable to face. I left Bid at 22.15 hrs on Friday, 29th January, and was back in Milkbank by 09.30 hrs on the Saturday. This time there had been no tumbling into a carriage, full of ale and with spirits bolstered. The table in the waiting-room at Preston Station was very familiar to me, for I had slept on it many a time whilst waiting for the main line express. This occasion must have been a particularly painful one, for spirits are lower in the early hours and mine were already below zero.

The unasked question uppermost as we held each other and said "Goodbye" was, "When shall we meet again?" There was another, far more sinister, whispered by a malevolent devil figure, leering in the shadows.

"But will you ever meet again?" it asked.

PART FOUR

North Africa
Egypt 1943 — Early 1944

For 'er sentries we stand by the sea an' the land
Wherever the bugles are blown.
(Poor beggars! — an' don't we get blown!)
Take 'old o' the wings o' the mornin',
An' flop round the earth till you're dead;
But you won't get away from the tune that they play
To the bloomin' old rag over'ead
(Poor beggars! — it's 'ot over'ead!)
The Sons of the Widow by Rudyard Kipling

CHAPTER XV

My search for adventure, experience and advancement, begun four years ago when I took the King's Shilling, now entered its fourth phase. I arrived at the port of Greenock from Lockerbie on 28th February, 1943. Here I was left in charge of a party of about a dozen men. Our task was to help in loading on to a freighter our Regiment's vehicles, equipment and the twenty-four guns which formed our complement, and to travel with them. During the voyage we were to man and operate the anti-aircraft guns. Technically I was responsible for everything which concerned 22nd Field Regiment RA, and once on board was answerable to the ship's Captain. All other personnel of our Regiment, I learnt later (for we were told as little as possible) travelled on a troopship which was much faster.

Our ship was the *Empire Rowan*, a 'Liberty' ship of some ten thousand tons. The place for which we were destined had not been revealed but it was pretty certain that we were bound for some distant foreign shore. It had not escaped me that there was a real possibility that I might not return. I had been engaged to be married for just one month.

At first we were housed in wretched billets on shore, in a most depressing insalubrious area near the docks. The food was some of the worst we had ever encountered. We worked long shifts in our roles as supernumerary dockers. Why did the union not protest? Sometimes we were kept at it through the night, once from 02.00 hours until 13.00 hours, a strange allotment of time, surely arranged by a particularly viperish overseer. Great arc lights illuminated our progress as we went about our unaccustomed duties. The huge empty holds rung hollowly as load after load was lowered down by cranes and manoeuvred into position.

As the ship filled, with every space utilized by experts, the reverberations of metal on metal became more and more subdued. We laboured for about a week. Our own not inconsiderable bulk of cargo went into one corner. Lines and lines of other vehicles and stores disappeared below. I was most astonished at and impressed by the bulk of goods which could be stored on a vessel of this size; and could not attempt to assess the value, although I knew it must be great. I was not slow to note that there were a great many drums labelled 'High Octane Fuel', cases of bombs for aircraft, shells for many calibres of guns, and assorted high explosives. All were slung below and eventually battened down. The fact that we lived and slept right on top of this giant explosive device was not conducive to greater repose later on, in the open sea, when U-boat packs gathered round and enemy aircraft threatened us.

Our work done as stevedores, we went on board and were given a cabin to share aft. My Certificate of Service states that from this day, 10th March, 1943, I became a member of the BNAF, the British North Africa Forces. Now we began to experience supreme luxury. Each of us had a comfortable bunk in this snug, warm place. Our food was, to us, of the highest order. Tea, coffee and sugar were in abundance. Hot meals came regularly from the galley. One memorable dish was an immense apple pie served in a great rectangular tin, at least six inches deep. Our compliments went to the chef. We even had a beer ration, cigarettes and tobacco.

We set sail after standing off-shore for a day. Ireland was visible on the port bow, the Mull of Kintyre on the starboard. Sixty ships, at least, had been collected in our slow convoy. Destroyers shepherded us on the perimeters as we headed out to the open Atlantic. Immediately, I was ordered to organize watches. Throughout the voyage we went on watch for four hours and 'stood down' for four, occasionally eight hours. This procedure continued with such regularity that it became monotonous and very tiring. We gunners manned the Oerlikons, the twin-barrelled guns used mainly against aircraft which were mounted round the boat-deck and at other strategic points.

On my twenty-third birthday, 17th March, we were five hundred miles out in the Atlantic Ocean, tossed about by a storm which was to last for days. Our vessel rolled and heaved and lurched about. Some of us were seasick, but I still managed to address my meals with enjoyment, probably because they were too good to miss. Over on our port beam was a very strange looking craft. She stood very high in the water and could have been mistaken, on a hazy day, for a large, dumpy, old-fashioned bath-tub. She tossed and reeled all ways, up and down, side to side, fore and aft. it made one queasy to look at her. She was a flak-ship. Later, under aerial attack, this gallant little tub burst out in one crazy firework display. She dropped down in the water with an alarming jerk from the downward thrust of the concentration of fire-power on board. Even under such an ordeal we had to laugh. We speculated that the whole crew must have been one mass of bruises and beset by frightful digestive troubles.

On our own stern was mounted a peculiar cannon. It looked like a prize from some distant Asiatic war which had been requisitioned as a desperate last resort for use at sea. There was a rack beside this quaint piece of ordnance which contained solid shells, deeply corroded. As Master Gunner responsible for the protection of the ship, or so I understood, I was required to organize a practice shoot, so that should a U-boat surface across our rear end we could 'poop off' at it. I posed myself the questions: How would these ill-maintained projectiles behave when rammed up the rifling of the cannon? Or was there rifling? It was so obviously the relic of bygone wars. I peered down the piece from the muzzle end. It looked very dank and corroded down there, when it should have gleamed. If there was rifling it had almost worn away.

Two or three packing cases had appeared ready to be thrown over the stern by some super-optimist, as targets to be blown to pieces, as would the submarines which would eventually emerge from the deep and present themselves. There were no sophisticated sights to be mounted. The ship was rising and falling about thirty feet from lowest to highest point. We should have to summon from the shades some veteran Gunner who had served at Trafalgar, to establish anything like a hit under such conditions and with this equipment. I tried in desperation to communicate telepathically with Sergeant Artificer Bickle. There was silence. Fate stepped in, though unfortunately I cannot remember in what guise. Was it that the breech was seated with rust, thus preventing the loading of this antique weapon? Was it that there were no cartridges to supply propulsive power? Was it a muzzle-loader and was the ramrod or powder mislaid? Whatever the reason, we were certainly saved from being 'hoist with our own petard', possibly blowing up the ship and part of the valuable convoy in the process. Submarine commanders conning us through periscopes ceased to tremble, as we ourselves did. The embarrassing packing cases were returned to their lodging. I was confident with my own cannon, on land, but these strange encounters with grotesque ordnance, in bizarre circumstances in unaccustomed places tended to unsettle me.

Back in the cabin the furniture creaked alarmingly and anything which was insecure was flung about. Even the bolts seemed on the point of bursting out of the steel girders. We slept, played pontoon, chatted, smoked and ate prodigiously. At regular intervals we donned oilskins and reeled off on watch and to man the Oerlikons. The boat rolled and rose and fell unbelievably. Standing out the stern, the bows would appear in the distance beyond the funnel, seemingly right up in the air, as the stern sank down, down into the depths. Then the reverse would take place, leaving one's stomach behind. Great care had to be taken when moving about the ship in the open, for massive waves endeavoured to wash one overboard. Guide ropes (for want of the correct technical name) had appeared. To these we clung as we moved from place to place. Succulent hot dishes, fresh from the galley, could easily disappear when carried by hands unused to the lunatic mood of the sea.

All the time, sleeping lightly, awaiting a violent awakening from the sudden arrival of a torpedo or bomb, lay the concentration of highly lethal material beneath us in the holds. Always, always, whatever we were doing, wherever we were (and we could never stray far) we were only too aware of our fearful travelling companions.

The throbbing of the engines went on and on, day in and day out. Mind you, we could not complain about this, for had they stopped our chances of survival would have been very slim. Once I was taken down into the engine room. The poor devils who spent most of their lives in their huge shuddering metal hall beneath the level of the sea, surrounded by hideous noise from the countless moving parts, were coated in sweat and grease and oil. These were taciturn men, lean and wiry. They supervised their vibrating world and took little heed of the transient visitors. This was the most vulnerable part of the ship, through which torpedos could stab their deadly sleek snouts with consummate ease. I was unhappy too at the amount of boiling water and steam in those great stretches of pulsing pipes, and was glad to ascend the long metal ladders to the open air.

There were warnings of imminent submarine attacks, for we in our convoy, slow-moving at twelve knots, bearing vital cargoes for North Africa, were prime targets. On some ships, of which ours was one, were fitted structures above the bows on which were perched fighter planes. Each vessel carried one aircraft. As we steamed nearer to the Straits of Gibraltar, German planes operating from airfields near the French coast, at Cap Ferret or Cap Finisterre, could reach us. Air attacks escalated. We gunners, strapped in our seats, would rotate and depress or elevate our twin barrels and cough at the enemy as he spat at us or tried to position himself to drop his bombs. As they came in at mast height the helmeted heads of the fliers were clearly visible. Sometimes a glance at the sea below would show momentarily as if a very sudden, immensely fierce hailstorm were in progress. We knew then that fire was coming back at us as the planes flashed past. The whole convoy gave voice. Not the least vociferous was our little, valiant flak-ship, which erupted in its comic act, not at all comical in reality.

The convoy had to cease firing to allow our pilots to take off. We watched our own young man clamber into his aircraft. With admiration tinged with some anxiety we spellbound onlookers saw him catapulted off. Like a bullet he sped up into the sky to engage the German planes. He was never seen again. Rumour had it that, assuming he survived, he would make for a North African airfield. He certainly could not return to his forlorn, forsaken perch.

We watched at least one enemy plane go down and looked on, utterly helpless, as a neighbouring ship was crippled by bombs. Helplessness and frustration was more pronounced here than on land. Often there were the sounds of depth charges in the distance. It was not uncommon to observe a destroyer whipping past in the opposite direction, way out on the edge of the convoy, flinging depth charges with all speed. It was reassuring, but we knew what lurked out there, and what they were after.

A week after my birthday we entered the Mediterranean. We had had a stormy crossing, but although the weather was still bad it was soon to become calmer until, welcome experience, the sea was still. I leant over the rail and saw the phosphorescent wake at night and watched the dolphins leap and play as they followed. I saw the coastline of North Africa for the first time.

CHAPTER XVI

We proceeded, tortoise-wise but intrepid, past Oran, then Algiers with its white buildings against the blackcloth of the Atlas Mountains.

By this time we were being attacked frequently. Stretchers had been ordered on deck soon after we sighted the African coast. I recalled my first firing-camp on Salisbury Plain in the summer of 1939. The ambulance had slipped into its place behind a copse at a respectable distance from the gun positions. I knew only too well by now that when meat-wagons or stretchers appeared there was a good chance of getting knocked off.

For two days we kept our heads down when we could, crossed our fingers and pressed on eastwards. On the second day I was on duty, strapped into my Oerlikon on the boat-deck, on the port side standing in for one of my men who was seasick. I was quite high up and there was no cover. The alert was on and anti-aircraft fire came from all directions. All the percussion instruments in our orchestra were playing a series of counter-rhythms which ranged from a rapid stutter to a slow controlled series of solemn thuds. Here and there torpedo-bombers, Heinkel 111s I think, appeared from nowhere and droned and swooped like great stinging insects. I spotted one flying parallel to the ship but moving in the opposite direction. He was close to the waves, almost skimming them in fact. He might have been half a mile away but it was difficult to judge. I remember depressing the gun to its maximum and opening fire. It was a struggle to get the barrels low enough. As I was so engaged (and all this must have happened in a matter of seconds) there was a tremendous explosion right below me. It was the worst I have ever heard. It seemed to burst within my head and my body. The explosion stayed with me a long time. I still think that some trace of it lingers, after forty years. The whole ship shuddered and lurched. The last thing I saw was a plane heading nose down towards the sea, as I was snatched right out of the strap which attached me to the seat and was sent flying through the air. I never did discover whether the aircraft crashed or whether it was taking evasive action. It must have been the one which hit us.

The next episode is hard to believe. Sometimes I myself wonder whether it did really happen. Over the rails I went on my own short aerial trip. Sternwards I flew and fell on the deck below. I landed on my back across a raised metal girder which was let into the centre of the deck, running from bow to stern. It was fortunate that this part of my landing platform had no square edges but was slightly rounded, with only an inch or so proud of the deck, or I must surely have broken my back. As it was I never even felt stiff afterwards, although I did have other problems to occupy me.

I pride myself that even if I did not land like a cat, I leapt up like one. It would have been better perhaps had I not moved so quickly. For immediately I regained my feet, the engine-room doors, which were a few feet away and which I now faced, burst open. A great sheet of flame engulfed me. It all happened so quickly that I had no time at all to react. Just as quickly as the flame had come, it went. It was either sucked back into the engine-room or there had only been this one burst. I felt no pain. There was a distinct stench of singed flesh and scorched hair. It was me, but I was too shocked to realize.

The ship had stopped and was listing. There was a strange silence. The sound of other ships' droning engines and gunfire were becoming more faint. The rest of the convoy had gone, slogging onwards. We had become a very lame duck and this was not good. The subsequent sequence of events is blurred. I remembered my watch, which Bid had given me, was in the cabin. I went back to retrieve it, and to see that everyone had escaped for it was only a short distance away. The watch had been flung off the table, or the hook where I had left it and was not to be found. Someone else had come to the cabin. We snatched bits of kit and turned to flee. The door of the cabin had slammed tight and we were trapped. My companion volunteered a most useful bit of knowledge. The doors on ships, he said, had escape panels which could be kicked out in an emergency. We kicked, crept out and ran. My greatest desire now was to take wings and fly off this potential bomb. Why had she not gone up, anyway? She might, at any moment. I slid down the starboard side into the water, for she had listed sufficiently for me to do so. There was oil floating about and I was aware that this could catch fire. Whether I wore a life-jacket or not I have forgotten, but it is very likely that I did. If I did not there were no problems, for the sea was calm and I could swim. As I was making all speed to get away, a ship's boat approached and I was hauled in. There were still signs that the enemy was in the area and it was a consolation to know that we could not be very far from shore.

A miracle occurred. The Royal Navy arrived in the form of a corvette. This relatively small vessel hove to and took us on board. I was told later that the young officer in charge had stretched his orders by stopping for us. Come to think of it, he may not have stopped entirely, for we were hauled over the side with scant ceremony like bundles of wet sacking. Immediately the ship picked up speed. Below, in the crowded sleeping quarters, bunks lined the sides. I sat, dripping wet, on the edge of one of these bunks and shook from head to foot. I looked at my shaking arms and hands in disbelief. Hanging from them were what appeared to be bedraggled elbow length gloves, like those worn at balls by Victorian ladies. These of mine were not of kid or satin, nor would their condition have done justice to any social occasion. It was my skin, shredded and in strips, with here and there raw flesh showing through a film of oil. A cigarette was placed to my lips, ever so tenderly. It was an effort to keep still whilst it was lit. Then I had a great effort to hold it. I drew on it. When I took it away from my lips it stuck, and bits of skin came away with it. A pint mug next appeared. In it was a very fair ration of Navy rum. No one can really claim to have lived until he has experienced this singularly potent alcoholic beverage. On the other hand, if this well-tried method of resuscitation fails, take it from me, you are dead. After the first sip my quaking body was still. The vibrations of my internal organs subsided and I began to feel good. The cigarette in my hands, stuck to my fingers, no longer trembled. Slowly I finished my medicine and by the time I had drained my mug I felt carefree and could almost have burst into song. Had I been given a mirror I daresay I might have been startled. Or would I even have realized that I was looking at myself?

Time fled. Almost before the voyage had begun I found myself being escorted along the quayside at Philipville, the North African sun warming my back, and my mind comfortably shielded from horrid reality by an alcoholic haze. In appreciation, for I never had the chance to thank them, I owe those great fellows of the unknown corvette a most glorious pub-crawl. One thing was certain; whatever I drank later, it would never match that Navy rum. From the dock at Philipville motor transport whisked me away to the 100th General Hospital where I was to stay for six weeks.

CHAPTER XVII

On my arrival I was put to bed. I was not allowed out of it for a fortnight. During the next couple of weeks I experienced misery, discomfort and considerable pain. It was the first time I had been inside a hospital, except when I had visited my grandfather in Preston Royal Infirmary when I was twelve; it was certainly my first time as an inmate. I had never suffered from any incapacitating illness or injury in my life. So here I was in the manner of the rawest recruits. My training was to be arduous and most enlightening. This was no ordinary hospital either, for its fabric, as far as I could see, was entirely of canvas and its function was almost solely dedicated to the treatment of wounds incurred in this major battle area.

On my first night in the 100th General I was shocked, burnt, and suffering from a stupendous hangover. Any one of these visitations would have given me bad vibes, but with all three united against me I was down for the count. The night was interminable. I emerged slowly from my alcoholic state to face a 'king-sized' post-alcoholic depression. I felt icy cold. Should a very stiff dose of very potent rum be administered, I wonder, to one suffering from severe shock and superficial burns? I really must ask our daughter Susan, who at the time of writing supervises the Burns Unit at the Birmingham Accident Hospital.

The situation was this. When I was torpedoed I was in 'shirt sleeve' order. My shirt was open at the neck and my arms were bare to well above the elbow. Long trousers or slacks protected my legs. I probably wore a steel helmet but that must have left me at the time of impact.

I now discovered that in that second or two when I was subjected to the blow-torch treatment, every exposed area of skin had been burnt. Even the lower strips of skin round my ankles had suffered, where my short socks had not covered and where my slacks had ridden up. They adorned my lower limbs like bracelets. My army socks, with constant washing, had followed the irritating habit of shrinking and shrinking until the tops of the socks had disappeared into the tops of my boots.

My appearance had not been improved by the disappearance of my hair. Mirrors were very skilfully kept out of my way, but I was aware that my head was as bare as the proverbial billiard-ball. There was a difference, however, for when I ran my hands over my baldness (the palms of my hands were unharmed) little clouds of charred hair appeared like tiny tufts of thistledown. Shed a tear for my bonny fair hair, all wavy and thick.

The chorus of professionals closed in on me. Gliding wraiths who turned out to be Sisters in the Queen Alexandra's Nursing Service, with a doctor as Overseer, lavished their skills upon my injuries. They took slivers of skin off me like fastidious predatory birds picking at a carcass. They worked unceasingly on my hands and arms, face, nose, lips and ears and even on my bald and singed pate. These gentle but persistent tormentors encircled me and leaned close. I did not appreciate their intimacy with any of the ardour which they deserved. Nor was I stirred by their fresh female scents. The stench of burning still stayed in my nostrils and now it intermingled with a strong tang of disinfectant.

I longed for the Sisters to go away, and with them the intense young man in the white coat. Unintentionally, unavoidably, they caused me pain. Nerves, numbed until now, began to make their presence felt. Apart from the stripping action of the tweezers I became more and more aware of a burning sensation which increased, causing restlessness and a general feeling of mental and physical uneasiness. This went on for some days, after which the symptoms subsided gradually.

When I was peeled to the satisfaction of the staff, they paused momentarily in artistic approval. Then they swathed me in vaseline gauze, held in place by a complex system of tapes and bandages. All the affected parts were covered completely. Bits of my body which I had been wont to take for granted had grown to many times their size. For instance, my lips which were considered to be so thin as to be almost non-existent, particularly when I was piqued, now felt like two large skinless sausages. Mercifully they were hidden from view. I was grateful that I was not Al Jolson. My ears, those projections which had been suspended unobtrusively on my head for twenty-three years, tingled and pulsated as if they were charged with electric currents. The bloody irritating appendages, I could have pulled them off had my fingers been capable. But these were also in dressings and as the new delicate skin formed it tightened and made movement very irksome.

During the days which followed I tried to disappear through my bed, to become invisible in order to escape the Swans of the Corps de

Ballet who danced attendance upon me with their dressing trolleys, vaseline gauze and the ubiquitous tweezers. Stretches of new skin, transparent, pink, shining, fragile and tight formed in patches under the dressings. Unfortunately, these dressings stuck in places and had to be teased or manipulated until they became detached. This procedure was likely to bring tears to my eyes. Hence the quaking feeling when the trolley approached.

Nights are always the worst times in hospital. I lay awake, night after night, watching the little light where the night sister sat. Sometimes she would glide between the beds on her rounds. There would always be someone who needed special vigilance. If a group of people, doctors and sisters, entered the ward with hurried steps, it meant that a crisis had occurred. For instance, a wound may have broken down. Once an artery, recently stitched, had burst open and the patient was bleeding to death. Often a new patient would be manoeuvred into a bed, already prepared for his reception. The ward never really slept. After each interminable period of darkness it was somehow reassuring to see another dawn break. I would probably drop off to sleep then, only to be awakened a second or two later for my liquid breakfast. It was two or three weeks before a pre-breakfast wash could be considered.

When I drank, driblets would escape and seep down on to my raw chin under the bandage. I became encrusted in that region and felt unclean, which, of course, I was. As the burns healed I itched. The itching and irritation was as much psychological as physical. I had a great urge to plunge back into the salty sea from which I had so recently emerged.

The bedpan was something else which previously had not entered into everyday life. Sitting there on my unsteady throne, more humiliating than regal, I surveyed the other inmates of the ward from this superior, pontifical position. A visitor, on entering, must have observed a giant panda-like creature, or a snowman. Wrapped all in white I stared through the apertures in the dressings. All I needed was a pipe and a dented billy-cock hat.

Our ward was a great marquee. During the day the sides were rolled up and I felt the warmth from outside and saw the cloudless sky and strong sunlight. When I did step outside, rather warily, to savour this marvellous climate, it was only for brief spells at first, for I was charged most strictly to protect my new pink covering of skin. I had to discipline myself severely for I had always been an inveterate sunbather. Quite soon I was able to sit out on the beach, which was near.

I learnt that the *Empire Rowan* had survived after all and had either been beached or brought into dock. She had caught the full blast of the explosion in the engine-room, as I had suspected, which accounted for the backlash of flame which I had encountered. I thought a good deal about the probable fate of the engine-room crew.

Almost from the time we had steamed out of Greenock one of my party had been utterly prostrate with seasickness. He lay in his bunk and ate nothing during the whole crossing. Naturally, he was in a very bad state when we were hit. On top of this he had suffered some other injury and this or the shock had resulted in his death.

The majority of the patients in the 100th General were wounded who had come straight from the line. I saw at first hand that men could still live after having been dealt the most terrible disablement. On one occasion on my way to lie on the sun warmed beach I met a party of men accompanying and bearing a poor wretch who was laid out on a stretcher. This young man (nearly all of us were young) was no longer strong, no longer rejoicing in his young manhood. He was emaciated, wan and shrunken. He wore a desperate look. From the sides of the stretcher tubes hung from under the blankets. To these tubes were attached bottles containing dark, clouded liquid. The bottles were carried very carefully by members of his entourage. What tragic thing had befallen this fellow, I asked, and what were the bottles? The patient, I was told, had been hit in the pelvic region and had lost his genitals. The tubes were attached to his bladder and other places. The contents of the bottles were his waste products. I shuddered inwardly. Another item of horror clicked into my subconsciousness, ready to project itself into the conscious when I was in a situation where the same ghastly injury could so easily come to me. All these nasty experiences accumulated. I was collecting quite a library. Two or three years ago I knew it could not happen to me. At Dunkirk I still clung to this belief, although afterwards I thought that it just might. Now I had first hand experiences that it not only could but had. I was moving on soon, probably back into action. Wherever I went the memory of the young man and his bottles, the shock of the explosion and its consequences, together with further unpleasant incidents which I collected, followed me as *doppelgängers* . . . .

I met a guardsman, one of the 2nd Coldstream, who had been 'shot up' at Longstop Hill. A burst from a Spandau had got him. An angry red weal ran up his side from hip to armpit and the marks of the stitches were to be seen clearly on either side. He would rejoin his Regiment soon and somewhere he would face a similar situation . . . and another . . . and maybe, another.

Holding a basin for a Sister, I looked over her shoulder and wished that I had not. She was attending a fellow who was lying face downwards on the bed. In his back was a great, deep, suppurating wound as big as a dinner plate. He had been hit by a large fragment of mortar bomb.

With these gunshot wounds, (GSW), be it from bullet, bomb or shell, there was always a distinct risk of infection from gas gangrene, and this, I was led to believe, was a killer. At about this time, although I did not know it, and I suspect few did, a medical team had brought to this very hospital, which had been earmarked to receive wounded from the Sicily landing, a new drug which was to save countless lives. It was called Penicillin.

I had seen men wounded and I had seen them dead. At Dunkirk, it will be remembered, I had helped to carry badly hurt men on to a ship. My curiosity had not gone beyond a cursory glance at bandages, however blood encrusted. Here I saw what lay underneath. I held the legs of one who was being mummified in plaster from top to toe. His spine was broken. I did not see the worst. We convalescents only helped out on the fringe, so to speak, and were kept well away from immediate post-operative cases.

There were a few Americans here. They were always prefixing their remarks with “Shit”. They bore on their persons a superfluity of candy, gum and ‘Camel’ cigarettes which they were very ready to distribute as gifts. The ones I met were good-natured and good-humoured. All, to a man, carried a set of dice. Their national pastime was played with these articles. It was called ‘Shooting Craps’, an American version of Sgt. Jordan’s ‘Pokey-Die’.

All had been injured legitimately, either in action or in accidents — except one. He had fallen prey to greed, or his inquisitive nature had got the better of him. Rummaging about on an abandoned German dump, he had been the victim of a booby trap. The Afrika Korps were crafty and very resourceful in planting these devices, which abounded in many forms. The Allies had taken a great deal of trouble in alerting the troops to take care, but there are always some who do not seem disposed to listen.

This Yank was tall, stooping and very thin; his movements were so lethargic that he seemed always to be on the point of total collapse; his face was young but cadaverous. This character with the unusual combination in his features, the languid movement, and what I took to be a Southern drawl, really deserved a porch attached to a wooden shack, a rocking chair, spittoon, corncob pipe and a jar of moonshine. I see him now, sitting hunched on the foot of my bed. He held up his mutilated hand of which only the thumb and little finger remained. He contemplated mournfully his odd looking appendage and with his uninjured hand he took a long, slow drag at his Camel. "Shit," he drawled, "shit. Me an' ma buddy was sneakin' about on this l'il ole Kraut dump, lookin' fur souvenirs. Ah lit on this l'il ole anti-aircraft bullet and the cock-suckin' bastard blew off'n ma f . . . . n' fingers." Apart from the irreparable damage to his hand he had another cause for despondency. He faced a court martial into the bargain.

Towards the end of my stay my mail caught up with me. For nine weeks I had had no news at all and it was a relief to know that all was well. Back home they would be unaware that I had been hit, for I had never been considered sufficiently ill to have warranted one of those ominous telegrams.

My eyes were tested, I had a medical and was passed A1. My hair was growing again but was never to be as fair as it had been. There were no scars on my face. On my elbows and fingers there were lighter patches than the rest. Traces still remain to this day.

In the first week of May I was discharged from the 100th General Hospital. Farewells were made to the doctors, sisters and orderlies for whose sympathy, friendliness, competence and dedication I was truly grateful. I said 'cheerio' to the chaps who had all like me, been brushed by a feather of the Angel of Death and who had survived. These chaps swam across my consciousness for a brief moment and were gone. I never saw or heard of any of them again.

I started on my travels. The roundabout journey back to my unit (wherever that was, for no one seemed to know) began in the company of chance companions. Our route lay between transit camps, which are depressing and lonely places. Still, I was in a vast continent which I had always wanted to visit. The sun shone fiercely all day and every day. The heat increased. There was plenty of opportunity to sunbathe and, quite often, to swim. The rations were wholesome and there was usually ample fresh fruit to be had. What more was there to ask?

I was unaware of it at the time, but I must have been mildly 'bomb-happy'. I was isolated from anyone I knew and felt lonely. I went through a period of despondency. It did improve to some extent but, using hindsight, the most enjoyable days of my soldiering were behind me. This was not just because of my association with Bid. When I did get back to my unit there had been changes and somehow it was never quite the same. Or had some subtle transformation occurred in me?

When air raids occurred, at or near the places we passed through or stayed at on our journey from the 100th General, especially in the vicinity of Algiers, I was disturbed by the sounds of the descending bombs and waited tensely for the explosions, though I knew the action was some distance away. Even the flak was less commonplace and acceptable than it had been.

"Roll on the boat," we 'old' soldiers would say as we lay almost naked on our groundsheets and blankets, in small tents we called 'bivouacs', with the flaps open and the sirocco blowing in from the Sahara, like the blast from a hot oven, "roll on the bastard boat." This saying was a familiar one, passed on by countless old soldiers who had served in India or some other far-flung outpost. It was a cry from the heart for the arrival of that so longed for and so often dreamed of trooper that would carry us home.

"Roll on my f . . . . g six," I would intone, meaning the expiration of my six years engagement with the Colours. I was into my fifth year with the Royal Regiment. The first three years had gone like a flash and I still had no other career in view except soldiering. I did not really want my Colour Service to end.

Sometimes, sprawled out on my blanket, sweating, I thought of my mother, living alone in her quaint quiet cottage with its resident ghosts. She rose at an indecent hour to set forth on her bicycle to deliver mail to the village and the outlying districts. She would be wondering about me all the time, and worrying too. I thought of my young lady an awful lot too. My yearning was particularly bad when the moon shone, full, big and close in a velvet sky. I thought of the same moon in a northern hemisphere under which I had dallied with someone very close, who looked in no respect like any of my present tent mates.

Mosquitoes 'dive bombed' us. We usually had mosquito nets. We were dosed with Mepacrine tablets which coloured our urine and turned our skins yellow, but this did not show under our mahogany tan. We even had cream to apply to our bites. All our aids did not deter the marauderers who, with the tenacity of the German pilots, got through the defences. Malaria was a very real menace which decimated our ranks. Another visitation to be reckoned with was dysentery. It was always lurking, ready to pounce. There was one type, called amoebic dysentery, which was very nasty and dangerous.

Ours was a flies' world. They were everywhere. They settled on our mess tins and plates in droves. They congregated, buzzed, crawled and settled on any bare part of us, given the slightest opportunity. Flies are notoriously attracted to excrement and there was a lot of this substance about, both animal and human. I hasten to add that the British and Americans did not contribute, for very strict rules of hygiene prevailed. Some units I could name, of other nationalities, were not so fastidious. One began to think that it was hazardous to eat anything. Fruit and vegetables were cheap and plentiful. But we had to dip all our purchases in a solution of potassium permanganate. The intake of sand had an abrasive action on the bowels, or so we thought. When a light wind was blowing, and often it was, we could not avoid a sprinkling of sand alighting on our rations.

Whatever precautions we took with our food, which, again, did not really amount to much, most of us developed diarrhoea which was often loath to depart. Although I escaped both malaria and dysentry, I had short bouts of diarrhoea. When we settled in encampments, our latrines were deep slit-trenches over which strong boards, poles or even slim tree trunks were placed. On these supports we balanced in a row, under the open sky. There were no ladies to spy on us and I should have thought that only rogue males of a particularly perverted type would have been interested enough to pause and look. This was no place for delicate dispositions. I wondered how those few shy youngsters of my schooldays who had cringed into the background when changing for games, had faced this primitive arrangement which was a perfectly normal one in Army life. We balanced on our poles, our haunches well over the supports, and reached the stage where we voided nothing but hot gases, for there was nothing solid left to pass. We suffered soreness and irritation.

In the villages the flies were all too evident, gathered in clusters round the infected eyes and sores of children and old folk. They harassed cattle. Once, out on the open desert on the edge of the Sahara, we pulled up for a short rest at a nomad encampment. On the side of a tent there hung what looked like long bunches of small dark skinned grapes, drying in the sun. One of the inhabitants happened to brush against these bunches. I was shattered to see the 'grapes' disperse into the air. They were hordes of flies, feeding on, and no doubt infecting, the long strands of fowls' intestines, which were in the process of being cured in preparation for their ultimate incorporation into appetising soups. I thought of the French Army cook and his knuckle-bone at

Sissone and retched instinctively. We soon found that we lived with a paradox. In this great beautiful country, in a marvellous climate for those who like a bit of heat, living outdoors in clear, fresh air, with ample facilities for swimming and other sports, fed on wholesome food, there was a price to pay in forms which ranged from minor to major irritations to exotic, unexpected and fatal disease.

CHAPTER XVIII

I began to travel in the manner of the French military and her allies when on French soil, namely, in railway trucks adapted to house *huit chevaux* or *quarante hommes*. Soon we were relegated to just a platform on wheels. This was no hardship during the daytime, but it was chilly travelling by night. We trundled along pleasantly and placidly, complete with our rations, mainly corned beef and biscuits, and our few possessions. I travelled lightly, for I had lost most of mine. We dangled our legs over the side of the truck, marvelled at the vastness of this continent we were in and drank in the changes of scenery which were often of sublime beauty.

We passed through Philipville, and stopping at every little station or halt, finally arrived at Constantine, the 'city built in a rock'. After staying in a siding until after nightfall we jolted to a start and slowly made our way to Setif. I have no idea who my travelling companions were but they were few in number and were from different units.

At one of the stops, where we slid off our transport to collect boiling water from our amiable engine-driver in order to make a brew, we were accosted by a young but efficient pimp. He was about a yard high and somewhere in the region of eight years of age. These youngsters seemed to start their training very early and were efficient operators at about the time when they would, in our society, be thinking of moving up from Primary to Junior School.

He began, without preamble, by offering us his sister for sale.

"You jiggy-jig my sister, she very good."

He made a grimace suitable to the occasion, and an appropriate gesture with his arm. We declined his offer. He then produced some eggs from beneath his tattered robe. These guys never gave up. He probably had some dirty postcards secreted about his person. The eggs were exchanged for a few cigarettes, one of which, after begging a light, he proceeded to smoke with the air of one accustomed to the habit. We indulged in some light badinage and accused him because of his garment, of being a *mademoiselle*.

"You *m'moiselle*," we said. He bridled.

"Me no f . . . . n' *m'moiselle*," he replied with great vehemence. He pulled up his long loose garment to prove his point. What he said was true. Here, indeed, was no *mademoiselle*. On the contrary the evidence which was revealed caused surprise, admiration and not a little envy among us. We were unanimous in assuring him that he was obviously chosen by Allah to provide ecstasy for such young ladies as he might favour with his uniqe endowment, in the not-too-distant future.

At another pause on our route, a line of trucks moving in the opposite direction lunged to a halt. Opposite us, perched on their belongings, were three very tough looking 'cookies'. They were bearded, burnt black, muscular and lean. It would be better to keep on the right side of them for they were soldiers of *La Legion Étrangère* — the celebrated and notorious French Foreign Legion. They were affable to us. One of them wore a very fine-looking pair of jackboots, familiar to the German forces but not to the Legion. With great courtesy I enquired how he had come by these fine-looking boots.

"*Eh bien, mon caporal, où avez-vous trouvez les bottes, s'il vous plait?*"

"*La Boche, la*," he replied, scarcely moving his lips from which the loose-made equivalent of a Gaulois hung. "*Je lui ai donnè le grand rire.*" *I gave him the 'big laugh'*.

He lifted up his chin and drawing the back of his hand across his throat, nodded in the direction of the fighting from which they had just come. He and his mates exchanged knowing half-smiles. It was fortunate for me, I felt, that I displayed no such splendid footwear, or his cronies might have given *me* the 'big laugh'.

Five kilometres from Algiers is Hussein Dey, where that night we slept in the open, in a stadium. A half-moon rode in a cloudless sky. The stars shone with a keen, brilliant light and seemed near enough to reach out and touch. The palm trees were silhouetted. Frogs croaked in great chorus. It was a night for lovers' meetings, but alas my love was a long way off, utterly inaccessible. Just one more night 'wasted its sweetness on the desert air'.

Next day we came to rest at No. 1 GRTD. What did this mean? The last two letters stood for 'Transit Depot'. Like all transit depots, it gathered all the 'flotsam of war' — the odds and sods. All the rogues, vagabonds, sturdy beggars and drifting lost souls hovered in these sterile places, then passed on.

We were only a few miles across the bay from Algiers. I went in the sea frequently and swam about under the water among the rocks and boulders, which were festooned with plants. The sea was clear, warm and unpolluted. I took up running again. My body turned a deep brown all over with this abundance of sea and sun. Could I have foreseen the future I would have known that it was to be another ten months or so before I slept under a roof.

One thing marred my stay here. There were air raids over Algiers at night. The position of the bombers, unseen but droning away overhead were difficult to assess as were the destinations of the bombs. We lay in our tents and waited for the screams of the descending bombs to terminate in the explosions. One night there was a direct hit on a family of Arabs camping near by. Nothing was left except a fair sized crater. In Portsmouth in 1941 I had experienced far worse, almost every night. Then I had been able to shrug off most of it, now I was far more on edge.

Happier sounds began to intrude in these Algiers raids. Suddenly, the anti-aircraft fire would stop and soon afterwards we heard with relief, our own night fighters up above. At this time, the first week in June, the battleships *King George V* and the *Howe* were moored at Algiers. The anti-aircraft fire put up by these great ships was truly formidable, Mr Churchill and General de Gaulle were also here. On a brief visit to Algiers I saw General Chartreux pass by, escorted by a detachment of the Spahis Algeriennes riding past on their magnificent horses. The spahis, rifles held across their arms, had cold piercing eyes and looked very hawkish, dangerous and supercilious.

The surrounding villages, Jean Bart, Maison Carree, Ain Taya all stank. Many cafés sold rot-gut at exorbitant prices.

'First mind you steer clear of the grog-sellers' huts for they sell you fixed bay'nets what rots out your guts,' sang Kipling. Wherever the soldiering is, the wide boys move in. There was a fair share in North Africa. There were brothels in the larger villages and the towns. I never visited them, for I had no inclination to follow hard on the heels of someone else. I had seen some of these brothel-bints hanging out of windows 'hawking their mutton' in the Casbah in Algiers, and the only feeling I got was revulsion. I would have shied off anyway for I had heard enough and seen enough to be frightened off for life. I never forgot that one of mates had got a 'nap hand' just as we were off to France. He never appeared in our midst again. Now, in North Africa, later on in the year, back with the Battery, a couple of our best gunners were sent off on a 'course' to the 'College', our euphemism for 'VD Hospital'. They climbed into the 15 cwt truck, throwing in their kitbags nonchalantly. They were big men, well built and very strong. Joking about their 'cold in the cock' they were driven off. On their return they were not so nonchalant; not so given to humour. As they almost fell out of the truck someone remarked that they were 'mere shadows of their former selves', a cliché which fitted admirably. It seemed an effort for them to manage their haversacks, never mind their kitbags. They never did regain their former strength and fitness. It was put about that the dreaded 'hockey stick' treatment had been meted out to them. This entailed a barbed instrument being passed up the penis. The very mention of this never failed to cause a tremor of revulsion in the loins of most men. There was no way of checking the validity of the rumour but one would have thought that some less drastic method would have been discovered. Or was it still used '*pour encourager les autres*'? Whatever had taken place our comrades were certainly subdued and did not appear over-hasty to make a return visit to the 'College'. Apart from discomfort and danger to health, pay and allowances stopped during treatment and I am pretty certain this meant pay allotted to wives.

Sgt.-Major Prior's final word on the subject, to which there was no answer, was snapped out in 'parade ground manner' at the end of a Parade as we stood to Attention, poised ready for the command "Dismiss".

"Remember, keep your pricks in your pockets and piss through a hole in your slacks," was his terse comment, followed immediately by "Parade, dis-miss." His eccentric statement never failed to raise smiles. If it was not couched in the elegant prose of say, the House of Lords, it was still very sound advice. It was a pity that there were always a few who chose to ignore it.

In the colourful villages, seething with activity, everyone was a character to be marvelled at. The women were heavily veiled so that only their eyes showed. It was unwise to look too closely at these females in their shapeless, often black garments reaching right to the ground; for protective and frightfully jealous cutthroats, sporting an array of outrageously wicked looking knives, were often in attendance. All the older men reminded me of my great-uncle. He was a villainous looking old rogue who had the most unspeakable array of bad teeth I had ever come across until now, whose proud boast was that he never took a bath lest it should disturb the natural juices of his body. He was, however, in spite of his appearance, very kind, and below the surface tender in disposition. Were these aged men, I reflected, of the same good nature as my great-uncle, despite their evil looks, the only difference being that they were denizens of L'Afrique du Nord? Teeth ranged from yellow to black, from green to brown. All were twisted, some protruded and many were broken or jagged. Always the latter species were black; all seemed to be promimently displayed through open, cavernous mouths. It must have been both a challenge and a nightmare for any enterprising dentist who was bold enough to endure in full frontal horror, so many bad breaths.

Once, walking with one of our officers, bent on some errand or other, we saw an inhabitant scurrying along in front of us. He had bare legs which were the thinnest imaginable. The officer tilted his peaked cap backwards a little and tapped his fly-whisk against his leg. "Gad, Sergeant," he said, "that's a fine leg for a boot." I fell about, laughing.

From the GRTD I set out by road with some of the 77th Field Regiment, RA. We bivouacked for the night at a wine farm where there were some enormous vats. Next day we travelled up into the Atlas Mountains and rested the night at El Aghir — in, of all places, a little schoolroom. We barricaded ourselves in in case we were attacked by brigands, for we were the only British soldiers, and probably the only Allied troops in the area on that particular night. We went on to Constantine (I seemed to be always dropping in on that ancient city) and then on to Souk-el-Khemis, where I rejoined the 32nd Field Battery, and was reunited with my mates. I was particularly pleased to see Earle, who, if he was not a Sergeant already, was soon to become one.

The Battery was bivouacked in a eucalyptus grove, on the edge of the battlefield where the Afrika Korps had surrendered so recently. We were 27 kilometres from Beja, 128 from Tunis. It was 19th June, over a month since Tunis had fallen.

The Regiment had disembarked at Algiers on 23rd March, four days before we in the slow convoy were torpedoed. They had been transported on the *Oriana*, a large P & O liner converted to a troopship. From Algiers they had gone to Rouiba, then to Bone by 3rd April. It was here that they learned that we had been attacked, that the ship was beached near Philipville, that most of the vehicles and all the guns were on board and that it would take some time to unload them. It was not until 17th April that the Regiment had been re-equipped with guns and essential vehicles. They were just in time to take part in the final phase of the battle which resulted in the fall of Tunis on 12th May, and the end of the Afrika Korps.

At Testour there had been some confusion. The 'recce' had become temporarily separated from the guns on 21st April and one of our

Captains had passed the line to the guns by compass, a skill which he alone of those present knew how to perform.

There was a big barrage on 7th May starting at three in the morning. Three hours later 600 guns had fired nearly 17,000 shells but what part we had played in this I cannot discover.

The 11th Hussars reported entry into Tunis with no enemy in sight later in the day. On the 8th the Battery went forward to a concentration area in Cap Bon. They were, in theory, supporting the infantry in 'mopping up' operations, but it seemed that they did not need any help. It was the day on which I was discharged from hospital.

About a week later, whilst I was in the process of being shuffled about in transit and was at Cap Matifou, across the bay from Algiers, Captain Babington had, to use his own words, in the company of BSM Prior, managed to liberate a high powered motor-cycle combination near what seemed to have been some sort of German HQ. "Unfortunately," he goes on to say, "when we returned to camp, the BSM driving and self in the sidecar, we passed on opposite sides of an olive tree and that was that!" This same BSM Prior was the right-hand man of the 4th British Division in the Victory Parade at Tunis.

Here at Souk-el-Khemis I had an interesting experience. I was back in business as Sergeant-in-Charge of a Guard of twenty-nine men, over a big prisoner of war cage. Behind the barbed wire were both Germans and Italians who were housed in separate compounds, for they did not appear to get on too well together. Neither did the German troops seem favourably disposed towards us. There were some hard-bitten looking fellows among them and some were aggressive, truculent and very displeased at their captivity, which was not surprising.

Stray dogs had become such a nuisance that we were given orders to shoot them. One of the young gunners fresh out from Blighty drew my attention to a little frisky-looking terrier which I promptly shot, at the same time tearing a most terrible strip off my gunner for his own inadequacy. The corpse was taken away and buried in an unmarked grave. Soon, but alas, not soon enough a Second Lieutenant appeared in quite a 'flap'. The canine friend of a high-ranking officer had gone 'absent without leave' and it was imperative that it should be found. Its description fitted that of the deceased. In spite of frantic efforts by sundry officers from Captain downwards, no hint was ever revealed as to its demise, or its wherabouts. No action could have been taken against me, officially, but it is always better to avoid risking the unofficial ill-will of superiors. I did, however, gain a certain notoriety within the Battery, for it was a praiseworthy thing to succeed in taking a swipe at Authority. The secret was kept closely within our ranks and never, I am sure, reached the ears of anyone of commissioned rank. I may add that I took no pleasure at all in killing that little dog; and that there were a few humans which I would far rather have knocked off.

An entry in my Diary states that when I returned from guard duty the guns had come in, so I can only draw the conclusion that these were our own, salvaged from the ship at last.

Changes had taken place within the Battery and for me it was never the same. New faces replaced the familiar ones of previous years. There had been a mysterious redistribution of officers, mysterious to me because no explanations ever reached my ears. BSM Prior had been transferred to 33rd Battery, which must have been a great upheaval for him and BSM Blackman became our Battery Sergeant-Major. My sponsors, so to speak, Major Lucas among them, who had encouraged me and who had shown more than a passing interest in my potential and development were gone, and it seemed that there was no place for me. A new Sergeant had appeared during my enforced absence, and had taken over my Gun.

I could not help feeling that the new Major held me in some way responsible for not bringing our own guns and equipment safely into North Africa on time. I know it was ridiculous to have this 'persecution mania', but somehow things were not quite right. I expected myself to be posted to another Battery, or even to another Field Regiment, but I stayed, in charge of Headquarters' Troop, which had sixty-five men as its complement. It was certainly no sinecure to be in charge of HQ Troop for I had a mixed bag of surveyors, signallers, clerks, storemen, drivers and cooks to supervise. Drivers, even those in the gun troops, could be 'bolshie' and some needed constant surveillance. One or two would have turned out on parade like the oily rags which they were so fond of flourishing, if they were not kept on a tight rein.

It must be understood, however, that in making this appraisal I in no way intend to denigrate these admirable folk. Undoubtedly they were first class men at their jobs. The prompt action of 'Fishy' Burbanks in France exemplifies their expertise. It may be that these drivers, probably the best turned out men in the Battery as they preened themselves astride their horses and proudly led their six-horse teams in horse-drawn days, suffered a metamorphosis in the new mechanized army. They seemed to take a perverse pride in steering just short of being disciplined when they appeared in the ranks. One character, nameless yet known to all, harried the Sergeant-Major so much by his mischievous insistence in appearing with side-hat worn from ear to ear in Napoleonic manner instead of fore and aft that he became a legend in his own lifetime.

The cooks were marginally worse. If they were turned out on early PE parades or on full parades when they had to dress (oh Lord) in best uniforms, instead of their smoke-begrimed, greasy garments, they showed their malignity and churlishness by taking reprisals. When the Battery was served its next meal the point of mutiny was almost reached. Strange unpalatable and lukewarm mixtures were slapped viciously into mess tins. The tea dixies were even more impregnated with onion flavouring; the grease which floated on the surface was appreciably thicker. The Orderly Officer and his attendant, the Orderly Sergeant, were inundated with complaints. One wag, I recall, when asked if he had any complaints replied, "Only a mess tin full Sir," and came within an inch of being put on a charge for 'dumb insolence'.

My mail caught up with me. It was like another birthday or Christmas for I collected fourteen letters in one delivery. There was always mail to answer, in the hope that one would get replies in about a month's time.

My duties in action would now be at the Command Post as CPOA, Command Post Officer's Assistant. Targets were worked out on an Artillery Board by means of angles taken from an instrument we called a Director in much the same manner as a surveyor would obtain his data. We at the Command Post did our sums and gave the necessary information to get the guns pointing in the right direction and at the correct range.

The permutations of fire called for depended on the nature of the target, from the use of a single gun to a section, from a section to a troop, a troop to a battery, on to a regiment, on even to the 72 guns of the Divisional Artillery. There were various means of control, from 'Gunfire — Gun Control' to 'Salvo', right on to the full scale Barrage. As there were so many subtle tricks to master, laid down in detailed procedures in various Manuals of Gunnery it is far beyond the intentions or limitations of this book to pursue the matter further. Sufficient to say that I was for the moment engaged on yet another skill which was an integral part of the whole.

I had had some training previously at the Command Post for it was the policy to have substitutes to replace casualties. I could not complain, for to be versatile and experienced in more than one role meant that I stood a better chance of promotion.

From the eucalyptus grove we set out from Tunisia to Algeria to a camp site near Bougie. We were astir by 04.45 hrs, took a hasty breakfast, packed our kit (much of it had been stored the previous day) and sped away 86 miles in convoy and bivouacked *en route* in a cornfield near Guelma. That evening I smoked my pipe which Bid had sent to me and penned a delicate letter to her. Next day we were off again soon after 05.00 hrs, and journeyed another 140 miles. I drove quite a good part of the way. Now we found ourselves on the plains, 15 miles from Setif. I mounted the guard. Diary June 29th. 'Wonderful mountain scenery between Setif and Bougie. Roads cut on edge of mountain. Sheer drop to river valleys thousands of feet below.'

Our next and last leg took us 60 miles on to the beach just outside Bougie. Here we set about erecting battery lines, which meant putting up tents to an organized plan for living quarters, stores, offices, cookhouse and dining areas. The guns were in the Gun-park, the vehicles in the wagon lines. It was the last day of June.

We were to camp here for three months until the first week in October. During this period the sun shone all day, every day.

I shared a tent with four other Sergeants in HQ Troop. They were Swaz Burman, Colclough (Colly), Ginger Hatton and Pete — who was Pete? I cannot recall him for the life of me. We would lie on top of our blankets, near-naked under our mosquito nets and talk of home, or the progress of the bloody drawn-out war — this and that, until it went cooler sometime after midnight and we could get to sleep. We rose early and were on parade shivering in our khaki drill shorts and shirts almost before the sun was up. We performed our duties and when we were in camp, took a siesta from 14.00 — 16.00 hrs when it was very hot. Three or four times a day, we swam in the clean, clear, warm sea. Some of us climbed hills which were really small mountains. Once panting and dripping with sweat I reached the crest, beaten by just one other. The sea was fifty yards away across sand which burnt one's feet, the mountains just across the way.

In spite of our healthy way of life, strange things happened. Sgt. 'Ginger' Rogers, quiet, inoffensive and apparently at the peak of fitness, slipped, fell and grazed himself whilst climbing. He was taken to hospital and began to waste away. The doctors seemed to be mystified by his sudden deterioration, for he was sent home without further ado. The last word we received was that he 'was in a very bad way'. Crosses behind the 69th General Hospital, on our way to Bougie grew in number every time we passed. I thought later that they may have taken in casualties from Sicily and Italy. Nevertheless, it was rather demoralizing at the time.

Septic sores were, to say the least, a nuisance. Small cuts, incurred whilst shaving were loath to heal. I took a toss from my motor bike on rough ground and bruised my bare knee. Flies settled on it, sand blew on to it and it even attracted some oil from my bike. This relatively small bruise went on for weeks, even though it did get a lot of salt water treatment.

Each soldier was responsible for his own cleanliness and turn-out, which meant that each man did his own laundry. A routine was established whilst in camp, but when we were out on exercises, which we often were for a week or so at a time, we had to snatch a few minutes when we could. Khaki drill, washed in the heat of the day, with the sun burning down, would be dry in a few minutes. We pressed our shorts and slacks by folding them and placing them between our blankets and sleeping on them on a flat stretch of sand.

We snatched relaxation whenever we could. In the evenings we had to roll down our shirt sleeves and change into slacks, so that there was less bare flesh exposed for the mosquitoes to attack. After washing and shaving we might write letters home, or go for a stroll, often finishing up in the Mess for a jar or two. Our Sergeants' Mess was a tent erected right on the shore of the Mediterranean, looking out to sea. Here we would gather and drink the sickly, oily dark wine which we called muscat. Our glasses were thick and coarse for they were really the bottom three inches or so of wine bottles which had been cut to size. Being more often than not used to drinking pints, we did not sip our wine as one might Chartreuse or Cointreau. I could not imagine 'Bam' Anstee, for instance, at a cocktail party with his tiny glass poised, holding forth on the emotional effect of the superimposition of bare fourths and fifths in Impressionist Music. Mind you, I consider him none the worse for that.

On one of our more boisterous evenings, a Senior NCO, showing signs of advanced inebriation, stripped himself naked, and wreathed in only a mosquito net, performed a pseudo-oriental dance whilst we intoned an ancient Indian melody to the words:

> Six long years you f . . . . . my daughter,
> Now you jaow to the Blighty Sahib,
> May the boat that takes you over
> Sink to the bottom of the panee, Sahib,

Ya, ya, the tum ya, yah,
The Bombay bibbi bot atcha.

We clapped in rhythmic accompaniment. As the 'music' throbbed out its constant repetition in the hot night, the gyrations of our performer became more frenzied. Perspiration dripped from all of us, but most of all from him. He was cooled off by the simple expedient of pouring sticky wine over him, from a large earthernware jug or chatti. Apparently the sudden discomfort was too much for our terpsichorean comrade, brought suddenly to some sort of temporary sobriety, for he made a speedy exodus seawards, his dark-stained robe billowing round him. Soon he was completely submerged in the Mediterranean.

We all followed like lemmings, bellowing and exhorting each other as we went, not bothering to strip off our clothing until we too had plunged out of our depth.

'Shall we make the welkin ring? Shall we raise the night owl with a catch that will draw three souls out of one weaver?' was the plea of Sir Toby Belch, who has always appealed to me because he enjoyed roistering at midnight. It was at such times of revelry as this that the rose-coloured spectacles really came into their own. One felt how good it was to be young and healthy and strong; good to be one of a band of such companions; good to be able to laugh down adversity and to treat hardship as a joke.

Staggering and laughing, wringing wet, we made our way across moonlit sands to our groundsheets and blankets.

Next morning, on early morning parade some of us swayed a bit and screwed up our eyes, which were sensitive to the keen light, as we stood to attention.

Yet no one remonstrated with us so long as we did our job; no one from the Temperance League was lurking ready to pounce and plead with us to mend our ways. If there was such a person, he must have thought better of it after stealing a look, and taken a smart about turn.

A pleasant interlude was afforded us when the Royal Artillery Band under its Director of Music, Captain O'Geary, came to play for us at Bougie. We sat and drank our muscat outside an estaminet (or its North African equivalent) overlooking Bougie Bay. We listened to the strains of Strauss's *Voices of Spring* and in conclusion, our own Regimental marches. For a few moments I was back on Woolwich Front Parade, on a beautiful day in early summer in 1939, when, as one of the participants in that ceremonial parade, I marched off to these marches, behind this very band.

Occasional forays by two or three of us were made at night to a nearby vineyard to steal a few bunches of grapes for our suppers. Our excursions were made for the slight excitement it gave us, rather than for the spoils themselves. Vineyards and acres of tomatoes were round about us and there fruits were to be had almost for the asking. The whole point in our visits was that great stealth was needed to avoid being shot at by at least one trigger-happy native who was always on guard. He was armed with a shotgun which appeared to have a squat, thick barrel. I saw him in silhouette as he stood motionless at the end of a row of vines, but he must never have spotted me.

We estimated that his weapon would use a fair-sized propellant charge. As the recoil might be fierce we propositioned our Sergeant-Artificer who was skilled in such technical matters to capture the lone watcher and fit his cannon with a miniature muzzle-brake of the same pattern as we had on our 25prs. The Sergeant-Artificer was derisory about this project so it was shelved.

A legitimate commando-like raid was arranged to keep us on our toes and to test the efficiency and alertness of the neighbouring encampments, which included Regimental Headquarters. Our small party of volunteers went out at night, wearing gym shoes. We did not need to darken our faces, for they were almost black anyway. I sneaked past tents with open flaps in which sleeping forms were just visible. Past these lines of tents was a grove which seemed to be empty except for one solitary camp-bed on which lay a figure stretched out under a mosquito net. Near by was a folding table on which stood utensils and toilet accessories. This must be the Officers' Mess *en plein air*, but if it was, it was thinly occupied. I picked up a shaving brush, razor, and I think, a small folding mirror off the table as proof that I had penetrated so far without a challenge and returned to my own lines with all the stealth I could muster.

Next morning, when I handed in my spoils at the Battery Office, there was not as much enthusiasm as I had expected. News had already been received that the Colonel's batman had taken the Colonel's shaving water nice and early, so that this VIP could prepare to present himself to his satellites in a neat and soldiery fashion at the start of the new day. Behold there was no razor, shaving brush or mirror. Wild cries of alarm had already been transmitted. Apparently I had committed a most terrible breach of etiquette. 'In that he, during the early hours of . . . . being of sound mind, did knock off his Commanding Officer's shaving gear, thus creating a most fearful stink . . . . '

My zeal had overreached itself. I, personally, received no official admonishment but there was a definite chill in the air. There were to be no more organized raids. Guards were doubled or trebled throughout the Regiment, and so tight and impregnable became our respective encampments that even the mosquitoes seemed, temporarily, to restrict their nocturnal activities. For a short time I became unpopular with some of my colleagues, who, like myself, found themselves on guard every other night. I was even sworn at for my youthful zeal. After a week or two the pressure was reduced and a normal routine was resumed. After this little episode I thought I would fade into the landscape when they wanted volunteers to execute their bloody hare-brained schemes.

CHAPTER XIX

Looking back in my pocket diary for 1943, the only one which survived the war, I see that I had been attending specialist classes in surveying at Lockerbie early in the year. I note that on Valentine's Day I surveyed the Battery lay-out and examined gridded pictures. Another time I was on Beattock ranges when I 'drew a panorama and registered targets'. My knowledge of trigonometry and logarithms which I had studied to Sixth Form level at my Grammar School held me in good stead. I had acted as Troop Sergeant-Major and Battery Sergeant-Major and had mounted an awful lot of Regimental Guards. Taking marching drill seemed to have been a speciality of mine, and I see that I was detailed for this unpopular duty at Bougie. The unfortunate and reluctant other ranks were marched up and down, halted, about turned, moved to the right in threes and shook up generally; and if the delivery of mail was thin I gave my charges more fierce attention. Gun-drill in all sorts of situations and on various sites had been no stranger to me since my Woolwich days.

I could and did drive every type of vehicle in the Battery. The only area in which my skill was slight was in Signals, although I had been on a wireless class just before our move to the port of embarkation. In retrospect it does not seem so strange that I found myself with the Command Post Staff for almost the rest of the year.

The events related in the previous chapter were merely short interludes between long stretches of training. We went out for ten days at a time, forever practising coming in and out of action and firing on imaginary targets with all the preparation which these manoeuvres entailed.

Continually we rehearsed, and nearly always we moved at night without lights save for one small bulb under each vehicle. Our routes led over some very rough ground, over which I now rode my new mount, an Ariel 350cc motor cycle with the ominous number MC.13.

On our return from one particularly harassing, sand-blown, fly-harassed trip I flung myself across the sand into the sea and did an exuberant dive into six inches of water. I saw a myriad of stars and found myself sitting at the water's edge, half-stunned. Jock, our Medical Officer, diagnosed a severe sprain. I had a blinding headache and for a few days could not move my head at all. By the time I was operational preparations for a big exercise were in hand.

There was checking of troop stores, inspection and checking of weapons, maintenance of vehicles and the packing of equipment on the vehicles. There was chasing and running round and about in what seemed to be utter disorder. Yet we found ourselves lined up, every truck, Quad and lorry in its correct place at the precise time appointed, ready to move off. Miracles like this never failed to occur and one never quite knew how they happened.

Away I went on MC.13, clinging like a limpet behind the Major's Staff car. The Humber Snipe took ploughed fields in its stride but I did not take so kindly to the furrows. Every time I went over one my neck ached and jarred.

One moment we might be speeding along a reasonably metalled road. Then the Major would decide to do a reconnaissance to right or left. Abruptly we would turn off over sand or hillocks or patches of scrubland.

One never-to-be-forgotten journey took place during the night, when I travelled for hours behind the Staff car, keeping close on its tail and its tiny rear light, always tense in case of sudden halts or changes of speed. When we pulled in to a 'hide' at dawn I fell off my bike with stiff neck and exhaustion. My eyes were sore with staring into the dark. I examined them in my little metal pocket mirror and saw that the rims and what should have been the white parts were like raw meat.

So it went on, up with reconnaissance when on the move, at the Command Post when static. We were not anywhere near the enemy out here, but it was obvious that we were being kept up to the mark ready for some close encounter which was not far off.

Whilst we were out on these jaunts our menu never varied. Breakfast was bacon and beans (a cowboy's breakfast we called it), for dinner about the middle of our day there was bread, jam and cheese and our tea (or supper) was bully beef stew.

So the summer went on under the burning sun by day, the hot sirocco at night until the temperature dropped in the small hours before dawn. On we went with our long spells away and our short respites back in camp at Bougie.

Towards the end of September the first showers fell, yet it remained warm. The Italian Campaign was well under way, we were advancing and there was a flap on that we were moving — to where? The whole Battery was in an uproar, and as usual the favourite 'secret information' which came on the 'grape-vine' was that we were being shipped back to Blighty for the Invasion.

Some stupid oaf out on a practice run had crashed my motor cycle and from now on I had to sit at an angle, for the forks were bent and the handlebars twisted so that the machine pulled very hard to one side. Sergeant-Major Prior, he with the coveted spur of the rough-rider for his prowess with horses in India, had regaled us when we were travelling in convoy by standing on the seat of his motor cycle and with hands outstretched to help his balance, would chug along the outside of the column, swaying gently and overtaking slowly. He had set his controls so that the engine ticked over at a fixed speed. I doubt whether even the accomplished Sergeant-Major would have been able to perform his celebrated act on my ungainly steed.

It seems that whilst we were at Bougie the inveterate planners were at work. We were earmarked for an assault landing called Goblet which was to have been made on the south-west coast of Sicily. It was cancelled. The Division was relieved of an active role. Men were sent to fill up empty spaces in other divisions. A thousand troops went as labourers to the supply and ammunition dumps at Bone.

My Diary mentions that on 30th September Sergeant Halton was at Bone with a party. I have a vague impression that when he and they returned much rancour was displayed at having been used as dockers. I myself was not affected.

When we did move, at the beginning of October, we went along twisting coast roads where there were in some places drops of hundreds of feet. The scenery was spectacular but I did not enjoy it. I was too busy grappling with my wayward vehicle which was doing its best to live up to its unlucky number and throw me over a precipice. It was a relief to arrive at our new camp area four miles from, I quote, 'the stinking little one-horse town and port of DJIDJELLI'.

We moved into these, our winter quarters, or so we had been led to believe, on 6th October.

All were set to work in one way or another to level, drain, put down gravel and set up the camp. There were heavy showers and thunderstorms. As the ground was wet but we were still under canvas, I arranged for a crude wooden bedstead to be made for me, with a wire-netting base. It was uncomfortable as there was no mattress to protect me from the wire, but at least it lifted me above the damp, uninviting bare earth.

When the sun shone it was still warm, like a good summer's day in England. The nights were cold. We dug drainage trenches round our tents, of course, and a barbed wire fence was erected to deter marauderers among the natives. There was some illicit trading in kit and blankets for those who were not concerned about shivering through lack of protection in the chill night air.

These extra jobs went on alongside the constant round of maintenance, cleaning of weapons, checking stores and weapons, training, guards. Our normal routine never stopped but the navvying was superimposed.

A Sergeants' Mess was under construction. The supporting framework was provided by the Navy, from discarded masts from their landing craft. Walls were large ration tins flattened out. What constituted the roof I cannot remember, but I should think that it was of the same material as the walls.

We had formed a good relationship with the Chief Petty Officers at Djidjelli docks. I went down several times to their workshops and helped to saw up and transport the posts we had prepared.

The rains came with a vengeance. Swaz Burman, among others, went into 'dock' with malaria, a malignant type being very prevalent here. With the rainy weather the droves of flies diminished, nerves became less threadbare, tempers less prone to flare up.

By the end of November we had become settled once more into our new home; the Mess was inhabited; there was even an open fire, wood-burning, reminiscent of home.

Naturally, as was only fitting for Gunners, we had our own bar. Versatile as we were we could not conjure up our native brew and pull pints straight from the wood.

There were still strange, uneasy stirrings from High Places, filtering down to us humble folk on the ground. I found myself in charge of a Gun — No. 1 of 'A' Subsection, 'B' Troop, the right of the line of the four guns. I must confess I was happier in this role, for I enjoyed the strenuous physical activity, the precise compliance with fire orders, the close comradeship of a detachment and the freedom from the supervision of my motley crew in HQ Troop, which was not subjected to the more 'regimental' requirements in a Gun Troop.

On my first exercise with my new detachment I showed off a bit to the young gunners straight from home by extending my clenched fist to measure the degress, before throwing the trail over and letting it thump down on the ground, so accurately that the gun-layer had little to do in the way of traversing into line.

A further indication that we were preparing for action in a known geographical situation was an exercise which was one of the most strenuous I had ever been required to do. This took place two or three days after our celebrated party with the Navy, about which I will tell shortly.

For twenty hours I was on my feet, directing, heaving, pulling, hauling, manipulating the Gun down a precipice on to a narrow ledge about twenty feet below. The wire rope attached to the winch on the tractor worked overtime, as well as the drag-ropes. Great metal spikes were driven into the ground at strategic points, using sledge-hammers. Trees were used to give a firmer purchase. Gunners swore and perspired as the monster lurched down, always perversely catching its curious projections whenever it could on every possible obstacle. Once in position, perched precariously, we dragged the bastard up again.

Whatever food there was to be had, I took standing up. Not often did I feel exhaustion, but after that ordeal, hard on the mind and body together, I was dead beat.

We were on our way somewhere — somewhere with steep drops down mountains on to almost inaccessible ledges — or somewhere with terraces — where, oh, where could it be?

I took over as Sergeants' Mess Caterer for a spell. This duty, worked on a rota, was not very exacting. The money which we contributed between us was spent on wine and extra items to supplement our rations. I saw that the meals were prepared at the times arranged, that the fire was lit in the late afternoons and that the orderly kept the Mess clean and tidy. In order to carry out this supervision I was excused some other duties.

As a tribute to the generosity of our Naval friends and to celebrate the completion of our Mess, it was voted that we should hold a party. I was despatched to Djidjelli to tender a formal invitation to the Chief Petty Officers. It was a Sunday. The midday meal was almost ready to be served and the CPOs were indulging in their most important ritual of the day. Rum was being distributed. They were taking their tots. I tried to excuse myself and said that I would return later but they would not let me go. They led me to the place of distribution. Each of my friends came up in turn, offered me his tot and said 'Sipper Sarge' or 'Sipper Tommy'. Etiquette required that only a sip was to be taken from each glass. To drink more would have been a serious breach of good manners.

Although I had felt the effects of their notorious drink previously as you may remember, I thought that such tiny amounts of alcohol would have little effect. However, there were several who came and showed their friendship and the cumulative intake reacted on me very quickly. It may be thought that I just had not the head for drink. This was not so, for I had been raised in a hard school and had even stood my ground, almost, with Bam Anstee himself.

This stuff was lethal. Half-pint men back home in the Shovels Hotel, Hambleton, just would not have got past the first heat.

Very soon, for the tempo of living increased, the momentum of events speeded up and I became marvellously content, somewhat hazy and not a little unsteady on my feet. As if observing myself from above I watched myself being led to a place at a table already prepared for me. Here I ate two huge dinners in rapid succession followed by a great helping of duff covered in custard or white sauce. What a meal. Never could I remember enjoying such a repast. Belching to show my appreciation, for I was in Africa after all, I bade a reluctant farewell and staggered out into the daylight. It was drizzling, so I manipulated my groundsheet in the manner of a bull-fighter, in an effort to get it round my shoulders.

A 15 cwt truck pulled up, one of our officers leant out on the passenger's side and offered me a lift. Blinking, I pulled myself up and gave him a smart salute, or the best attempt at a smart salute that I could muster. The effort caused me to fall over the bonnet. The officer saw nothing amiss, or appeared not to do so.

"Jump in the back, Sergeant," he said. Jump in? I teetered round and fell over the tail-board. For the moment my elasticity had gone. Back at camp the officer was dropped off at the entrance and it was left to the driver to help me out.

I reeled into the tent, slept for six hours, woke with someone else's head and experienced a terrible thirst, which, when slaked made me drunk again.

The purpose of my visit must have been successful, although I had no recollection of submitting the invitation, for a few days later the CPOs arrived in force. Though in no way resembling the Wise Men, they bore gifts, which was not inappropriate for Christmas was not far off. The gifts were in the form of rum.

"Oh Christ," I muttered to myself as I stationed myself behind the bar and set about pouring out of the black bottles containing muscat into glasses with the thick sides and still thicker bottoms.

We relaxed, smoked, drank and exchanged yarns. As the atmosphere rose in conviviality a sort of cabaret show began to emerge.

Individuals stood up to perform. It seemed to be a good idea at the time, although now I think it was a kind of desecration, when I decided to add a splash of rum to the wine to give it a little more body.

I raised my glass, looked over towards Anstee and gave him a toast.

"O for a draught of vintage, that hath been
Cool'd a long age in the deep-delved earth,
Tasting of Flora and the country green,
Dance, and Provencal song, and sunburnt
mirth . . . . " I intoned setting a dramatic stance.

"F . . . off, you little bleeder," said Anstee. Evidently he was not in the mood for Keats.

Voices were raised, but not in anger. Perspiration began to show. Some sang, but not many, and of those few only one or two displayed a true concept of tunefulness. Others gave recitations or told stories, all bawdy and mostly based on the favourite theme. I still kept up with my work at the bar, quite often taking two drinks where others took one.

The CPOs had made a Sipper's Badge and a little metal mug which they presented to me, accompanied by a short speech. This ceremony called for more drinks. Some of our officers called in for a while to pay their respects. When requested to give a turn, I sang a slow solemn air, which, though in the manner of a folk-song, is not to be found in the National Song Book:

"As I was walking down the street
A fair young lady I did meet,
She said "Hallo, how do you do
How would you like to play with
My Ring-a-dang-do?"

Inevitably, as she is no better than she should be, she falls on hard times and her lack of virtue results in utter destitution. The song was a favourite of mine, which I had first heard sung in the NAAFI by an enormous gunner when I was at Firing Camp with the Territorial Army at Redesdale in the summer of 1938. I had been overwhelmed by its vulgarity and bewildered by the complete indifference of the young women who were serving. They might have been in the presence of some elderly spinster in a village shop for all the notice they took.

So well was I received that an encore was demanded. Supported physically by comrades on either side, for I was no longer capable of keeping myself upright, I sang the 'Rose of Tralee' in honour of my Irish grandmother. In a mellifluous tenor, a legacy from my grandfather on my mother's side, which only came out when all inhibitions had been removed, and pitched at least a third too high, I let fly.

Gunners on guard duty, looking outward through the perimeter fence were startled to hear a continuous series of high-pitched sounds and almost turned out the rest of the guard; lean, dark-skinned predatory creatures lurking on the other side of the barrier, waiting to do business of a shady sort with one or two of our own boys, cast even more furtive glances at each other, and marvelled at the strange rites which were indulged in by the 'sahibs'.

As I reached the climax, "Oh no, 'twas the truth in her eyes ever shining that made me love Mary, the Rose of Tra-lee . . . . " I went up to the octave, feeling the strain in my loins as I did so, clawed at the top note and strove to sustain it. I was pulsating near to top A. Amidst waves of applause I bowed and fell forward. Earle stooped, picked me up, popped me over his shoulder and carried me to bed. I was not to know it, but it was my swan-song. Never again would I enjoy a night out with the comrades of 32nd Field Battery RA, with whom I had lived side by side for so long.

There were only a few months left for me; well within a year from now Earle would be dead.

Next morning on awakening, damp and bleary-eyed, I leant over and saw on my mosquito net which had been carefully tucked in round me, a small circular mass like a Christmas pudding, which had strained itself through the fine mesh and left a red stain on the floor. I had parted with the contents of my stomach during the night.

Within a few days mail and presents came from home. There were cards, Air Mail letters, books from my mother, Abdulla cigarettes, a pipe, hand-knitted pullover and a large photo of herself from my fiancée, Miss Nield.

On 9th December there was another move in the pipe-line. We blew all our Mess kitty and celebrated Christmas a week early. In the middle of December we handed over all our equipment, guns and vehicles. The 21st Tank Brigade had left us and was to be replaced by the 28th Infantry Brigade.

With Captain Peter in charge and myself as his senior NCO, we set off with an Advance Party through Bougie, Algiers and Hussein Day and finally arrived at Blida, which is not far from Algiers. The camp at Blida was erected by Italian prisoners under our instructions. It was raining and the ground was sodden. On the morning of 23rd December the rest of the Regiment arrived. We spent an hour or two on the Eve of Christmas, in the afternoon, in a bar in Blida. Most of us were depressed — fed up, f . . . . . up and far from home — at Christmas. This was the worst Christmas of my life and the place we were in did not help. Some wild boys who had been in the desert for about three years came into the bar. They had originally been with General Wavell and had fought their way up with the 8th Army. Their long sojourn mid sun and sand showed, for they were prone to sudden unpredictable whims and changes of mood. The old Indian soldiers would call them 'Deolali', or say that they had a 'tap'. They had few inhibitions and were not averse to throwing glasses or jumping on tables and dancing, but as we were at least half-way to their condition we didn't mind.

It was on this Christmas Eve that I was subjected to the one and only attempt at homosexuality during my service in His Majesty's Forces, or indeed anywhere else. On this night I shared a two-man tent with another sergeant. He was known to me as an acquaintance only, a lonely, taciturn man with few friends, who had served a long time in India. There was a rumour that he had a fancy for boys, but I knew of no evidence to support this. Swaz Burman had said jokingly, "Keep your hand on your ring, Badge." I took his remark lightly for I was no boy. If anyone fancied me he would be pretty hard up, for I couldn't have come up smelling of violets after a few days on the road with no chance to change or bathe.

We lay side by side on our groundsheets on the damp earth, with a couple of feet between us. Our night-light was a candle in a bottle and this was placed between us, about a foot from our heads. The light was blown out and I turned on my side away from the other occupant and listened to the melancholy patter of the rain. We were fully dressed. As I was drifting off, probably concentrating on an erotic fantasy set right on the west coast of Lancashire, near Knott-End-on-Sea to be precise, I felt that a hand was seeking to unfasten the top buttons of my slacks, for I had probably loosened my belt for greater comfort. I allowed the groping hand to commence to gently ease down my slacks. Stretching out and yawning, I put my right hand above my shoulder, grasped the bottle and struck where I thought the head of my would-be-ravisher would be. There was a nasty thump, a grunt and then only the sound of breathing. My companion wasn't dead, so I went to sleep.

Next morning I was up first and was already at breakfast in a marquee when he came in. The bridge of his nose was swollen to such an extent that his eyes were just visible, like two buttons sunken in purple dough. People round about questioned him as to what had happened. His tale was that he had walked into a marquee-pole in the dark. A likely story, for he was one of the few who did not drink. There was a good deal of derisive laughter but nothing was ever said; no questions were asked. But these fellows we soldiered with were no fools and would have no difficulty in putting two and two together.

We embarked on a troopship on Boxing Day and slipped our moorings at Algiers at 18.00 hrs. 'The bloody trooper turned right instead of left and we belted hell for leather in convoy down the African coast' says my Diary. I slept on 'C' Deck away down where it was hot and claustrophobic and where I had plenty of time to think of such things as torpedoes. We passed within 150 miles of Crete, but no enemy harassed us.

By 31st December we were off Port Said. Up the Suez Canal we went and greeted the New Year in complete temperance, anchored on one of the lakes. Then we proceeded southward and disembarked at Port Tufik. There we were greeted with the news that bubonic plague was rife at the moment — or was it always?

Our 'most secret' move to Egypt was to prepare for a possible assault landing on the Greek Island of Rhodes. We collected yet another lot of guns and practised yet another series of combined operations at Kabrit. The proposed onslaught on Greece was cancelled. It did not affect us ORs one bit for we were oblivious to both the intention and its abortion.

The 28th Infantry Brigade joined the Division. The 2nd King's (Liverpool) Regiment and the 2nd Somerset Light Infantry had come from Gibralter where they had been stationed since the outbreak of war. The third battalion of the Brigade, the 2nd/4th Hampshire did not arrive until the end of February, 1944. They had seen action in Tunisia and the Sicily and Salerno landings.

Officially, I was in the Middle East Forces from 26th December, 1943 to 13th February, 1944. We were under canvas in the desert, this time in big tents with fly-sheets for extra protection against the sun. The sides were rolled up all the time. Was it the copper sun which caused me to hallucinate, or did we really subsist on a ration of minute mutton chops and sweet potatoes?

Amorous thoughts troubled me, intermingled with loneliness and frustration. It was pretty certain that Bid would have to hang on a bit longer for that wedding ring. I hoped she would. As for me, well, I had no option.

The sky at night was black velvet, relieved by brilliant stars, almost close enough to touch. With the desert stretching out all round we attended our outdoor cinema and watched a film which was thrown on to a huge screen. The Division's history says:

> 'Almost everyone had the chance of a short leave in Cairo, and there were cinemas — Shafto's Shuftis — and a few clubs; but nothing could make life in the desert enjoyable.'

Shafto's Shuftis knew me not; neither did even one club of the few. The only glance of Alexandria I got was from the troop train on my way to the boat.

On rising I tapped out my boots in traditional 'old soldier' style. At least one scorpion fell out. Captain Peter 'persuaded' me to box an 'exhibition' round or two with him in order to encourage the ORs to take a little healthy exercise in the pure desert air. I chose to believe that Captain Peter and I had established that rapport between officer and senior NCO which did so much to foster a good spirit in the Troop.

The Regiment demonstrated firing in an upper register in the first week in February, 1944. All too well do I remember us digging a deep pit on two levels. The Gun was lowered carefully using winch and drag ropes under my direction. It was a tricky business, for if this Chap slipped He could crush someone to death. The wheels were brought to rest on a level platform about three feet down and the track was another yard lower down. The piece pointed skywards like a big mortar. When we fired, the recoil system at that elevation gave a sharp, short vicious kick. The compensating system was so devised that at a flat trajectory the recoil was longer; at a higher one it was shorter, to stop the breech mechanism from stabbing into the ground.

Soon afterwards we dumped our guns, entrained in the desert and chugged off to Alexandria. It was 'pick up your parrots and monkeys and face the boat'.

We had no such pets, we were not bound for Blighty either. On 15th February we embarked on His Majesty's troopship *Ascania*, and were soon steaming into the Med.

PART FIVE

Italian Campaign, 1944

An' 'er troopers you'll find with a fair wind be'ind
That takes us to various wars.
(Poor beggars! barbarious wars!)
The Sons of the Widow by Rudyard Kipling

CHAPTER XX

In the third week of February, 1944 we disembarked at Naples. The Italian Campaign had been under way for some time and the Allies were pushing northwards, slowly but doggedly.

For me the fighting was to last for only two months. I won no medals for bravery; no heroic action is recorded. I did my job as a professional soldier as did many another. Hundreds of thousands endured worse conditions and for much longer, yet for me, in these few weeks was to be contained the most traumatic experience of my life, and it left its mark.

As we fell in on the quayside I looked round with some discomfort and apprehension. Ships were lying partly submerged or on their sides. There were all the signs that there had been a heavy bombardment, but I did not know when. I was back at Dunkirk but did not now possess the reckless disregard for danger which I had at twenty.

We had come across the Mediterranean from Alexandria under grey skies, when we saw them, for we were housed deep down in the hull. The seas were grey and forbidding and a heavy swell caused much disturbance.

Our mess-decks were awash with vomit. Galvanized tubs and buckets were placed round and about and sounds of retching filled the air. It was a very rough crossing.

Our spirits, not good, were made even worse when against the night sky we saw on our port side what appeared to be a giant cigar-butt in the sky. The far-travelled among us stated with certainty based on experience that this was the volcano Stromboli in Sicily, and that we were steaming through the Straits of Messina.

No indication had been given of our destination, so there was always a chance that this time we were really going home. But deep down we knew, because of certain recent changes in our training that this was a false hope.

Did we get off the boat in our khaki drill? I rather hope we did, for it would have been the Classic Touch. After all, we had just come from the Sahara and here in sharp contrast it was cold with a leaden sky.

As we passed through Naples, poverty, ruin, devastation, decay and hopelessness lay all about us. Groups of little old emaciated folk with pot-bellies accosted us. Their average age could not have been more than eight years. These had no eggs to barter; no sisters to offer for sale. They closed round us, looked at us fixedly with huge, sad, lack-lustre eyes. They begged for food, and being soldiers we gave it, contrary to the strictest orders.

Suddenly, I felt a lot older. There was not much to cheer about now, but I had a feeling that there were far more unpleasant things in store.

We were going into action. To crown it all it was raining.

We travelled in lorries by road north-westwards about thirty miles to Teano, passing through Capua on the way. There were all the signs of a war-torn and war-worn country. Holes were blown in roofs so that whole stretches of bare rafters showed. Tiles hung off, and rubble, still uncleared, was strewn about. The whole countryside looked run down, the inhabitants starved and cowed. I only met a few, and for a very short time, but these presented a guarded hostility. I was not impressed.

Certainly no *bel canto tenores* serenaded us or regaled us with arias from *Rigoletto* or *La Traviata* as we drew ever nearer to the line; no peasants ran smiling towards us to proffer vino. No doubt they did later, when it was apparent that the Allies were sure to win, but the time was not yet.

Our Division took over from the 46th Division. On 24th February we relieved a battery of 71st Field Regiment, RA, in the line. Our position was in the Suja area, overlooking the River Garigliano. It was a relatively quiet sector, far more so for instance than the battle areas a little further north, closing in on Monte Cassino. We stayed here for about three weeks, first supporting 28th Infantry Brigade, the one which was new to our Division, then 10th Infantry, an old comrade of ours going back to Shorncliffe.

We were now in our battle-gear, battledress and greatcoats. From now on our steel helmets were constant companions. After travelling so far by tractors, droning away one behind the other, well spaced, in the night, we alighted and walked carefully the rest of the way to the gun position. Though the path had been swept for mines by the Engineers, as the white tapes which ran along the edges showed, there was just a chance that the odd schu-mine might have been overlooked. When one stepped on one of these the best one could get away with was mutilation of the legs and lower part of the body.

There were no shells coming over, but an uncanny sinister feeling was present, as it always is in battle areas. It is an atmosphere indescribable until experienced; one never feels secure. Vigilance is constant, as if an unseen eye is watching, hand poised ready to strike.

Intermittent bursts of small arms fire could be heard up front, and there were flashes on the horizon, sometimes accompanied by the dull thuds of explosions. These signs of battle could escalate very rapidly, and die down just as quickly. Having experienced it before, I knew what to expect.

The Gun which I took over was dug in, nice and snug in the lea of a terrace, and it was camouflaged with a net on hollow metal poles. Here was my new baby, or rather old lady with forked tongues, for she had fired a few rounds by the look of her. She appeared like an old lady tonight, sitting there as in a wheelchair, immobile, but this was only a crafty disguise. The muzzle pointed towards the River Garigliano, which we could just see shimmering in the darkness and over which we would fire. My opposite number, battle-worn himself, handed over quickly and efficiently, gave me one or two hints and pushed off.

It was at such times that the malicious side of my nature showed. I wished to wave a magic wand and transfer instantly from their safe warm beds in the Village of my Birth or its environs, one or two blokes whom I disliked to join me, still, of course, in their night attire. Would I give them a rough ride.

The Gun was on a fixed line, ready to put down harassing fire. I organized the guard rota (the Gun was guarded always), chose a sheltered place, put down my blankets and got my head down.

Not far away, invisible but certainly there, were our infantry, and just beyond them, a very tough, efficient and stubborn enemy.

Next morning there was a conference in a room adjoining the Officers' Mess, which was in a requisitioned house to the rear of the Battery position. The officers and senior NCOs were all there, and a Captain assessed the situation.

Well known faces from 'A' Troop were there. Swaz Burman and Bam Anstee stood near by. I myself had been sorry to leave 'A' Troop, for I had known it a long time. Still, I supposed, these changes and transfers were common in wartime.

The Captain stood and in a nonchalant but efficient manner appraised us of the situation.

I speculated that the casual approach which disguised the courage, leadership and professionalism of his class, could be an extension of qualities displayed by ancestors in the regiment through the First World

War, the Indian Mutiny and maybe back to Waterloo.

"Sergeant Bowman," he said, looking across at me and smiling as if he were about to reveal some practical joke, "Sergeant Bowman, you on the right of 'B' Troop appear to be specially favoured by the Hun. He seems to have ranged in on you," (I had noticed some ominous black gashes in the terrace round about), "and he also has a nasty habit of bringing up an SP Gun (Self-propelled 88 — mounted on a tank) after dark and pooping off. Better keep your heads down."

My colleagues laughed a bit and I joined in with a wry smile. None knew that my stomach, probably not over-full to start with, had dropped into my intestinal tract.

We got a few shells back during the day in reply to our own fire. This counter-battery work was standard practice. We fired, they fired back — they fired, we tried to stonk them. Though flashless cordite was in use, which meant that the flash of the muzzle blast was less easily visible, gun positions and single guns could still be picked out. Sound ranging was an effective way of discovering us. As soon as we opened fire they would start to find us, just as we would endeavour to find them.

Shells might come over spasmodically or being the methodical Hun (now know as 'Tedesci') he might give us a few rounds every hour, on the hour. It varied.

In Italy we were usually recipients of big stuff, like the 150 mm (15 cm), weight of projectile 250 lbs, or the smaller very spiteful 88 mm (8.8 cm) Flak 36 dual purpose gun with a very high muzzle velocity, which was fond of firing air-bursts at us.

The thing about this was that unlike the 'big stuff' where the whine of the trajectory gave warning of the approaching projectile, even though it might only be a slight one, with the high velocity shell the savage crack of the explosion came slightly before the last split second of the sound of its flight. "Bum — choo", it went as the round fragmented twenty feet above and splattered us. But being shot at with anything was always unpleasant.

There were also the 'nebelwerfers' which were mortars or projectors firing a fixed number (5, 6, 10?) of large rocket-like projectiles simultaneously. Their range was short compared to 'legitimate' artillery and they were no good for pin-pointing targets. They were deadly though at putting down blanket fire on a given area.

That night we heard the sound of a tracked vehicle moving forward. How still it was, exaggerating the sound on which we all concentrated. It stopped. I stopped breathing. We got under whatever cover we could grab, praying that no fire orders would come through. For then, whatever else was going on, we manned the Gun. Furthermore, when we opened fire he would pin-point us better.

When we were fired on we crouched frozen in fright, in the cold, black night. Our small close-knit community, guardians and serfs of our rugged overlord the Gun, (masculine once more), were, when we were being shot at like this, also single vulnerable units, lonely and alone.

Tonight the German gunners were satisfied with a few rounds. We were glad when the SP gun went home. I had a strong desire to live, not just to live to fight another day, but to live, full stop.

Back home little Miss Nield, my young lady with the snow-white skin, waited for me. I longed to look upon my white-skinned maiden after being so long deprived in these countries of the dark-skinned.

'Sche was well more blisful on to see
Than is the newe perionette tree;'

I escaped into a dream-world, with confidences exchanged in whispers.

'How silver-sweet the sound of lovers' tongues by night.'

My girl and I had fed a little on honey-dew but not quite drunk the milk of paradise. I had developed a great thirst and I wanted to survive so that we might quench it together.

I did hope so much that she would wait for me. But news of rejection came daily for someone. Such depressing tales I assimilated at first with dismay, until I realized that another old adage was faulty and that absence did not always make the heart grow fonder. It might have worked all right for a weekend at Scouts' Camp, but it certainly did not function here. Cynicism was a part of my nature. Now through experience, it deepened.

Shattering letters, telling of unfaithfulness and adultery arrived relentlessly. They were called 'Dear Johns', a marvellously descriptive term taken from our American cousins who have an instinct for the right expression.

'A fool there was and he made a prayer
Even as you and I
To a rag and a bone and a hank of hair
The fool he called her his lady fair.'

How Sergeant Artificer Bickle would have smiled at this. I thought of him, brewing up on his cherished primus stove as we crouched under a hedge in France and watched the Jerry bombers moaning over, drove after drove, with no opposition to be seen. Had Sergeant Artificer Bickle had a love affair, a great romance, which like Franz Schubert's had never been allowed to come to fruition? His personal life was never revealed, but some experience, probably several, had left him super-cynical, and I was his admiring disciple.

But now I, who had quoted Kipling to my mother and sworn that I would never marry, had a 'lady fair' of my own. Somehow I could not see things in the same way any more, and I wanted to believe that *all* women were not alike, and that there were some good ones — a few.

'Dear Johns' or not, the war went on.

We on the ground had our own special problems. I do not deny that sitting helpless in a bomber, anticipating 'flak' coming up from Hamburg or Berlin would for me have been a relaxing evening on the town. Nor would I readily have exchanged with those constantly at sea, in surface ships or submarines. But in these circumstances, failing stark tragedy, there was usually the regular hot meal and the dry, snug bed.

We were always exposed to the weather. Never in action, and rarely out of it during a campaign was shelter afforded us, save that which we found for ourselves. We slept rough by the Gun. Sometimes I slept under it.

If there was a tarpaulin sheet or canvas cover it was one which had been 'won', not issued. When the big, sturdy gun-cover was not cloaking our charge, and it never was, in action, we drew it over ourselves.

When it rained there was no means of keeping dry. Boots became water-logged, as did battledress, equipment and especially greatcoats. These latter, once soaked, never seemed to dry out, and if it rained incessantly, as it seemed to do for the next two months, we remained wet — very wet.

We used groundsheets as capes and also to sleep on. Gas-capes, superfluous for their planned purpose, were also worn to keep out the rain but both garments hampered our movements and caused us to perspire even more violently.

Constant wet weather wore us down in an insidious way, just as a long, hard winter wears down the old.

More often than not we were dirty and mud-caked because of our job. Oil and cordite impregnated our clothing. We stank, even though we kept to the disciplined ritual of washing and shaving at least once a day.

Quite often we stood for our meals, and these were scarcely Cordon Bleu. Doubtless our cooks did their best, occasionally pulling a miracle out of the bag, but they could not always provide something hot. It became more and more common to rely on Compo Rations, a composite pack which we prepared ourselves.

I digress here, to reflect on cookhouse dixies. They always seemed to be seasoned, whatever the present contents, with a strong flavour of onions. My mess tins, one for tea, the other for everything else, always tasted of onions. Even the rice pudding flavour was curiously enriched by the onion's distinctive taste. Rumour had it that a preparation, unspecified, was added to our tea to subdue our brutal sexual urges. Could it be that the onion contained such unwelcome properties, or did it disguise a more sinister additive?

A covering of grease covered all the liquid we consumed. However much I scrubbed my utensils or scoured them with sand, the ubiquitous grease was there.

All of us, whether Signallers, Command Post Staff, Drivers, Cooks, everyone was united with one purpose and this was to see that our shells hit the targets quickly and accurately in order to do the maximum damage. We on the Guns were the last in the chain. The projectiles were gathered round us, rammed up the breech and sent on their way.

Somewhere in England, in some improvised Sergeants' Mess I came across an old book on the Gunners, which I felt at the time should have been in safe keeping at Woolwich. Browsing through it I came across this verse:

'We have bartered our souls to the Guns,
Every fibre of body and brain
Are we trained to them, chained to them, serfs?
Aye, but proud of the weight of our chains.'

Positively Kiplingesque and archaic you may say? Nevertheless, there is a lot of truth in it. We Regulars who had been trained at the Depot were taught to believe that the only way to leave a gun in action was on a stretcher. I never knew anyone or heard of anyone who left in any other way. We wanted to, no doubt, but we didn't. There was a great bond of loyalty and comradeship and these qualities were transmitted to the recruits who had been called up and who had joined us. There was certainly strength in numbers and one man's weakness would diminish that strength.

The philosophy stated by A. E. Housman in *The Day of Battle* may also have had a steadying influence on us.

'But since the man that runs away
Lives to die another day
And cowards' funerals, when they come,
Are not wept so well at home,
Therefore though the best is bad
Stand and do the best my lad:'

I always felt sorry for the young and not so young men who had been conscripted, especially those who had left a settled marriage and a family. They coped splendidly, although their minds must have still remained at home. They had been uprooted from a stable domestic environment. From their mental suffering I learnt a great deal; and some of it was unpleasant as I shall reveal.

As for me, there was no one to blame but myself. I had made my own bed and could not grouse about lying on it, and had no wish to do so. Come to think of it, I was a rather rare bird, being young and single, for most of those left from Shorncliffe days and France were reservists who were quite a bit older and mostly married as were those who had been called up. My responsibilities domestically were negligible.

Domestic troubles or not, our purpose must take priority. Young or older, married or single, whether beset by cares or relatively carefree, we had to tend the Gun.

Our foe across the way was eminently worthy of our attentions and indeed (inexplicable to civilians) our admiration. His aim was the same as ours, and he retaliated very well.

Our search for each other was relentless and it went on, not just from nine to five but round and round the clock.

With puckish humour the Gun continued to turn on me as a lion does occasionally on its trainer; still tried to pin me against hard, immovable objects; still remained inscrutable as it did so, ugly great bastard that it was.

We had a steel hawser attached to a winch on our Quad. It was used a lot, so we were experts in running it out and in, just as we were experts in daubing it with grease to keep it in good working order. Another of my jobs was to supervise its use and to convey my intentions by hand signals to the driver, who was handling the gears. Close co-operation was needed for there were some very risky operations where people could easily get hurt. Steel spikes were driven in with sledge-hammers to gain more leverage. We dug wheels out of sucking mud. Drag-ropes were employed as we joined in a frenzied tug-of-war with our monstrous, inanimate object which changed its image frequently and at such times became a vicious, uncooperative living thing.

Sweat poured from us on the coldest days. When it was wet, moisture from our bodies mingled with that coming through our clothing.

More often than not we had to dig in, and fast. First of all a pit would be dug, into which the Cannon was eased, all nice and snug on its platform. Then there were slit-trenches, weapons pits for small arms, in our case Bren-guns, and finally we would improvise places in which we could rest or sleep as safely as possible. But we might, according to the surroundings and vulnerability, have to slap the Gun down in action temporarily and put up a big hessian camouflage net on big strong poles, stayed and pegged down like a tent, and tightened. This alone could be quite a task, particularly if it was put up in the dark with a strong wind blowing, with a rush to beat the dawn. The meshes were apt to catch any awkward projections, like the dial-sight or corners of the shield. The net, if wet, was heavy, for it had green, brown and yellow strips tied on it which caught the moisture. Furthermore, the rain dripped through when we were knelt waiting for fire orders.

Lorries laden with ammunition came up to the gun-position under the supervision of the Quartermaster Sergeant and his staff. We slung the metal boxes, four twenty-five pound shells to a box, like feather pillows. There were boxes of cartridges, more cumbersome but not so heavy. Usually this unloading was done at a crazy pace for the vehicles with their lethal loads, were very much sought after by the Hun. It was in our own interests to get those large lorries away. There was another reason for our haste and that was the Quartermaster Sergeant. When he came up the line he was always later than late for another engagement back where he lived.

Poor man, he was never happy with us, and I must confess that there were times when our perversity replaced our consideration for our own safety and we employed delaying tactics. We delighted in playing on his impatience which merged into a marked uneasiness and restlessness. Where did the Quartermaster live? I never really knew, although I did know that gun positions were not his natural habitat. I thought he must rest in a snug nest of surplus blankets and dry greatcoats with access to a whole store of rations and even rum. There he would lie, curled up like a dormouse, whilst we would be crouched, dripping wet, round our Monster ramming shells up his great hungry maw.

We piled shells and cartridges as near as we could to the Gun, throwing them in an endless chain, some of us stacking the pile as it grew. Incessantly we cursed, using one familiar word as a constantly recurring motif as it were, round which we wove the most colourful textures. We vied with each other for the most varied flow of language. Blasphemies of the most luried kind were incorporated. To be a Supremo in this skill gained one added respect, for all were artists except for those few who had religion, and who indulged in their own private vices to relieve their tensions. The Gun did not take kindly to them for he really did need Macho-mates as his companions.

I suspect that our bra-burning sisters, Ms X and her chums with more than an inclination to support Women's Liberation, would like to challenge us to a competition on our own ground. Sergeant Anstee might not have welcomed them with honeyed phrases had they joined his gun detachment on a pitch-black night in the rain or sleet, with the spade dug in up to the handspike and the platform tilting so that the Gun had to be run up; with fire orders coming through on a completely new line of fire; with possibly a misfire to deal with for good measure. Oh! and just to add a little interest to a mundane existence, Jerry chose to drop a few of his shrieking horrors to liven things up a bit. We had our moments all right and we became coarsened. When we got home, those of us who did get home, our poor wives and sweethearts had a lot to contend with. It took me years to realize that my tender young wife was not, apart from certain delightful differences, just a smaller version of me. I hope that eventually I was restored to some degree of gentility.

Always, always we listened. Whether resting, eating or writing letters; whether shaving, relieving ourselves (especially then) or washing our meagre stock of linen we listened. Our ears were finely tuned when we were firing, and the Gun itself was making a good effort at blowing off our heads every time the firing lever was pulled; but then we were helpless for we could not take evasive action by flinging ourselves into whatever cover we could find. The Gun came first. If we were sprayed with small pieces of metal He came off best, for He could take a few hard knocks.

Our ears never rested. Nor did our eyes. They roved about the landscape continuously, with acute vigilance. When we pulled out of the line for brief rests, there was still no respite from our watchfulness. These heightened senses were still with us back in England. For years we would be ready to fling ourselves to the ground at the sound of a faulty exhaust.

Tex Bell, in a letter to my mother sent later in the year after the worst of the fighting was over in Italy wrote, 'Please don't think that my nerves have gone or something, although I'll admit that when I hear thunder I instinctively duck down, but a lot of us do that. It will wear off.'

There was one redeeming feature, if it can be so described. Unlike other battle-zones, for instance France or North Africa, or at home in the earlier stages of the war, there was no threat from air attack in Italy.

In this penultimate decade of the twentieth century all sorts of people wear ear-muffs. It is the fashionable thing. Tractor drivers, engaged in ploughing wear them, men at small arms practice, using what is now known as a hand-gun, are so equipped. We never wore ear-muffs. Granted, ear-plugs were issued but I do think they were very popular, for we needed our ears as much as our eyesight. Quite apart from what I have said above, it was vital to hear fire-orders clearly.

It is only fair to mention that a Tannoy System was introduced, probably in 1942 before we went to North Africa. Each gun detachment carried a speaker attached to a cable which was run to the Troop Command Post on coming into action. The system was not used if a short stay was intended and there were certain other occasions when it was impractical to employ it.

'And gentlemen in England now abed.' My embitterment towards certain privileged young men in my part of Lancashire who had been so adept at evading anything approaching discomfort or danger was also joined by my contempt, for I could not see how any fit person could stand by and watch when Freedom itself was at stake. Still, it was more their problem than it was mine. I wondered whether, beneath their arrogance, they found it difficult to live with themselves. Others made up for their insularity.

News came with almost every letter that someone else I knew had joined up, had become engaged in the fighting — had been killed.

From my Sixth Form at school, a high percentage had entered the Services at the outbreak of activities. Some, as was inevitable, were already dead. Tommy Fairhurst, he of the golden hair, known for his headlong flight on his motor cycle which always seemed to be leaking oil, had thrust his fighter plane towards the Luftwaffe and perished in the full exuberance of youth . . . golden boy if ever there was one. Terry Lendrum, youthful athlete and Victor Ludorum had gone down with HMS *Hood*.

I have a booklet containing the names of old boys who served in the forces. At the beginning it states:

'This list of seven hundred names is not to be regarded as complete.

It is, however, as comprehensive as possible and includes the names of all Old Boys known to have served in HM Forces up to VJ Day.'

After the war those who had been and those who had not mingled in the bars of pubs. We, the far-travelled were catching up on lost time; we had a backlog of pints to sink. They were not in such a hurry. We, who tended to drift off occasionally to gaze at distant horizons, saw by their eyes that they were lacking in hardship and suffering such as we had known and seen. They had lingered with the girls with the scent of haytime round them, with all the time in the world for dalliance. Whilst we . . . ?

A great gulf had yawned which could never be spanned. There was no doubt about it. We were different from the rest who had stayed behind.

Where was my Youth? It had gone. I never knew when it went, or how, but my Golden Years had sped, and I was one of the fortunate, for there were many who were dead before they had lived.

CHAPTER XXI

From our position under the terrace we moved the next day to a similar one, further to the left. Here we were raised up on a terrace, with others rising behind us. We dug in as well as we could, for we were more exposed. There were some small trees obstructing our arc of fire, so these had to come down. It would not do at all to hit one of these unless we were bent on suicide. The ground was rocky in places so I dug my own slit-trench on the terrace above, behind the Gun.

In the early evening when it was already dark we 'took posts' and opened fire. Our target was well over to the right, and 'B' Sub., the cannon on our left, was firing nearly across us. We could feel the muzzle blasts and the shells were far too close for comfort. Suddenly there was a terrific crash. Our Gun and the next were silhouetted momentarily against the flash. Fireflies flew wildly about and made spiteful hisses. We ducked instinctively and swore, even though we were busy.

Christ! What was it? A secret weapon? We never knew. It was said afterwards that someone had fired into a tree, as we were really well over the prepared field of fire, and it was dark. Another opinion was that it was a premature, which meant that a fuse had been faulty and the shell had burst just outside the muzzle. This did not happen often, but there was always the exception. Somehow this unwelcome visitation did not act or sound like anything we had experienced before. The odd air-burst had started coming over, but this one was not quite right. Miraculously, no one was hurt, but it did not help to soothe our nerves. The rain continued to fall steadily.

When we 'stood easy' I left Gunner Smith to keep watch. He was a willing young Cockney who had been called up and who had a young wife back home. I retired to my slit-trench, which resembled a shallow grave. In the bottom of it there seemed to be about six inches of water. I put down my groundsheet, a futile act to be sure, and wearing my soggy greatcoat I lowered myself down and drew my very damp blanket over me, covering my head. I always felt more protected and cosy when I did this.

It had been put about that enemy paratroopers might attack our position from the rear. I did not find this possibility comforting; nor did I find any comfort in my sleeping place, so I decided to move. Wearily I took up my bed and slid down the terrace on to the path behind the Gun and put down my groundsheet as near as I could to the steep incline. Stretched out at ground level, I had just closed my eyes when the most plaintive voice I have ever heard intruded on my privacy.

"Sarge," cried Gunner Smith, "the f . . . . n' breech 'as fell out." I sprang up and reached Gunner Smith in record time. There he was crouched with bent knees in a most uncomfortable position, holding up half a hundredweight of breech-block which was on the point of crashing into the mud at his feet. How he got into that position I never did find out for he was very reticent about it. I could only assume that he had decided to carry out some maintenance, which was laudable but misguided considering the conditions. My admonishment, carried out in a low voice, was charged with deep emotion. There was no threat to put him on a charge for we kept such happenings in the family, and he was a good lad.

Just as we had slipped the breech-block back into position fire orders came through. The target was in a completely different direction. The spade at the extreme end of the trail, which digs in with the shock of recoil, had buried right in and was embedded deeply into the stony path. Sometimes we fitted a box which did not penetrate the ground. But in this position, with the box fitted we should have slid, platform as well, right back against the vertical wall of the terrace. The handspike was in its socket above the trail-eye, but part of it was embedded in mud. I grabbed it and lifted but the spade was dug in firmly. I shoved my arms, bent at the elbows, under the handspike, bent my knees and heaved. Gunner Smith was doing what he could at the side of the trail. I made the biggest heave I can ever remember making and almost gave myself a double rupture. Time was not on our side, for orders were being reeled off throughout. There was a great sucking sound and the spade came out. I felt proud that I had made a lift worthy of Anstee. Anstee, by the way, was probably using his giant strength on a similar task. Why had we not arranged things better between shoots? The answer is simple. We had been on a fixed line on the previous target ready to put down harassing fire immediately and we daren't move the Gun.

The rest of my detachment had appeared on the scene by this time, for the whole procedure had occurred in a matter of a few seconds. We set our instruments, traversed and elevated, loaded and fired. Air-bursts rent the air not far above our heads and round about us. This game of retaliation was played constantly, so we were not really surprised, but just scared stiff.

On 28th/29th February 32nd Battery had a DF (Defensive Fire) Task called Stinker.

When things had quietened down and the Gun was resting, its barrel too hot to touch comfortably, I returned to my bed. In the middle of my groundsheet, about where the upper part of my body would have rested, there was an unwelcome visitor. It was a jagged shell-splinter about six inches long, firmly embedded and sticking up like a dagger.

We did not stay there much longer. Having crept out the way we had come in, again at night, but this time taking our guns with us, we travelled once more through run-down, war-scarred villages or small towns. Wherever I went in Italy (granted this was not very far) there were buildings leaning at crazy angles, with great holes in them. It was obvious that this was not a very rich country, but war had just about put paid to it completely.

Allied bombers dropped over one thousand tons of bombs on Cassino on 15th March. The New Zealanders made the second attack, which failed. Our role was a diversionary attack during the night. The 1st Infantry Brigade (Guards) had joined the Division for the period 10th March, 1944 — 21st March, 1944.

We passed a battalion of the Guards who looked as if they were on their way up the line. Our tractors were grinding forward slowly, well spaced out with guns and trailers rolling behind. I was looking out of the aperture in the roof of the Quad, scanning the surrounding country. It was a bleak, depressing day and there was nothing much to see except desolation and devastation.

By the roadside were standing some tall heron-like creatures, silent and motionless under their dripping groundsheets. The rain ran off their steel helmets. Their weapons were covered as a protection against the moisture. Mist and drizzle partially enshrouded them. They were the 2nd Coldstream, splendid fellows who had a reputation for keeping themselves to themselves. They took very little notice of us as we passed. I took a lot of notice of them though, for I was intrigued at what they were eating. That they were taking their meal standing was not unusual, but what they held in their hands and put into their mouths was. Each had an enormous Cornish pasty which looked as if it had come straight from the bakery. My mouth watered so much that I must have left a trail of saliva behind me.

We were not in favour with the Guards just at the moment, for during a shoot a stray round had fallen perilously near their cookhouse, causing bad feeling but fortunately no casualties.

There was ample visual proof that this cookhouse was fully operational, and I was very envious.

I stood on a hill looking northwards towards Monte Cassino. Today most young people have never heard of it, are unaware of its existence, its whereabouts, know nothing of the slaughter and destruction that went on, either in the Monastery itself or round about.

It was early morning, and for once it promised to be a beautiful day; for once there was an unexpected tranquillity. Our world, which never slept, must have nodded off. The sun was rising. With a great home-sickness for my loved ones and my birthplace, I wondered whether I should live to see the sun rise again. Such sunrises I had witnessed many a time as I ran over the fields to work as a farm labourer at Land Hill Farm. It was scarcely normal when a young man was moved to wonder whether he would last out the day.

On this hillside, not far from the Gun, never far away from the Gun, I experienced some understanding of the tremendous waste which war brings. But it would go on, of course. I was only one tiny link in an immeasurably long chain stretching from the distant, distant past, through the present, into the endless future, who had experienced, would experience and was still to experience such emotions as mine were then.

Soon the bombers came over, on their way to Monte Cassino which was in the process of being destroyed.

The monotonous intonations of the cohorts of planes were high overhead. I was washing a vest in water heated in an empty ration tin. There was a tremendous shrieking sound, like a coven of witches screaming in on broomsticks to a Sabbath. Instinctively I flung myself under my father-figure, the Gun and landed on His ribbed platform. There was a mighty explosion. This was surely bigger than we had ever encountered. Nothing else happened so I crawled out. At a respectable distance there was a very large crater. The Yanks had allowed one of their bombs to escape, thus causing me to have feelings similar to those of the Guards' Colonel about his cookhouse. I cursed as I picked up my bedraggled vest and rescued my diminutive wash-tin.

There was a light rain falling and mist was lying close to the ground. The Guns were dug in just off the churned up road and their snouts were leering out at the files of the 2nd Battalion, the Bedfordshire and Hertfordshire Regiment as they passed by. This was the same Battalion to which we had given support many times, one memorable occasion being the counter-attack on the bridge-head at Escanaffles in 1940. They were on their way up a hillside. There was no shelter awaiting them there except the sangars they would have to build out of the stones and boulders round about, unless they were fortunate and some were still intact.

These poor harassed foot-sloggers wore sandbags round their legs for extra protection. They seemed to be of little use for the soldiers were encased in mud from head to foot. All carried a weapon of some kind; all had additional accoutrements hung about them. There were those among them (selected it seemed for their smallness of stature) who laboured under the weight of mortars and their bases and of course, the cases of bombs. The Infantry bore all their goods on their backs. It was small wonder that they slipped and slid about under their burdens.

One of the troglodytes spoke with a Lancashire accent very well known to me.

"Hallo, Edwin," it said.

"Edwin? Who or what the bloody hell is Edwin?"

My detachment and indeed all in the vicinity voiced this question. Of course, I am Edwin, but not here. Like most others, I had a pseudonym, not nearly as refined as Edwin. My comrades seemed to see me in a new light. How should I live this down? I felt that I should be leaning over a wicket gate in some Victorian garden, singing 'Come into the Garden Maud'. Alas. I am not dressed suitably for the part and furthermore the scenery is all wrong.

The infantryman who greeted me was Teddy Hornby, who came from a rural setting of almost unbelievable quietness not far from where I lived. He was a couple of years younger than I was, and we had attended the same village school together. Now Teddy was scarcely recognizable, festooned as he was with his battle-gear, and disguised as he was beneath a thick layer of mud. I suppose it was his voice which gave him away. We exchanged a few words which were all we had time for. We remarked that even the Fylde, damp as it was, was surely never as bad as this.

Teddy moved on to the very unhealthy spot allotted to him; whilst I stayed in mine. Under the circumstances I was pleased to remain, but it was surprising that the Infantry did not normally care to linger where we were. They jeered at the relatively long distance there was between us and the front line, and called us the 'Nine mile Snipers', but they seemed to move faster when they saw the shields and the barrels and muzzle brakes sticking out. The Beds. and Herts. probably got the message that Jerry might range in on us (he already had) and might decide to put down a stonk. Later on we heard the incessant rattle of small arms and the thump of the mortars. When we popped over a few rounds as supporting fire, I imagined the screaming of the shells and I said to myself, "Here she comes Teddy," and hoped that none fell short.

On St. Patrick's Day, my birthday, I felt despondent. Nowadays my condition would probably be diagnosed as an anticipatory bout of premature male menopause and I should have been prescribed tablets. Had I gone sick here 'Jock' would have given me short shrift.

It rained steadily. We had to carry ammunition up a steep slope which was very slippery. Most of us struggled up this forbidding, unwelcome hillside, some carrying boxes of shells suspended by the handles in both hands. I tried carrying a box on each shoulder but the metal bit in and I was so twitched about on the uncertain ground that I rejected this method. Each box, as I have said previously, weighed nearly one hundredweight.

My battledress blouse had been removed and so had my shirt, so that above the waist I wore only a short sleeved woollen vest, soaking wet with rain and sweat.

Near the Gun a protective shelter had been erected out of discarded shell and cartridge boxes filled with earth. Our treasured tarpaulin sheet was thrown over to form a roof. Inside a fire had been lit, for though we were well up forward, we were at that time invisible to Jerry. Even a bed of brushwood had been spread over the floor of our temporary home.

On this improvised divan I reclined and read my mail which had just arrived. News from home was good. There was every indication of faithfulness and high regard from my sweetheart. My mother was taking no harm. These sentiments should have uplifted me out of my despondency, but the place and the weather did not help in ridding me of my loneliness. Furthermore, my physical discomfort was increasing. Our fire, made of damp wood and twigs, was throwing off a lot of smoke which could not escape, for there was no outlet in the roof. The heat increased in the confined space; my eyes smarted and watered. I ruminated on the plight of less sophisticated people like, for instance, the Anglo-Saxon serfs in their hovels. They must have been a pretty miserable lot, cowering over their smoky fires in the deep mid-winter.

Stretched out on my miserable pallet, feeling even less fortunate than the serfs, I lit a cigarette and inhaled deeply. Blinking with red-rimmed eyes, I watched the steam rise from my smelly, begrimed woollen vest with its buttoned neck, and mingle with the smoke. I thought that this was it.

Tomorrow I should be on my way to hospital in a meat-wagon, with double pneumonia, or worse. At least, there would be a respite from humping bloody ammo.

I never reached hospital, never caught a chill or a cold. Only my eyes felt sore.

This was a memorable birthday. I never had a drink.

There followed a shifting series of events, one pursuing the other in rapid succession and moving with increasing rapidity to a climax. It was like being at a Magic Lantern Show where, when the lecturer tapped with his stick, the assistant moved the slides from one to the next.

We were out in the open, on terraces, with no foliage at all to give us cover. 'B' Troop's four guns were in line below 'A' Troop, whose cannons were in position just behind us, on the higher terrace.

Familiar animated figures in steel helmets operated the guns which belched and roared, kicked and quivered as the recoil systems thrust backwards. These violent sudden movements could spell disaster for the unwary. Smoke and fumes, flashes and noise, loud metallic clangs as the breeches were opened and closed, these were the sensations and actions, attendant upon and familiar to our calling.

Cartridge cases, spent of their charges, were ejected and bounced off the trail, or, if the barrels were at suitable angles and if the breeches were operated by experts, flew back well clear of the trail-eye. These metal cases were red-hot, straight out of the oven so to speak, and it was prudent to keep out of their way. The Guns were hungry and in an angry mood. Two or three gunners to each Gun were kept very busy bringing up and passing shells and cartridges to the Nos. 4, the ones who loaded. Added to the cacophony were the sounds of metal boxes being opened, emptied and flung hurriedly out of the way. When the Guns were being served, there were no idle hands.

Each time 'A' Troop fired, which was with great frequency for each Gun was operating individually with each detachment loading as fast as it could, we in front and below were all too aware of the muzzle blast. Bits of debris from the propellant charges were blown on to us. They were like tiny pieces of charred papers from a bonfire and they were accompanied by the stink of cordite. This did not bother us much. What did worry us was the risk of a premature. Any one of the missiles, blown out at great speed and rotating immediately over us and just above, could explode if it was faulty and do us a lot of damage.

Such crowded conditions would not have been encouraged or tolerated by the Instructors in Gunnery at the School of Artillery. At least, I think not. Situations were sometimes bizarre when there was a real live enemy leaning on us. Deviations were often made; rules bent.

In which position was it, I wonder, where there was a little house or hut a hundred yards or so to the rear of our cannon? By it was parked a 15 cwt truck which we called a 'Monkey' truck because of the big letter 'M' on its side. It housed a wireless set and was, of course, operated by the signallers. Investigation of the interior of this vehicle, behind the tarpaulin flaps which were always closed to prying eyes, would have disclosed an interesting modification. Room had been made in the already confined space to store a large demijohn of vino in a wicker container. Gunner L — was esconced within. It could be guaranteed that his manner would indicate partial or advanced inebriation, for he had been like this since the early days in the BEF in France. Nevertheless, he and his pal S. — who operated with him, were both efficient and courageous. They could always be relied upon to go out and lay lines, day or night, whatever the conditions.

The demijohn and especially its contents were strictly against King's Rules and Regulations, but nobody spoilt L —'s pleasure by dropping a sly hint in the wrong place. Incidentally, here was one of us at least who never went short of a drop to drink. He was, however, in a much better position to get it for his duties enabled him to make detours, which ours did not.

There was a short whining sound followed by an explosion. Flames and debris erupted from the little house. Simultaneously there was a desperate exit from the truck. Gunner L —, upright but unsteady made a lightning tactical assessment and decided upon his route. He aimed with lurching gait to move round the corner of the house. Had he waited another second or so he would have been whisked away in the truck which the driver revved up and drove to safety.

There was another shell-burst, quite close to the dwelling. He was precipitated round the corner. We observers waited wondering whether we should call for stretcher-bearers. Suddenly, in the paddock on the far side we saw as in silhouette or caricature, a lean figure running at full stretch. For one not given to any form of exercise, he was doing remarkably well and was aiming to achieve a record sprint by the look of it. Long thin legs at full stretch, arms flailing, head thrust back, steel helmet flung to the full extent of chin-strap, he was intent on being first at an invisible finishing post. We sent up a cheer, for it was a good display he was giving. Back at the truck, exhausted by his ordeal, still mouthing frightful curses in his mother-tongue as he had when he propelled himself from the tree at Dunkirk, he was greatly in need of a stimulant. His rage was aggravated beyond all limits when he found that a large fragment of stone or shell had wrecked his demijohn.

In contrast to the hard drinking, there was Gunner Allman, probably Lance-Bombardier by this time. He had been my limber-gunner, and a jolly good one. He saw to all the greasing, oiling, assembly and checking of tools and the packing of them when we moved. This latter was quite a skilled task for we never had enough room under our covers on the shelf in front of our limber or in our limited storing space. He also had another important job. There were always light-fingered members of other detachments, all too ready to pounce on a muzzle cover or breech cover, or maybe a pull-through or spanners or a spare drag-rope. L/Bdr Allman was always on the alert for prowlers, for he was jealous of his property. It helped me a lot to know that he took his appointment seriously.

L/Bdr Allman approached me looking very downcast. At his best he was not given to untrammelled outbursts of humour. He was thoroughly reliable but taciturn with it. In his hand he bore a letter. It was a 'Dear John', saying that his wife had forsaken him for another. It turned out that she had also left him in debt to the tune of £800, which in those days was a lot of money.

He was wet and dirty. He was being shot at fairly regularly. His dream-world had been shattered, for his home which he had struggled to create was now disintegrating and he had no place to which he could return.

I sat on the trail, sipping a mug of strong tea, laced with a delicate onion flavour and a tinge of grease. I read the letter which he proffered. "Sarge," he asked, "what shall I do?" How could I answer? I had never lived with a woman, had no home of my own and certainly had no chattels for anyone to dispose of. I offered him as much sympathy as I could but I could not judge if it meant anything or not. Later, I arranged for him to see our Troop Commander who probably brought the matter before the Battery Commander. I knew myself that nothing could or would be done. Poor Tom Allman was only one of the great many who found themselves abandoned.

Talk about piling on the agony. This poor bastard had more than enough to contend with without his wife doing the dirty on him.

I finished my tea and threw away the dregs, thinking as I did so that the act of living seemed to get more grim. Quite a lot of human beings were not very pleasant or faithful, or at all reliable.

L/Bdr Allman soldiered on. He was fed up, f . . . . . up and far from home but he soldiered on. What else was there for him to do? A man of less strength of character would have kicked against Authority, or even deserted.

But he was as strong in spirit as he was physically and he carried on. And his example taught me a little more about standing up to adversity, and strengthened my cynicism towards human relationships.

We remained in action in the Suja area until the 20th March when we were relieved by units of the French Army and moved to a concentration area near Guiliano just north of Naples. Two or three days later we were off to San Marco.

We pulled in to a wooded area where we boiled out the barrels of our cannon and pulled them through with our giant pull-through to make the rifling gleam. (Incidentally, we did this frequently when we were in action.) Then we got everything ready for inspection including ourselves and our kit. There was a Gun-park inspection and the vehicles were also given a thorough look-over.

The preparations for these functions were not met with starry-eyed enthusiasm; nor were the attendant remarks about our leaders, from the Colonel downwards to the Sergeant-Major, at all complimentary. Barbed comments, uttered in undertones, but still intentionally audible, fell for the most part on the ears of shrewd NCOs who appeared to have been stricken quite suddenly with a mild form of deafness.

When we were in this place, 'resting', some sly dog brought from who knows where, a small bottle containing clear liquid purporting to have an alcoholic base. One more reason for my distaste for the Italian Campaign was that there was a shortage of strong drink, at least where I went. Granted, a gun position was not usually over-populated. No enterprising Italian appeared to the rear of the guns, vending booze in the same manner that peripatetics in England sell ice-cream. So when the bottle was passed round we reached for it eagerly and took a swig. One small swallow was enough. It scorched our gullets; burned all the way down our alimentary tracts; took our breath quite away. Even Navy rum had nothing on this. For hours we lived in an unreal world where great pile-drivers drove into our heads and where any exertion, like taking off a gun wheel to carry out maintenance, caused our visions to be eclipsed by multicoloured lights. A connoisseur thought it had been wood-alcohol.

CHAPTER XXII

After the Garigliano our next sector was grimmer still. Doom threatened round every corner of the tortuous roads as we climbed upwards into the wild and mountainous country to the north-east of Cassino. From 26th March we had entered the command of XIII Corps, 8th Army and were on our way to relieve the 3rd Algerian Division. As there was more intense shelling and mortaring there were more casualties.

Towards the end of March saw us in action at Aquafondata. It was at this location that the Regiment's War Diary refers to the signal lines of French units being employed, 'owing to continued breakage of the Regimental line by shellfire'. A little later the lines were laid to the forward Command Post, each by a different route. Two maintenance posts were set up. One gains the impression that it was with difficulty that one line at least was kept in operation all the time.

So we went into these very stark surroundings. Up, up into the mountains we climbed, slowly and as it were, with 'cat-like tread'. I did not like this eerie atmosphere. It seemed that we had entered 'Long Tom' country. These 'Long Toms' were big guns of the American Army. They were positioned just off the road, audible but often unseen. They boomed away like great funeral knells. Their echoes reverberated through the hills and hollows. As these tocsins sounded I seemed to be taking part in one great funeral service, in which I could very easily participate as one of the deceased. These macabre sounds went on and on.

Standing up in the Quad, looking out through the open aperture in the roof, I saw sheer drops with valleys, partially enshrouded in mist, lying far, far below. Sometimes we came perilously close to the edges. Back there, a few yards to the rear, ever present, ever our constant companion, lumbering along, was the Gun.

The ground was rocky, but by the roadside in one place someone had laboured to dig shallow, temporary graves. There were markers, improvised, to show where the bodies lay. Here and there a hand had risen as if in greeting.

As we are today, friend, so shall you be tomorrow, even today?

It was like the landscape on the moon, barren and unfriendly.

We dropped down to lower ground, rolling slowly but inexorably to the next inevitable position. From trees which covered the ground on either side of the road phantoms seemed to emerge from all directions. They were oblivious to the menace of our heavy vehicles, and seemed set on keeping to predetermined paths. Ashen-faced and covered in a dusty substance, they stumbled and shuffled through us. They dragged their rifles by the slings, and it was only the rattling of these weapons on the road surface that caused me to think that these were not supernatural visitations after all. All of us in the Quad must have been of the same mind for the silence of death was on us as well.

There were some women among them, it would appear, who seemed to be in the same trance-like state. The troops were Ghoumiers from Morocco and it was their custom to take their womenfolk with them wherever they went, or so I was told. They had just dragged themselves out of what must have been a terrible action. They should have been dark-skinned, but strain and exhaustion had made them pallid. Far beyond the limits of ordinary endurance, they glided and drifted past us, beyond us and away. What horrors they had experienced to be thus transformed, I could not imagine. For a good while afterwards a chill descended on us, such a one as is said to come when ghosts are present. No one spoke as we ploughed to the next goal.

I asked myself continually from the time that I arrived at Naples, was this Italy, home of the sun-kissed grape, beloved of English milords on the Grand Tour over a couple of centuries, applauded for the influence of some of the greatest musicians, artists and poets? Or was I being hurled hither and thither in all the wrong insalubrious places?

It was at about this time that we had a casualty which caused another sombre few hours. One of our young gunners, who came from the East End, was going about his duties, singing softly to himself. A young Adonis he was, prone to joking and laughter, strong and in glowing health. A stray shell splinter caught him and killed him instantly. No other marks were to be found except a small incision. There was little blood, I think, and no disfigurement. A temporary grave was dug by our latrine orderly, who doubled up by acting as mortician. This outdoor lavatory attendant stitched an army blanket round the corpse, which was still warm. More feeling was shown than would have been displayed by your average civilian undertaker though, for he lying prone in the blanket and he bending over at his devotions had been mates.

Within the hour our youthful soldier was stretched under his mound of earth, the same earth which he had trodden so blithely such a short time before. The War Graves Commission would move him to a British Cemetery later. Somewhere, up near Monte Cassino he will be there, perennially young, surrounded by thousands of others who never did have the chance to grow old.

This short, sharp lesson in annihilation also left its mark on me:

> 'Boast not thyself of tomorrow; for thou knowest not what a day may bring forth . . . . '

I carried two books in my haversack. One was my Kipling, the other the Holy Bible. It may be thought that this latter was a strange choice for one less than Godly. My mother, a devout woman, had probably pressed it upon me and I took it for her sake. There was a lot of reading in it, but it did not always soothe my troubled spirit. The text quoted above, for instance, was uncomfortably true.

> 'Thou shalt not be afraid for the terror by night; nor for the arrow that flieth by day . . . . '

I did, all the time.

One which I would have liked to place my bet on ran like this:

> 'A thousand shall fall at thy side, and ten thousand at thy right hand, but it shall come not nigh thee.'

Eleven thousand to one are pretty poor odds.

On an afternoon we pulled into a wood, raised up, overlooking the Liri Valley. There were muffled thuds of the artillery and puffs of smoke here and there. It appeared so harmless from where I was standing.

I looked down on a sunken road. Suddenly there was an unfamiliar jingling sound which rapidly grew louder. From my point of vantage, I watched a mountain battery going forward. The mules, harness rattling, screw guns strapped on their saddles were accompanied by the gunners. Mules and gunners walked at a very fast pace, mules straining, men looking intently ahead. Anstee, probably witnessing the same scene not far away, must have felt a twinge of nostalgia.

I have already referred to this élite branch of the Artillery.

They could get into otherwise inaccessible positions, drop into action incredibly fast and hit targets on the other side of high hills.

I was reminded of the account by John Masters when he witnessed such a meeting on the North-West Frontier of India.

Kipling also sang the praises of this branch of the Artillery:

'D'you say that you sweat with the field-guns? By God you must lather with us . . . . '

Neither to right nor left these gunners turned their heads — save one. He glanced up quickly, gave me an intent look, and was gone. In the same instant we had met and parted. We had both converged on this one spot, travelling a long way to do it, for he was not of my race, but we were united for one purpose. A. E. Housman must have experienced a similar momentary meeting which he recounted in his *Shropshire Lad*:

'What thoughts at heart have you and I
We cannot stop to tell;
But dead or living, drunk or dry,
Soldier, I wish you well.'

The lean and vulpine Swaz, he with the arresting display of tattoos seldom revealed, may not have been the most likely candidate to lead a Bible Class or a Revivalist Meeting. His piratical appearance at this moment suggested more an inclination towards deflowering young ladies than Flower Arranging; and that mothers in various places had cause to wish that they had boarded up their daughters, first having locked them in chastity belts and chained their legs together. It wouldn't have mattered much, for he would have seduced the mother instead.

Yet Swaz had many good qualities. He was very loyal to his mates, very efficient at his job as Sergeant I/C Signals.

We were up forward where the opposition was tough and numerous. Mr Smith, called me in and showed me the map laid out in the Command Post. We were surrounded on three sides by enemy artillery, and they were thick on the ground. The six-barrelled mortars, or Nebelwerfers, were not far away. To say that no one liked them would be a massive understatement, for they put down a blanket of large bombs which arrived simultaneously with hideous but brief sounds which made the flesh creep. They caused very bad wounds for they did not fragment very well. To put it another way, big lumps of metal flew about when they burst.

The telephone wire to the Observation Post had been severed by these mortars. There was no one available to go and repair the wire, particularly as one of Swaz's minions had been sent to the rear for treatment as the pressure had made him 'bomb happy', a new name for shell-shock.

Swaz kicked his motor cycle into life, nonchalantly settled himself into the saddle, offered some quiet aside, probably bawdy and certainly witty, said, "Be seeing you Bas," and chugged slowly away over the rough ground. He called most people Bas, short for Basil, a name which was for him especially amusing. I watched the back view of Sgt Burman disappear among the trees. When I think about it I can always conjure up the rear view of him astride his motor cycle. I mumbled "Nice knowing you Swaz," to myself, for I did not expect to see him again.

But he did come back, some time later, unharmed but dishevelled, having restored communications. There were no visible signs that the mortars had ruffled his composure.

A 'bad ram' had been made. The driving band of the shell had not engaged properly with the rifling and the rear end of the shell was not far enough into the barrel.

> 'No. 1 will not order his gun to be fired but will inspect the chamber of the gun to see if light is showing past the projectile. If this is so he will report his gun out of action to the GPO who will order him to remove the round using the ejector projectile.'
>
> (Gun Drill for Q.F. 25pr. Gun War Office Publication)

The Ejector Projectile had a very long strong pole at one end to which was fitted a metal cone like a large funnel. The cone was slid down the barrel from the muzzle end. It fitted over the striker cover on the end of the fuse. Once positioned a smart tap with a sledge-hammer on the end of the pole caused the shell to slide backwards, where it was caught when it came out of the breech.

Where was the Ejector Projectile? It was either broken or had been loaned to the other Troop and was being used. It may have been taken away for repair, but whatever the reason no Ejector was available. Bam Anstee appeared from nowhere, smelling trouble. He had already acquired a camouflage pole, made of metal and hollow.

"Get out of the way, you little bleeder," said Bam, nudging me so that I almost fell over. He slid the camouflage pole down the barrel and worked it with great sensitivity, as if he were defusing a bomb, and under the circumstances it was not unlike that procedure.

In the Handbook, Ordnance Q.F. 25pr. Land Service (War Office Code 11450) it states:

> 'it (the shell) with normally be ejected under the supervision of the gun position officer by using the projector.'

On this particular occasion the GPO had been called away hastily on a most important mission, and was nowhere to be seen.

It also says in the Handbook:

> 'the final adjustment to the ejector should be carried out by one person, all others being behind the muzzle, and care must be taken

> to ensure that the head of the ejector fits snugly over the nose of the projectile, clear of the fuse.'

All others were behind the muzzle — well behind. They had probably left the country. There was no funnel-shaped cone to fit snugly. Indeed, the hollow end of the camouflage pole only just cleared the striker cover. 'Bam' moved the pole about like a doctor trying to find a vein when he was setting up a drip. Eventually he seemed to be satisfied. "Hold the bleeder, Badge," he said, "and hold it bloody firm."

He took up the sledge-hammer. Always an impressive figure, he now looked like Vulcan. "Christ," I muttered to myself, "up she goes and the colour's red."

Sgt. Anstee tapped the end of the pole and the shell was caught as it slipped out of the breech. Another heart-stopping incident was added to our repertoire.

Once a strange twittering noise accompanied the sound of a projectile passing near by on its outward run, as if a flight of giant starlings had decided to make a very speedy migration. It was thought that some idiot had failed to remove the canvas muzzle cover, which fitted over the muzzle-brake. We were tuned to pick up any strange extraneous noise, for we were always on the alert for potential danger. We laughed about it and speculated that if the muzzle cover had spiralled its way to the Hun, wrapped round a shell and making the same curious noise, it must have caused him to make a superhuman spring into his slit-trench. In actual fact, it was probably some defect in the driving-band which affected the rotation of the projectile.

The whisky ration had arrived, which was a privilege accorded to senior NCOs. It was probably against the rules, but I proffered a tot to those in my detachment who were interested. After all, soldiers with far more service than I were given to boasting of their twenty-one years of undetected crime. I, with my five years of Colour Service behind me could begin to bend the rules slightly.

By this time the rifling of the cannon was becoming decidedly worn; the maximum number of rounds had been fired and the safety level had been passed. We had been briefed by the Artificer to keep a sharp look-out for the tell-tale swelling of the piece above the breech, which presaged an explosion if we sent off the next round. Every time we fired I checked, and this in itself was a strain at night when I could only use a small torch.

I make no excuse for what happened for everything to do with the Gun was my sole responsibility; nor do I put it down to the whisky for we only had a drop each. I only know that it happened on the night of the whisky ration which was a highlight in our work-a-day lives.

The loader, No. 4, loaded a second shell after the first in place of the cartridge. It was very dark, with only the faint light of a torch and I was keeping one eye on the piece. There was a crunch as the striker cover of the second shell hit the base of the first. The second shell stuck out of the breech.

I lifted that baby out and cradled it in my arms. Someone shone the torch and we saw that the striker cover was all curled and awry when it should have been cylindrical and smooth. It leered at us and looked as if it would enjoy sending us to oblivion. I knew that normally it would take the rotation of the shell to force the aperture inside the fuse to open and allow the striker to operate, but I also had a sneaking feeling that it might be very, very lethal, deranged as it was.

I laid it down ever so gently near the Gun until we got 'Cease Firing'.

All this happened very quickly and there was only a slight delay, so that no suspicion rested on us and retribution did not approach us in the form of an irate and over-inquisitive Gun Position Officer.

Harry Slack, Gunner Harry Slack, a small thick-set Manxman, who, in spite of the quaint tongue which he spoke, was a valuable member of the detachment, my limber-gunner I think, assisted me in burying the result of our shame, 'darkly at dead of night'. There was even 'a lanthorn dimly burning' when we put the shell as deeply as we could, by a hedgerow in a ploughed field. I only hope that some poor Italian peasant did not hoist himself to eternity by catching his ploughshare on that menacing fuse.

The position we next found ourselves in was a very bad one indeed, to such an extent that we moved about as cautiously as hunted foxes, with eyes and ears on full alert. It was to the east of Aquafondata and we were again in support of the 10th Infantry Brigade. We had entered by a pass through which ran the River Inferno. Did someone say this pass was called 'Il Diavolo' — the 'Devil's Pass'? If it wasn't, it should have been. To get to the valley where we were to place our guns, we had to run along the edge of a mountain. The rock surface which towered on our left was pock-marked with the detonations of enemy shells. There was a sheer drop on the right, and as we were overlooked by a heavy concentration of German artillery we ran the gauntlet, so we were well spaced out.

The Aquafondata-St. Elia-Cassino road was under observation, so that road reliefs of OPs could only be carried out at night. As jeeps were the only vehicles allowed to move by day, supplies, water, arms and ammunition were delivered in the darkness. Ammunition was restricted to 15 rounds per gun per day. The Regimental Diary goes on to say that 'there is no limit for ammunition used to repel the enemy.'

From the moment we dropped into action and opened fire the enemy started to range on us. We were all too familiar with this procedure. We were well forward up a slope at the far end of the valley, just below a low ridge. It was a position which had been chosen skilfully. The trees, some of them large ones, did not interfere with our field of fire. Nevertheless, the Hun found us. A few detonations took place down below us, near the road from which we had come. Down there, 'Jock', our MO (were not all Medical Officers either Scottish or Irish?) had set up his Regimental Aid Post in as sheltered a place as he could get.

There was a sinister spirit abroad in this place. We were subdued when we were given 'Stand Easy', and we did not stay above ground or without cover if we could help it.

It was here that I saw what I considered to be the foolhardiness of the old school of officer, last relic of the First World War. A Senior Officer came to have a look at us. He may have been a product of public school and the 'Shop', but his act was not based on wisdom in the opinion of us, the more lowly. He was referred to as the 'nutmeg chewing bastard', because of some sort of attraction he displayed to this aromatic kernel of an East Indian fruit. There he stood up on the hillside by 'A' Troop, raised as if on a podium, haranguing his junior officers who stood uneasily around him. He gestured calmly from time to time to accentuate his statements, whilst the enemy artillery put down a fearsome stonk round about.

Lying under the Gun as I was, I observed by glancing round the gun-wheel with its big thick tyre, that his disciples, though trying to appear unruffled and attentive, were really very restive. I felt for them. We lesser mortals took no chances if we could help it. But then, we had nothing to prove. Frankly, although I was under reasonable cover, (my mother-figure, the Gun) I was most decidedly ill at ease.

The British generals of Wellington's army in the Peninsular and at Waterloo would have seen nothing eccentric or foolhardy in the action of our Senior Officer, and would have ostracized him most severely had he behaved otherwise. Michael Glover in his book on Wellington reveals that 'A reckless bravery was one of the hallmarks of British generals, good or bad.' Beresford, at Albuera, unhorsed a Polish lancer with his bare hands; when at St. Pierre, there was an explosion at William

Stewart's feet, he merely remarked, "A shell, sir, very animating," and went on with his conversation. Officers who might have been applauded for being more circumspect in avoiding unnecessary exposure to fire were looked upon as shirkers.

In the middle of the night I was even more scared. There was no discrimination between day or night, there were no set hours for us and that is why we were always tired out and always longing for sleep — perfect, uninterrupted sleep.

It was worse in the night though, and on this one in particular Jerry was really letting us know he was there. In the darkness the shells seemed to be exploding above us and into the ground all round us. There was a lot of 'big stuff' coming over and this included a concentration of 210 millimetre projectiles or '210s'. Amid the frightful whines and crashes, each one potentially lethal, and the deadly insect-hum of searing fragments of metal, trees came crashing down and the most terrifying factor was that one was uncertain where they were going to fall. Again I was lying on the platform of the Gun, under the trail, close to one wheel. For some reason I began to shake like a leaf from head to foot. In some curious way, I became two separate beings, one lying trembling, spread-eagled and face downwards, the other suspended above, looking down in some bewilderment at my state. Was I cracking up I wondered, as others had done; would I be sent down the line, having failed the supreme test; would I be sent through psychiatric ward and Transit Depot (oh! no) to end up for the rest of the war in some nondescript post, killing time? How should I face my detachment, carry on with my duties? I felt ashamed, but still I shivered and shook and was glad that I was alone.

The GPO shouted 'Take Posts — Troop Target
H.E. 117 Charge III . . . . '

I stood up, still with the bombardment going on round me, still with the trees and branches falling in the neighbourhood. My tremors stopped. I supervised the settings, aligned the gun, gave the order to load. The projectile was rammed into the rifling with steady precision and when the breech clanged shut, I shouted "Fire".

Recovery was rapid and complete. It appeared that I just could not bear the boredom of lying around waiting for something to happen.

Today was Easter Sunday.

CHAPTER XXIII

On Easter Sunday, 9th April, 1944, those with any sense would still be asleep, their best clothes laid out the night before, ready for church. The womenfolk would still have managed to conjure up colourful utility Easter bonnets to add a temporary relief to the drabness of wartime Britain and to attract and impress the congregation.

Our Easter bonnets were less decorative. There we were in our battered tin-hats, balanced on a mound of shells as we laboured. We must have looked a pretty ghastly crew in our smeared, begrimed battledress, but we matched the surroundings. The Quartermaster, who had escorted a big truck filled with ammunition, was rather more agitated than usual on this early morning, and we ourselves did not think it expedient to enforce delaying tactics. We flung our babies about like men stricken with St. Vitus's Dance. In this place with the bad atmosphere we were very exposed and we were still suffering from the rigours of the night which had just passed. Our quips hid our underlying fear and as usual, we were ready to fling ourselves towards the nearest cover, each of us having assessed where that would be.

Into this scene there entered a character not often seen in such a neck of the woods as ours. It was the Padre. Would we care to come to Holy Communion? he enquired politely, looking up at us.

Once upon a time, in my sheltered youth, even later as a recruit at Woolwich, I would have considered nothing amiss in his request. Regular attendance at Communion was a ritual not to be avoided in my home. There was even a prize for being the most promising scholar at Sunday-school, signed by the Revd Joseph Gorwall, MA, himself. Now, whatever simple faith I had assimilated was gone. No longer could I accept a benevolent protective Diety when suffering, carnage, betrayal and heart-break stalked abroad unchecked in my grim world.

It was not the Army which was responsible. There were many devout believers who retained their faith and some who found that it was strengthened. I did not. I lost it. Later in life, well-meaning folk tried to convert me. I found tracts slipped into my pocket, and once a book entitled *Jesus Saves*, but I remained a lost cause. Do-gooders in droves flocked round me, eager to claim success in rescuing such a choice brand from the burning. I remained adamant, having to rely upon my own philosophy for assistance, and whether this is good or bad I cannot judge. It was therefore to be expected that I was taken aback at the Padre's untimely invitation. 'Communion,' I thought. 'Communion with what or with whom? Were we not communing with Nature, with the Quartermaster, with this great load of ammo, and most of all with the Hun?' I declined the Padre's offer, not very civilly I am afraid, and thought that I had overstepped the mark and might be up on a charge for 'an insolent attitude to one of God's servants whilst on Active Service:'

'In that he on this Holy Day did utter remarks bordering on the blasphemous, in the presence of, if not exactly to, one of the Lord's Spiritual Advisers on Earth . . . . '

I suppose I should have sprung to attention on my lethal heap, flung up a regimental salute and barked:

"Sir, as you will observe we are busily engaged on our military duties. It is necessary to prepare to chuck a few more thunderbolts at the Hun in order to lessen the risk of our own obliteration. We beg to be excused from attending the ritual aforementioned. Intercede for us in your prayers — and burn a candle for us, (but not at both ends)."

Such blasphemous and unkindly thoughts deserved just retribution, and it was not long in coming. It was probably accelerated by further peevish actions on our part, for we were soon getting rid of some of the projectiles we had prepared. We might have been doing a bit of 'sweep and search' or maybe we fired on a fixed target previously ranged on, with a few rounds 'Gun fire — Gun, control'. Whatever it was, the results came loud and clear. A series of heavy explosions took place up front and there was a lot of dark smoke. It looked as if we had hit a supply depot or an ammunition dump. I knew from experience that if you chose to stir up a wasps' nest you had to be ready to make a very quick get-away. Our refuge was a low stone hut a few feet behind the Gun. This shelter had all the appearance of having been built with the intention of housing pigs. I seemed to have been drawn to pigsties for succour. The occupants immediately prior to us had been the Germans who had, with their usual competence, reinforced the roof with sturdy tree-trunks, thus earning our grateful if anonymous thanks.

Immediately we had been given 'Stand Easy' we flung ourselves inside this dwelling. In the twinkling of an eye there fell on us and all round us a most powerful 'stonk', put down by a concentration of bigger guns than ours. This was 'big stuff' — 210mm no less, or so someone said, though they may have been 150mm. The hideous shrieks of the trajectories rent the air and finished very abruptly in shattering explosions.

I was thrown about like a rag doll and the pigsty disintegrated. Then I staggered about doing the 'chicken with no head' routine. I knew my head was on because I was spitting blood and dust and bits of black stuff which had the unforgettable taste of the chemical which exploded shells. Some teeth must have also been spat out for I never saw them again. It is just conceivable that they might have been gathered up and given a decent internment. If so, I was never informed and besides, I had a few other things to attend to. My vision was blurred and my legs wobbled about. It was a very odd feeling, and in my dazed state, struggling for survival instinctively in a pall of dust and smoke, I never knew what happened to the rest of my detachment, except for one. Years later I met Tom Allman in his native Cheshire, and heard that one other had received a faceful of stone and splinters, but I never found out how many had survived. I made the classic exit from that stricken place on a stretcher. Tin-hat on my chest. It was not an heroic experience. My friends and comrades were left to 'soldier on'. My last round had been slammed 'up the spout'. For the last time I had knelt beside the trail of a 25pr. in action. The peak of my fitness, toughness, training as a gunner had been reached and had been severed at the moment of the shell's impact.

I was carried a couple of hundred yards down the valley to the Regimental Aid Post, a short journey fraught with danger as we were still under fire. I was never aware of having lost consciousness, felt no searing pain. At this time I thought that I had been badly bruised and battered a bit about the face. When 'Jock', carried out his inspection he seemed to dwell a little on what looked like a shell splinter which was sticking out of my left side just above my hip-bone. Some sort of dressing was put on my face and I was whipped away in a 15 cwt truck which had been adapted as an ambulance and which had Red Crosses on the tarpaulin. We were driven along the treacherous mountain pass which was still under enemy observation. Although we could have been fired on (and I was still conscious enough to realize this) we were not molested.

Inside the truck two or three others were packed in. Someone moaned and rolled about but I never knew who it was, for I was beginning to lose interest. An uneasiness invaded my body. I began to drift in and out of consciousness.

It did not seem long before we arrived at the Casualty Clearing Station (Field Dressing Station, Field Hospital? — I never did know), and I was being placed on a trolley. "Does it hurt when I press here?" someone asked. A hand was placed gently on my lower abdomen. I had no time to reply to the question, for a pain shot through me as if a red-hot iron had pierced my entrails and I passed out. It was as if a black blind had been snapped into position and, had I had time to react I should have been very frightened. I have no idea what happens to the mind in such a situation, but although I thought about it a lot afterwards I could remember nothing more until I opened my eyes and found that I was in bed. A face bent over me, mystic, wonderful; a woman's face, most beautiful. She was quite short and on the plump side, not unlike my fiancée, and she wore battledress. I would have liked to have been taken in her arms and nursed. Soon another face appeared. A man's voice said, "How do you feel, son?"

I croaked some sort of answer, for I found it an effort to speak, and the sound which came out was weak and seemed to be projected from a long way off. This young man in the white coat, bending over me went on. "Look," he said, "you've had a bit of a bashing. I'm afraid your left eye is damaged, and if we don't take it out soon it will affect the other one."

"It had better come out then," I whispered. I didn't seem to feel a lot of concern and I could still see with the other eye.

My face felt as if it had been hit by a sledge-hammer, but apparently I was not disfigured, apart from grazes, cuts and bruises. I was bewildered by the array of bottles (later discovered to be filled with blood plasma) which were hanging by my bed, and by a little pipe which ran from a bottle and disappeared under a bandage round my left wrist.

I croaked for a drink but my Angel, Sweetheart, Substitute Mother, disguised as a Nursing Sister, gently declined my request. To drink at this stage of my injury would have meant death. But could I have reached any liquid I would have drunk it, for I had a raving thirst, such an overwhelming thirst that I never forgot it. Day after day passed, and I had nothing to drink. My lips were moistened but nothing more. It may seem a relatively trivial thing to bear, but to me, with the dry mouth and the parched lips, it was the ultimate in torture, and formed a major part of my ordeal.

When they took me to the operating theatre in order to remove my eye, I was unaware that this was my second visit within a short period, for unknown to me they had already performed a very difficult major operation. In the months to come, visits to the theatre for some of us became quite frequent, so much so that we referred to them as "going to the pictures".

On this, my first journey theatre-wards whilst conscious, or in the area bordering on consciousness, for I seemed to have side-stepped into a cotton-wool world just outside reality, where the binoculars were never quite adjusted correctly, I thought I glimpsed bins filled with (bizarre as it may seem) arms and legs, feet and hands, bits and pieces of people, flung in at grotesque angles. There were also fleeting glances of white gowns, of long rubber aprons heavily stained with blood, reminiscent of a butcher's or of an abattoir's, of head-gear worn by theatre staff, of short white wellington boots.

Back in the ward, the contents and extent of which I knew nothing, for I had up to now taken no interest in events beyond my own bed space, I was approached during a period of wakefulness. I was at this time ebbing and flowing between my own version of the real world contained hazily in about four cubic yards, and the black pit of oblivion. The young doctor bent over again, and using a little metal spoon which looked like silver, he carefully dusted some powder into the empty socket which had recently housed my left eye. This substance was called penicillin he told me. It had recently come from England and it was marvellous for clearing up wounds of this kind. I never did have any more trouble with that socket, and when the time came for me to receive an artificial eye, almost a year later, it fitted like a dream.

Sir Ian Fraser, writing on 'Penicillin; early trials in war casualties' in the British Medical Journal in December, 1984 states, under 'First foreign experiences' that before leaving North Africa in preparation for the invasion of Sicily, 'I visited Philipville and left the base penicillin team at a British general hospital there, which was to be one of the hospitals prepared to receive casualties from Sicily.'

It must have been at about the same time that I was in hospital at Philipville in 1943 and was probably the same hospital.

In the same article Sir Ian Fraser says 'Penicillin became available just at the end of the Eighth Army Desert Campaign (February, 1943) and was therefore in full swing and ready for use by the First Army for the invasion of Sicily and Italy when the attack took place through the "soft underbelly of the Axis".'

The treatment of my eye was only the first of a succession of incidents. New dramatic experiences piled one on top of the other in rapid succession. My Sister approached me and began, very carefully to lay me bare. After drawing down the bed-clothes under which I lay motionless, my strength gone, she laid back the wide strips of a huge bandage which encased me from pelvis to rib-cage. I was unbelievably sore but my Sister of Mercy *was* merciful. I looked down as best I could, straining my neck, and gazed on my bare abdomen. It seemed to have been replaced by a football with the laces showing, for an incision had been made from naval to pelvis and had been stitched with what looked like leather laces. This, I learnt later, was called a laporotomy. There was something else down there which at first I considered an hallucination, for how could the presence of an average-sized tomato, resting on my lower abdomen on the left side about four inches from my hip bone be explained away? Or had someone worked it up under this great swathe of bandages as a sick joke? It was no joke. This red shiny sphere with an incision in it was part of my gut, my descending colon to be precise, which had been pierced internally and which was now drawn out through a hole they had cut in my abdominal wall and which was stitched to the sides to stop it from slipping back into my abdominal cavity. This I learnt, was a colostomy, through which all my waste matter, or excreta, would pass from now on, or rather from the time they let my intestines start working again. My rectum and anus were still there but were out of commission. How distasteful, embarrassing and even emasculating this all was. I had not even the remotest idea that such a device as this existed. To say that it offended me is grossly inadequate. I shrank at the shame of it and did indeed feel that much of my manhood had been lost. However, in the true sense my manhood was intact; parts vital to future joys were still there, if not at the moment entirely rampant. So I came to terms after a fashion with my offensive, uncomfortable but necessary companion.

"You will soon be able to play football," they told me. Very slowly in my subdued old man's voice I replied that it was most unlikely, as I abhorred football and was proud to announce that I was quite useless at all ball games. They gave me their tired, sad smiles which I was beginning to recognize so well. 'Poor young bastard,' their smiles said, 'we're trying our best, and so are you, but it's a bit dicey.' They left me to disappear down a great whirling tunnel of light into my second existence, wherever that was.

I was wont to emerge just as suddenly as I had submerged, like a diver bursting through to the sunlight from the murky depths below.

This time when I shot through to the surface I was propped up on pillows and was vomiting with as much violence as my poor sewn-up guts would let me. I was bringing up copious flows of black liquid, and it still tasted of that explosive. There was an audience. Two or three gentlemen were gathered round, looking anxiously down at me. They wore long white aprons of a shiny material which reached almost to the floor, and these coverings were again smeared with blood. One at least wore short white wellington boots, which seemed to me to be quite incongruous but yet appeared to form part of a standard uniform. This was obviously a crisis, for they looked to be as concerned as I was. I felt very poorly indeed. Between great shuddering heaves which racked and almost burst me asunder with pain, I looked up and said as best I could between spasms, "Cough it up chum, it might be a gold watch." This was not the most brilliant *bon mot* I had ever uttered, but it was a saying we rough folk used among ourselves. I could think of nothing else to say, and no one else was talking. They forced wan smiles into their drawn faces and their eyes conveyed their intense sympathy. I knew my chances were not very great. Once more I thought that I was on the way out.

Next day I stopped being sick and I just lay back immobile, with no wish to move and with all remaining strength drained out of me. I felt dampness under my bandages. When the dressings were removed pus was oozing from the incision down my middle and the wound had opened on the stitches. The thick yellowish liquid with its characteristic sickly odour was seeping down between my legs. When I was a boy in the 1920s, I had heard tales enough of people who had contracted septicaemia and who had died inevitably. My mother was fond of saying that a person had "septic right through him". I thought I had. There was then no hope of beating such an infection. All my mother's acquaintances had died, but then they always did, of everything.

I said, "This is it then, I'm going to die."

"No," said my Sister, dusting me down with sulphonamide powder after cleaning me up, "no, it will clear up."

I did not believe her. I shrank right into the bed and felt very low.

In spite of my pessimism the cut on my abdomen dried up and formed a sort of yellow crust round the stitches.

The doctors were listening for a certain movement of my bowels which they called peristalsis. Oh! yes, I picked up all their terms relating to my body, and the doctors did not conceal anything from me. When the gripping, slithering actions of the intestines had been disturbed, as mine had, the nervous system took a little time to adjust. Anyway, this peristalsis was working and with it my red spherical friend was beginning to ooze some sort of excremental discharge, which, when I started to eat and drink, assumed the proportion of a normal bowel action. I also discovered (there seemed no end to it) that there was a suppurating wound just above my hip, where the shell splinters had entered and done the damage internally, and the thick, brown, offensive liquid which came from it added further to my discomfort.

Now that I was permitted to drink I was considered capable of washing down monstrous amounts of large, white sulphonamide tablets. The energy consumed in taking them stretched me to the very limit, and I would flop back exhausted immediately after gulping down the last one of each batch. It would have taken several large sacks to contain my intake of such tablets during my lengthy stay in several hospitals.

About this time, although I did not really know how many days had passed, I was moved to a more central position in the ward. As I began gradually to take more stock of my surroundings I saw that I was in a large marquee, as I had been in North Africa, but here the beds were very close together, so close that there was only just room for the nursing staff to attend to patients. To have been in such an urgent, tense place as this was indeed an experience; but there was a heavy price to pay for it.

A couple of my comrades had rushed from the guns to pay me a brief visit, but my vision was blurred, my mind wandered and I could never remember who they were. Now, after a space of over forty years Sgt. Stoker, who goes by the name of 'Smoky', states in a letter, just received:

'It's a long time since Bam Anstee and myself visited you in the Field Hospital after you were wounded . . . . '

"It's not so great leaning forward into a bellyful of lead," was Bam's terse comment, intoned in mock-western style to Smoky after these two rugged Gunners, hard and fit as I had been a few short days before, had looked down on me, helpless as I lay.

They hid their concern, bade me a hasty farewell and returned to their grim trade. Others were coming, but the war moved on and so did they. *C'est la guerre*.

There is a brief entry in the Regimental War Diary:

'Casualties. The regimental area was shelled by 150 mm and 170 mm enemy guns from time to time.

32nd Battery	1 OR killed	6 ORs wounded
33rd Battery	1 OR killed	2 ORs wounded
36/55th Battery		4 ORs wounded
RHQ	Nil.	

It so happens that Jock, our Medical Officer, then Captain W. H. M. Wilson, RAMC, had kept a diary, a forbidden practice which many chose to ignore.

For 9th April, 1944 he recorded:

4 Casualties	Jones killed.	Bowman badly wounded.

From this entry he continued in Arabic, presumably as the fighting was becoming more severe and there was a very great danger of his diary falling into enemy hands.

Every day bagpipes played the same slow march with the same sombre muffled drum. I could only assume that there was a temporary military cemetery near by, to which more and more casualties were being committed daily. Or were these sad, haunting sounds merely another manifestation of the state of my troubled, wandering mind? Dr Wilson now tells:

'Your Field Hospital would be the one in The Inferno — a very deep gully opposite Monte Cassino.'

Men died round me all the time, all young, all in the prime of life, or not yet at their prime. The beds were never allowed to grow cold, for as one young corpse was taken out a shattered body replaced it. The battle for Monte Cassino was at its height, the drive for Rome was on. Surgeons, doctors, sisters, orderlies, they were all tired, overworked, and the strain of the environment showed.

It was in this place, in this stark atmosphere with no escape, that I died three or four times, or felt the Shadow of Death brush against me so closely that it conditioned my attitude to living, so that I probably enjoyed the years that followed more keenly than the uninitiated. Happy occurrences were happier, setbacks, which many treated as momentous, seemed relatively trivial. But it was still a hard apprenticeship.

I had still a long struggle ahead. Tiny old men, clad in ancient garb and wearing beards, sidled up to my bed and peered up at me. They clambered up the tent-poles to get a better look. One or two of the more adventurous climbed on to the bed and leered at me. I brushed them off feebly, trying to move them away with my hands. The most persistent and most malevolent of them carried a little mug for some reason which I could not understand and he came right up to me. I pushed him off as best I could.

It was night-time. The lighting was dim and soft and it threw grotesque shadows as our dedicated attendants moved about among us. The gunfire could be heard, for we were not far from the battle which was raging.

On my left was a young paratrooper, eighteen years old they said. To say that he died of shortness of breath is no facetious statement. He had been shot through the chest. Every fibre of his being was concentrated on breathing. Most people breathe without knowing it, but his whole existence was devoted to taking his next agonized breath. On and on they went, these rapid gasps. Just occasionally he managed to intersperse another sound which I interpreted as "water". Sister and the male orderly tried to give him a drink, but he never did get one. He panted like a dog, ever more rapidly until the limit was reached and he gave up. In between sweeping my hideous phantom dwarfs away, I watched him die. When he was still I looked slowly and dreamily to my right. Here was a Guardsman who had been shot through the throat. He was unconscious and was making bubbling, gurgling noises. A stretcher appeared at the bottom of my bed.

"Is this the one?" someone asked quietly.

"No, but he's the next," was the reply.

There was a Union Jack over the young soldier on my left as he was borne away. The Guardsman died. The noises in his throat ceased very suddenly. He also had the Union Jack draped over him as he left the ward. Within minutes I had two new neighbours. The prediction at the foot of my bed which I had overheard never came true. They never came for me. The little folk went away in the night and happily they never returned. I began to feel better.

CHAPTER XXIV

Slowly I emerged from the strange hinterland through which I had travelled and began to eat, and even better, to drink as much as I wanted. Small amounts were given at first, but these were accepted with immeasurable gratitude. When I was served a small tin of salmon all to myself, a frugal meal by normal standards but to me a feast excelling those of Suleiman the Magnificent, I would have drawn my plump little guardian in close embrace had propriety permitted and had I possessed the strength. I would also have written her a cheque for an unspecified amount had I had a cheque book. It was fortunate that I had no such amenity, for the cheque would have bounced alarmingly. Anyway, the gratitude was there.

For the first time I thought about writing home. My friendly orderly, and he *was* friendly and kind and helpful, wrote letters to my mother and to my fiancée, which I dictated a little at a time. I told Bid that I had been wounded and that I had lost an eye. I intimated that if she considered this disability would intrude on our forthcoming marriage I should understand. It was a very difficult letter, but I knew that it had to be said, for she was only nineteen. Of course, I hoped as deeply as it was possible to hope, that it would make no difference.

No mention was made of my abdomen wound, for happily I had been told that once I was free from infection, my little red mound, by now working away and causing offensive odours every time the bed-clothes were raised, would be slipped back into my abdominal cavity, hopefully never to be seen again. To be truthful, I wanted as few people as possible to know about my little embarrassing secret down there.

A lot had been going on in that little bit of Lancashire where I lived. My mother had been sent a telegram from the War Office which informed her that I had been wounded in action and that I was on the 'Dangerously Ill' list. This rating was very bad indeed — only one less than 'Killed in Action'.

My mother cycled through the country lanes to tell Bid on that sad morning. What went through her mind on the journey one can only guess. She was very familiar with the route, for she had worked very happily when a young woman as a maid at a parsonage not far from where my fiancée lived. On this particular morning the beauty of the spring-time countryside of which she was so fond went by completely unnoticed.

My girl, as was to be expected, was overcome with grief when she heard the news, but there was not a thing to do except play the dreadful waiting game, which I always think is the worst ordeal of all. What would the next message be, the next telegram convey?

Quite soon there did come another telegram. It must have been a supreme effort to open it, and I would not have liked to have lived that thousand years encapsulated in that moment or two through which my mother lived. Fortunately, the news was better, for I had been upgraded to the 'Seriously Ill' list. (These telegrams were given to my elder son, a little while before my mother died.)

Then came the letters which I had dictated in Italy. Bid again was very upset and wept a great deal at the choice which I had offered her. It was fortunate that her uncle was there to explain that he considered that I had done the honourable thing under the circumstances, and that I myself had no wish to break off the engagement. She wrote a letter expressing her continuing love for me; intimating that whatever my injuries she would always stand by me. Soon afterwards my mother was told of my further improvement. My wounds were described as 'Left eye — enucleated — G.S.W. (Gun-shot wounds) Abdomen'. They began to breathe more freely back in the old corral.

Of course, I knew nothing of all these traumatic happenings. Obviously for much of the time I was not in a fit state to know much about anything. But I was slowly gaining strength, clawing myself back to convalescence, (or so I thought), and becoming more and more aware of external events.

My eye socket was healed. I gathered that apart from splinters which had grazed my face, knocked out a few of my front teeth and touched my eye, others had entered above my hip, driven into my gut, gone upwards and lodged just short of my spine. Years later a little suppurating wound on my left thigh appeared, high up, which eventually revealed a bluish hard object. I dug it out with a pair of curved nail scissors one Sunday morning in the kitchen. When I prised it out it clanged up against the sink with a metallic sound. Bid, looking on, then a wife and mother, cried, "Oh Edwin," and leant against the sink herself. It was a nasty looking jagged piece of shell splinter, and I still have it. That little wound healed immediately, but the one above my hip which I suffered from now was showing great reluctance to heal.

I had a bed-bath and for the first time my nurses thought it was time to have my toe-nails cut, a minor operation which I never enjoyed. My male orderly swore that they had cut my socks off and that grass had been growing between my toes. This was not beyond the bounds of credibility, for I must have soldiered for quite some time without removing my boots. He was also fond of telling me that he had been in the theatre when my intestines had been laid out on a nearby slab. I had a mental picture of this which I found disturbing.

Still, I was alive and making progress. Every doctor or surgeon who has examined me since have said that the surgeons who operated on me, and the nurses who tended me must have been supremely skilful. One surgeon, later, even went so far as to say that, "God's star was shining on you at that time." Remembering that all this went on in relatively unsterile conditions, I had been very fortunate indeed.

> ' 'Tis well an old age is out,
> And time to begin anew.'

I thought these lines were fitting for the occasion, for the time had now come for me to 'begin anew'. I was being moved to a higher place, on the mortal plane rather than that spiritual one to which I had expected to be called a few times in the previous weeks.

It must have been about the middle of May when I was transferred to the Second General Hospital at Caserta, but this is only an estimation, for I had lost all knowledge of the passage of time.

For the first time in over a year I was under a roof rather than canvas or the stars. The hospital was housed in a very long building with high ceilings, but I never knew what it looked like from the outside. I was allowed to visit the lavatory and to go and wash and shave. These major expeditions were very exacting at first. Nor was my strength encouraged to return by means of lavish over-feeding. We semi-convalescents, in fact all patients, seemed to be sustained on a diet of cold toast, which was not the best means of encouraging or reviving unpredictable or fickle palates. We must have been given more nutritious dishes, but these could not have been outstanding, for the cold toast predominates.

I was put back to bed for a couple of days whilst they laced up the incision down the centre of my abdomen which had burst open soon after my first operation. When the surgeon came round next day to have a look at his work I asked him if I gained consciousness whilst they were sewing me up. I distinctly remembered awaking in this strange place surrounded by people begowned and with instruments. I looked down on my belly on which they were working and behold, my football laces had reappeared. Then I fell asleep again.

The surgeon was very reticent but did not dismiss my question outright. I still think I came to on that table.

Neither I nor my ward mates were able to indulge in even the most gentle exercise. Those who were ambulatory creaked and staggered, hopped and slid, groped from bed to bed. There were an amazing number of limbs in plaster, out of which maggots dropped in profusion. They dropped out of the cavities between upper thighs and casts, the owners' legs being strung up on intricate devices constructed of ropes, weights and pulleys; they fell from arms, wrists and ankles. The plasters ripened like exotic cheeses, the colour deepened as they matured, and together with the all-pervading smell of disinfectant there was another distinctive sickly stench coming from these wounds, which connoisseurs will recognize. The owners of the plasters, or 'pots', experienced ecstasies of irritation as their tiny, restless parasites crawled about. Nevertheless, these little creatures had their uses for they fed on the discharge and cleaned the wounds.

In some instances it was decided that it was better to leave wounds open. Patients lay with their legs out of bed, great gashes gaping and full of congealed green pus on which flies were all too eager to settle and from which they had to be discouraged continually.

Then there were the stumps, which in this hospital were in the process of healing. They were many and varied. Legs terminated at the ankle or knee or lower thigh. In a few instances the amputation had been done not far below the hip. Mutilated arms ranged in length also. As I passed I saw raw wounds or partially healed ones with the skin sewn to overlap the stumps, for screens were not always used except for dressings of a more personal and private nature. Occasionally an unfortunate had to be wheeled to the theatre to have some more of his limb taken off, if the infection refused to submit and was endangering his life by creeping higher.

My problems lay hidden except for the regular dressings, but always I awakened to a rich, repulsive odour which arose from under my bed-clothes — a mixture of dark liquid which had oozed from my hip wound in the night, and from the excreta which had escaped from my colostomy. They say that a colostomy can be controlled, but I never learnt the trick. Maybe it was the wrong sort, or I did not have it long enough.

Again, I found myself observing my neighbours. The one on my left was a Lance-Corporal in the infantry who had been up with his platoon in the mountains in the FDL (Forward Defence Line). Up there in the dark, where every shadow struck fear, a young soldier, inexperienced in action and hearing a noise he thought to be dangerous, had fired and hit his own NCO. The one bullet had gone through the flesh of his upper right arm, passed through his stomach and lodged in his left thigh. Miraculously, no bones had been touched but he had his fair share of 'pots'. He was well on the way to complete recovery.

Ironically enough, the lad on my right had been brought in with, would you believe it, appendicitis. There was a lot of movement around his bed a day or two after his operation, for peritonitis had set in. Nothing was spared in the effort to save him, no consolation was withheld. I even heard the doctors tell him that he could have any delicacy, even at the expense of flying it from home. All to no avail. He died, very young.

How unpredictable was this process of living, or dying. Here he had been, the only one with what might be called a commonplace illness, surrounded by men who had experienced a diversity of injuries inflicted violently, and yet he had been the one to die.

Two of our officers who had been wounded by mortars were in the hospital. Someone from my Battery (I have forgotten him completely) who was a patient in my ward went with me to see them. The officers' ward was only a short distance away, but it was an adventurous journey which left us quite spent. There our officers were, in bed, treating their wounds quite nonchalantly, languidly exchanging pleasantries between themselves and with us. One more leg lay over the side of the bed; one more pus-filled cavity with in one place the shin-bone laid bare. Characteristically, flies were kept away with a fly-whisk.

In late May, when the sun shone with ever increasing strength and brightness I went home. Our hospital ship put in briefly at Gibraltar and then sailed out through the Straits, steaming through the night with all lights on. My wound was beginning to suppurate badly and my temperature, which had never really been right down to normal, had risen sufficiently for me to be put back to bed. By the time we docked at Liverpool I had to be carried down the gangplank on a stretcher.

It was 6th June, 1944, D-Day, just four years and one week since I had arrived at Dover from Dunkirk.

PART SIX

Home 1944-46

Ho, don't you grieve for me,
My lovely Mary-Ann,
For I'll marry you yit on a fourp'ny bit
As a time-expired man.
Troopin' by Rudyard Kipling

CHAPTER XXV

Had I been Bid, entering that ward in the Military Hospital at Southport a day or two after I had arrived there, I would have taken one look at me, given a shriek of horror and rushed out of my life forever, as fast and as far as I could go.

It has always been a wonder to me that she stayed, especially as her aunt had said when news came that I was dangerously ill that she should not worry too much as "there were lots of good fish in the sea." I did not hear of this until much later, for had I known I should have shown a marked coldness to 'auntie'. I was always aware, of course, not being entirely naïve by now, that there were a few fit chaps, well heeled with one or two 'creeps' among them, who lived in a different world and who would not hesitate to move in and take advantage of the absence of someone like me, about whose ordeals they knew nothing and cared less. Lying on my back here, I knew I was at a bit of a disadvantage.

The 'aunt' was with Bid on that first visit and so, of course, was my mother. It was a reconnaissance in force. My mother said afterwards that she had been shocked at my appearance and I had looked like a plucked chicken, which I thought was a very appropriate description of my appearance. I had also reminded her, she said, of my grandfather (her father) on his death-bed, this morbid preoccupation with death again revealing itself. She could not live without a tombstone or two for company.

Bid drew near and leant over me. She was a picture — everything that I had dreamt about and longed for in the long, long months that we had been apart. This fresh young girl, smelling sweetly of the promise of summer, smooth, white skinned, in the full flush of health, dark hair shining, eyes not at the moment mischievous but still bright, cool-looking in a light dress, leant over me, kissed me — called me 'darling'.

What was I? When I had last held out my arms to her I had been a very fit young man, confident, strong, not giving a damm for anyone. Now she bent over this 'plucked chicken' of a man. Thin and gaunt, semi-toothless, raw-looking eye socket fully revealed, hair dank and listless, perspiring, (for my wound was discharging copiously and I had a fever), and giving off a faint whiff of a very badly kept public lavatory. Ugh! I did not like myself very much.

There could not have been a much greater contrast. When I questioned Bid about this first meeting all she would say was that she knew that I would not always be like that. Bid had a lot of faith, a lot of hidden resilience, an immense loyalty and in spite of her placid demeanour a mind of her own. All these qualities I was to come to recognize and to treasure.

Bid *did* come back. Once a week at least she made a difficult journey by bus and by train, which entailed at least three changes. The visit took a full day. Into the ward she would come, bearing her basket containing delicacies, her neat little feet tripping towards my bedside, bringing radiance to a dark day.

My mother came when she could, usually on a Sunday when the trains were few and capricious, and she also bore gifts. My Uncle Ben came, fresh from his threshing machine or whatever agricultural pursuit he was engaged in at the time.

When I had arrived at Southport the ward had been nearly empty, as it still was when I had received my first visitors. When Bid came again, when my mother came, there had been a tremendous transformation and the ward was overflowing. I was back in Italy, with hardly enough space to move between beds, for the casualties from the landings in France were flowing in. There was little real rest to be had. The shaded lights at night were sufficient to reveal the familiar flitting restless shapes, the rustle of the nurses' uniforms as they moved about us. There were the whispered consolations to the new intake of poor bastards, shot up, not really knowing where they were and what was going on round them.

There was great activity on my right, for I was tucked in a corner bed, with hurried consultations of a professional nature, bustling, scurrying, great tension all at once. The freshly sewn artery in the thigh of a new arrival had broken down and blood was cascading on to the floor. There was immediate departure to the theatre. Did the patient die? Alas! yes. Did they do him the honour of the Union Jack? I do not know, for my horrible stinking wound was bringing me very low. I was perspiring all the time, had gone off my food and I think they were watching me keenly for the possibility of gas gangrene, a sinister visitor who came to victims of gunshot wounds and saw them off. It would be ironical if I were to succumb now, so soon after being reunited.

Since my first days as a patient in Italy I had been loaded with sulphonamide tablets to keep down and to overcome infection. I was rattling with sulphonamide tablets but they seemed to be losing their effect.

An elderly gentleman, a surgeon, gave directions for me to attend upon him in theatre so that he could see what he could do. He saw what he could do, and did it so effectively that I have never forgotten it.

With some difficulty I was manoeuvred into lying on my right side. It was an effort to sustain such a position for I was very weak, so weak that a frail-looking young nurse was instructed to support me. The elderly gentleman produced a long thin instrument like a button-hook, inserted it into my wound and proceeded to poke about inside me, hitting what felt to be my hip-bone a few times in the process. No anaesthetic was given, not even a local one. Every time he twisted his hook and touched something inside I jerked and arched my body as if an electric shock had passed through me, which in a sense it had. I forgot that I was in the presence of a woman and swore audibly and horribly whilst I gripped the delicate upper arms of the little nurse so hard that there were great purple weals on her white skin when I finally unclenched my hands. Sweat dripped off me and it probably did off the little nurse as well.

When my tormentor had satisfied himself on his next course of action he proceeded to insert, screw in and pack a long narrow strip of material which looked like vaseline gauze. Up, up, up as far as he could get it. Yards and yards of it seemed to disappear into my wound. I don't think I cried out, but I really ought to have had a bullet to bite on, for if ever an occasion required it, that was it. I changed my grip on my fragile, stoical help-mate and gave her some more bruises. Poor little soul, I have thought of her and wondered whether she had to be hospitalized too. My ordeal left me completely exhausted, and by the look of her she was also in a state of near collapse.

The gauze was kept in for a while, a few days at the most, and not surprisingly the discharge almost ceased, for with an amazing display of strength my elderly gentleman had plugged me so tightly that nothing could escape. I thought that there was a very real possibility that I might explode, which would have caused consternation and not a little discomfort to my immediate neighbours.

When the gauze was removed, another operation not as electrifying but still traumatic from which my little nurse kept well away, there followed a dramatic and to me miraculous decrease in the discharge.

When Bid came next time, her neat little feet did not make so much noise, for she approached me across a sun-lit lawn, on which I was reclining in a kind of basket on four wheels. I felt much better and appreciated her trim buxomness and her well turned legs and ankles and wished that the lawn had been bigger so that I could have savoured this vision for a little longer. I *was* getting better.

Very soon after this I was moved to Whiston Hospital, near Liverpool.

Lying in bed on that first Monday morning at Whiston, contemplating the new day before me which had nothing much to offer in the way of excitement except meals, dressing and tablets, I became aware of the arrival of a very dominant person. This immaculate darked-suited dapper gentleman, approaching middle age if not in it, swept up to my bed, and almost without stopping, flung back the bed-clothes and gave me a peremptory order.

"Get up," he commanded, "I want you fit by next Monday. I am operating on you."

There was not so much as a by your leave. That was it. The presence proceeded on his headlong flight, not once looking back.

No one seemed to know what this aloof person had in mind, so I spent the rest of the week wondering what was in store for me, and in taking faltering steps round the ward, steps which became more certain as the days passed.

As had been preordained I was duly conveyed to the theatre on the following Monday. What a relief it was when it became obvious that I was to be anaesthetized, for I was not all that keen on the 'button-hook' treatment. That which followed was pretty routine stuff. I felt myself going under, a soothing sensation which I had come to enjoy, then I woke up, tucked up, back in the ward. There was nothing to it, if they put you to sleep, and they usually did.

When the dressings were removed next morning, behold I had an incision fourteen stitches long running down my left side, right through where my wound was. Mr Bennett-Jones, (I had discovered the great man's name), did not believe in half-measures. Had he been a painter his choice, one felt, would have been large canvases with bold decisive brush-strokes rather than miniatures and the delicacy they demanded. This was no nervous, hesitant work of the amateur — here was professionalism.

Mr Bennett-Jones visited me later in the day and condescended to descend to ground level for a brief moment to explain to me what he had found and what he proposed to do next.

"You should be all right now. I removed a few small pieces of metal and some bits of battledress and belt which must have got in the way. You are better without them. When your stitches are out, and when your wound is seen to be free from infection I will slip your gut back in and you will be as good as new."

With a slight parting nod and an expression almost suggesting affability, which no doubt in such an eminent being *was* affability, he strode away, the Sister following two paces to his right rear like a destroyer accompanying a cruiser, taking two steps to his one. He had gone before I could thank him properly, or even begin to thank him, for I was so full of gratitude that I was bubbling over to deliver a long and boring speech expressing my feelings.

Mr Bennett-Jones instilled confidence. Here was progress, indeed. Here was good news to tell my young lady and my mother who would soon be coming to see me. I could tell them that the final operation was just round the corner.

It was somewhere round this time, on a beautiful Saturday in late July or early August, for the summer was advancing, that Bid, her sisters Margaret and Sheila and her future sister-in-law Freda cycled over from Newton, near Frodsham in Cheshire. Bid was staying with her parents who lived there. We went out of the grounds and enjoyed the sunshine in a field of corn which was nearly ripe.

The long incision healed with amazing rapidity, the stitches were soon out and preparations were made for the completion of my surgical treatment. I was given an enema containing some white liquid which showed up on the X-ray and told them that all was secure in that area.

I had lost count of the number of times that I had been wheeled to various operating theatres, yet every visit had its own piquancy, although the surroundings were pretty much the same.

Now I was given a spinal anaesthetic, which meant that it was injected directly into my spine. My body went numb about the bottom of my ribs downwards, I was placed on my back on the operating table and a small screen was erected a little below my chin so that I could not see what was going on down below.

The young surgeons on the team were a cheerful lot, and as I was fully conscious they gave me the *Daily Mirror* to read. I don't say that I read it from cover to cover and I certainly did not get to the sports' page at the back, but it was a friendly and assuring gesture.

I felt my body being jerked about whilst they worked, but apart from this there was no discomfort. It was soon over.

After the operation the nursing staff were very attentive for a while until feeling had returned to the lower part of my body, which it soon did, and until I had passed water. I made an uneventful recovery, was soon eating and, splendid 'red-letter day' event, my bowels began to work normally in the way that they were meant to work. I was whole again.

What joy it was to lie between clean sheets which would not be soiled, fresh from a bath in which I had wallowed on my very own, and smelling sweetly. What relief it was to be able to move around in the presence of Bid and to have her close beside me without feeling that all the time my biological odours could not be totally concealed. I was happy to feel clean in my mother's presence and in the company of all who visited me but it was particularly comforting to feel whole and wholesome for my young sweetheart.

A mould was fitted into my eye-socket in order to stretch it ready for my artificial eye, which was an improvement, and I had an impression taken for a partial upper denture to replace my missing front teeth.

Now that I was all in one piece, regaining my vigour and beginning to look more like my former self, my prospective wife and I put our heads together, literally when the occasion permitted and we could find a quiet corner, and began in whispers to plan for our marriage. We did not see any purpose in waiting any longer, for it was very unlikely that I should go out of England, and certainly not on Active Service.

I even sought an audience with the great man, to enquire if he thought that I was in a fit state to get married. He granted me a second or two of his crowded day to state brusquely that if I saw no impediment he saw none. I managed to thank him for allowing me to see him and for all that he had done.

Bid's mother came from Cheshire by way of Runcorn and the transporter bridge, taking time off from supervising her large young family and bringing me an apple pie, freshly baked. Uncle Ben and my cousin Arthur came, fresh from the flat rural area of the Fylde where no enemy action had invaded their relaxed rusticity. They were ill at ease amid this strange exhibition of torn bodies and I thought it best to take them out of the gates to a pub round the corner where we sank a jar or two.

Ah! halcyon days. Not only were there regular visits from my wife-to-be, each arrival bearing the promise of joys to come, but also there were excursions to pubs in the area which were an important part of the process of rehabilitation and did much towards accelerating my convalescence. The Sister was most considerate and lenient and we who were on the mend were given liberal leave of absence for a few hours at a time.

We found a very friendly pub where the 'regulars' were glass-blowers from a local factory. Their calling gave them monumental thirsts, and we who were still really very young, who were still surprised that we were not dead and who were beginning to display an overwhelming and sometimes unrestrained *joie de vivre*, took great pleasure in joining them. They were great fellows, very friendly towards us, and we enjoyed their company. We got carried away and gave the piano a drink or two, as well as the pianist. Now, I would consider such an act a desecration of a criminal kind, but mine host did not seem to mind. He probably did not understand the damage that liquid can do to the felt pads.

Nevertheless, in spite of my happiness, I did suffer from bouts of depression which were not brought about by hangovers. To counteract these, it appeared that there was another kind of rehabilitation besides girl-friends and pubs.

A person in charge of this occupational therapy or whatever it was called approached me one grey afternoon as I was going through a bad patch, and thinking about my prospects for the future. My unease had nothing to do with my forthcoming marriage, about which I had no doubts at all. Rather it had to do with how I should earn a living for my wife and myself, as I could no longer continue my career in the Army.

This fellow who disturbed my thoughts caught me at a bad moment. He bore a large tray containing material out of which I was expected to construct a purple elephant by sewing felt together, which had been previously prepared, and then stuffing it. At first I could not take in what he was trying to explain, but when I did I reacted violently. First of all, I loathed sewing, I hated purple and had no interest at all in stuffed toys, particularly elephants. The one thing that would be guaranteed to send me to a nut-house at the double would be the manufacture of stuffed toys. I took his tray, stood on my bed, reached up and tipped tray and contents through the open window.

"F . . . the f . . . ing elephant," I said, "and f . . . you!"

He sped away to report me, but I heard no more. I went to him later and apologized on my own volition, for they were not honourable things that I had said or done.

My reaction had been effective. I was never asked to make anything for anybody ever again. They left me alone to my fits of gloom and I pulled out of them. When I gave Bid an account of this happening, watered down, she laughed and said that I was a naughty boy. In one or two directions, this *was* a naughty boy she was getting.

I went twice to Bid's parents and met her father and her flock of brothers and sisters for the first time. On the second occasion I had to stay the night, for Cheshire became fog-bound.

All arrangements had been made for the wedding, and on 23rd October Bid and I finally stood side by side at the altar of Kingsley Parish Church. It had been a long and perilous haul but jointly we had achieved our greatest wish.

My cousin Arthur was my best man and Bid's father gave her away. Little Miss Nield wore a brown dress and a wide-brimmed hat, and to me she looked very young and demure and very beautiful as she came up the aisle on her father's arm. She *had* stood by me, *had* supported me when I needed her most. I felt a great love go out towards her. A photograph of us taken on our wedding day lives on the chest of drawers in our bedroom. I often have a look at it and think how little she has changed. When I mention it I am told not to be silly, but I still say it sometimes.

After a reception at her parents' home, my wife and I went on a short honeymoon to a bungalow which we had been given the use of for a few days.

It was over all too quickly. Bid went back to look after uncle and the aunt, whilst I went back to hospital at Whiston.

CHAPTER XXVI

I began to go home for weekends, mainly through the kindness and ingenuity of the nursing staff who covered up for me by the old device of placing a pillow in my bed.

It was a strange feeling at first, to return to the quietness of the Village of My Birth, untouched by the presence of the military, to feel the warmth and snugness of my mother's cottage where I had spent my youth and to go on to Bid's uncle's to enjoy unaccustomed comforts which a man on a professional salary had built round him.

As the Ribble bus from Poulton-le-Fylde turned the corner to go down Shovels Lane, with the Shovels Inn on the left, I thought what a good place it would be to run up a 25-pounder and fire a couple of rounds of HE over open sights, and how their arrival at the fence of Ryecroft Corner would liven things up a bit. The inhabitants *would* draw back their curtains more than slightly to see what was going on. What a roguish ungentlemanly act to consider. But then I was no gentleman, only a soldier. Psychiatrists may make something of it but I never tried. Maybe I needed the attentions of a social worker or a concentrated course in stuffing toys?

Walking up 'the village' towards my mother's cottage, a relative of a soldier who had recently been killed in action on the Continent leaned over her garden gate and asked me accusingly why it was that I had returned unharmed when her dear one was dead. I replied that there was no convincing answer as to why I was still alive that I could think of, but surely even she must be aware that my journey had not been entirely without incident. She flounced up the garden path, whilst I went on my way, thinking that it was impossible to please everyone.

Everywhere else I was well received.

When I had settled down at Bid's place and had time to look round, I found that she had been very mindful of me whilst I had been abroad. Make no mistake about it, my little wife, as well as being an excellent cook and housekeeper was also very skilled with her fingers and her work was now displayed for my approval and appreciation. She had embroidered some delightful miniatures of country scenes, a fire-screen and also a large Artillery Badge, and all had been framed. All these were to grace our future home and are most cherished possessions. Bid had also worked a small Artillery Badge which I had seen previously, for she wore it on the breast pocket of a navy blue dress, and I was very proud of it.

I was home for Christmas. Popping down to my mother's, I collected some small loaves freshly baked. Always I was surrounded by good cooks. There had been my grandmother (up to that time the doyen of them all), there was my mother, now there was Bid and there was also Bid's mother. Carrying my loaves, still warm, I made a quick detour by way of the Shovels Inn for a swift pint, and then caught the bus to Knott-End-on-Sea. To my great shame I left the bread on the bus and there were loud recriminations from both sides of the family.

This Christmas was a marvellous one, which included a sumptuous dinner at my mother's on Boxing Day. Bid and I went dancing. It was in complete contrast to the previous one, spent miserably at Blida, waiting for the boat.

What a momentous year 1944 had been, a year in which I had both tasted the bitterest dregs and quaffed the sweetest nectar which the gods could offer.

I paid a visit to Liverpool early in the New Year where I was fitted with my artifical eye. Soon I was sent to Crosby Hall to complete my convalescence, and it was in this stately environment that I spent a very comfortable few weeks. Of course, I would rather have been with my wife, but if I had to be separated a gentleman's residence was not a bad place to choose. It was a very hard winter and a group of us took walks through the snow-covered woods. As the lakes were frozen solid it was safe to go on the ice. It was there I donned ice skates for the first time, tried my hand at skating and enjoyed myself, even though I did have a few mild falls. Much to the surprise of the cowman on the home farm, I milked a cow by hand, the first time for about five years.

I was sent on my travels again, this time to the RA Barracks, Woolwich. The wheel had turned full circle. Six years after my debut as a recruit I returned to the home of the Regiment. The barrack blocks were still there, the squares were there, but now no squads were being marched up and down incessantly, no boots were tramping in unison, no crisp commands barked out by efficent NCOs sounded in counterpoint. The squares were empty.

No trumpets sounded the familiar summons, no bugles sounded

faintly from the Lower Barracks where the young soldiers had performed to 'Pedro the Fisherman' through what seemed to be all the hours of daylight.

The Depot was populated only by the ghosts of the many gunners who had passed this way, and by present gunners in transit, gliding themselves like phantoms gathered from every theatre of war and forever moving on.

The young, resilient, boisterous recruits who had filled the Barracks with energetic action in my day, were now old men in their mid-twenties. The urgency and drive had gone.

The brooding melancholy, almost itself approaching the supernatural at times, hung over the Depot and was presided over by the ruins of the Garrison Church, last seen by me in its full regimental splendour when I had carried the collection plate up the aisle. The Church had been destroyed except for the outside walls by an enemy bomb in 1944.

Apart from the uncharacteristic inertia of the Depot there was a menacing danger which aggravated my uneasiness and discontent. Air-borne projectiles called doodle-bugs and V2s were being hurled across the Channel. The V2s gave no warning at all of their arrival. They just exploded violently on impact and did a lot of damage. The barrack room where I slept was placed high in an upper storey and every time a missile arrived the whole building rocked. Some of us who were fragile through over-exposure to such sudden violence took to 'kipping down' in the stables under the verandas and lower barrack rooms in another square.

I dined in the Sergeants' Mess in which the Mess silver, or some of it, still shone. How was I to know whether it was all there, for the last and only time I had been allowed to glance into this hallowed place was when I had just finished scrubbing the tiled floor of the Mess kitchen.

Mess waiters in their distinctive uniforms hovered round us whilst we dined.

I visited the Main Guardroom where the Sergeant-in-Charge of the Guard turned out to be a member of my old squad in 1939. I mounted a Guard on the Front Parade in the same place where I had stood to attention as a very young gunner, and had been selected as the smartest and best turned-out man on parade.

The wheel had indeed turned full circle.

It had been one of my ambitions to return to the Depot some day as an Instructor and I probably would have done. Now in 1945, under the circumstances I was glad to get away, for the frightful intruders were having a very disturbing effect on me. My posting came through to proceed to 175 Field Regiment, RA, stationed at Hartford Bridge, Bedlington, near Newcastle in Northumberland.

Standing on Woolwich Station, waiting for the train to take me to the City and then on to King's Cross, I witnessed my last blast of my war. Just down the road, in full view from the station there was a tremendous explosion and a great plummeting cloud of dust and smoke. So near and yet so far. The further north I travelled, the safer I felt.

175 Field Regiment, RA was yet another collecting place and haven for gunners who for some reason or other, mainly wounds, injuries or mild mental disturbances had found themselves here.

Yet there were several of us, who though unable to withstand the rigours of active service, could surely have been employed in some useful capacity in our own trade. We were highly trained and experienced NCOs, yet we along with all the other wastages of war had been bulldozed on to the scrap-heap, without any effort to recover and make use of the components which were still serviceable. Maybe we were just written off as a loss, precalculated. I never felt bitter about it at the time, nor later, but strangely enough, having thought about it at a distance of forty years, there is a certain sour taste in my mouth. You can say that my first and only redundancy came when I was twenty-four. I suppose I shouldn't complain really for matters were moving favourably in another direction.

As I was showing some interest in teaching as a new career I was directed to the Education Office where the Education Officer, Captain Tester, held sway. He proved a good friend to me, for he encouraged me to give lectures to the troops, came and listened to me and advised me on how to correct the errors in my presentation. It was splendid preliminary training and I appreciated it. My audiences were thin at first for there were not many residents in the camp, but once the ex-prisoners of war from Japan started to come in it was a different story.

Sometimes I shudder at the thought of my first attempts at talking to a couple of hundred men whilst standing exposed on a raised platform, on a topic about which I knew very little. Various subjects were chosen for their topical interest, or on government schemes devised to assist readjustment to civilian life.

I cannot say that my students were uncooperative. It would be more true to say that they were utterly neutral or passive, for they never showed any objection to, or voiced any criticism on my feeble, ill-prepared, superficial travesties of scholarship. Emaciated soldiers with lack-lustre eyes, sat in rows looking at me but not seeing, no doubt thousands of miles away, reliving horrors about which I knew nothing, horrors which few could imagine even, until the truth came out.

There was a Gun-park at Hartford Bridge but I never saw any detachments at gun-drill there. I went and sat on the layer's seat of one of these guns and manipulated the hand wheels. The Gun had lost its dignity and its drive like so many of the torn souls who for the moment passed round and about it. It looked shrunken and ashamed. I remembered It, roaring and belching flame from Its formidable throat, strong and defiant against the night sky in Italy. I patted Its barrel with affection, an action which will be sneered at by many, but which will be understood by some, and left It with a consolatory word. I never went back.

It must have been in early April that Bid escaped from her housekeeping and came to stay with me for a week. I had arranged lodgings for us with a pleasant lady in Bedlington who took in paying guests, and it was no trouble for me to get a sleeping-out pass. My hours of duty were by no means oppressive and I had no guard duties whatsoever.

We considered this visit an extension of our honeymoon. How idyllic it was to have some time entirely to ourselves. The local buses took us to Morpeth, Alnwick, Blythe and Whitley Bay. Never have I forgotten the sight of Bid running bare-foot over the sands (in April?) laughing as I pursued her, eventually to catch her and pull her to the edge of the sea, where, still laughing, we both got our feet wet. She seemed to be like a young bird which had just been released from a cage, and without being malicious to anyone, she was. Whatever rigours I had met, I had owed allegiance to no one, had been free to go wherever I pleased outside the duties which went with my profession. This way of thinking may seem incomprehensible to many as I said at the beginning, for I was in the King's service, which was considered so restrictive that one's life was not one's own. I had never felt it to be like that. I was an individual and was allowed, even encouraged to be one. For Bid it had been different, for she had never had the opportunity to be free in her own environment, either domestic or in the small, inquisitive, conventional though friendly society in which she lived. When she returned to the Fylde the aunt began to display bad feelings towards me and to make it very difficult for Bid who was being pulled both ways. It was natural that she should feel some allegiance for her aunt and uncle with whom she had grown up, but she was not going to continue to listen to unfounded recriminations against her husband.

When the aunt realized that she could no longer command full and prompt attention from her maid and housekeeper *par excellence* she did not take kindly to the change. The aunt also had a peculiar idea that anyone who took more than a small sherry at one session was an alcoholic. It was not surprising that I, who unashamedly and without giving it a thought, often came into her presence with the smell of alcohol on my breath, was classified as a dissolute man 'who was no good to anyone.' It followed according to the aunt's philosophy that if I was dissolute in one thing I would also be dissolute in the other. She wouldn't be surprised she told Bid, if I was 'carrying on with other women.'

This was too much for Bid who sent me a telegram asking me to come home. Captain Tester, to whom I gave the facts, summed up the situation very quickly and sent me on short leave, described as 'compassionate leave'. The Captain told me to be firm and to put my foot down.

There was not a lot of compassion flying about as, tight-lipped, I stepped on to the train in Newcastle. If anyone had got in the way just then I might have shouldered him on to the track. It was certain that if anyone had upset Bid, and at the same time perpetrated seditious rumours about me which were completely untrue, compassion would be in very short supply. I had been brought up in a hard school, where, if you turned the other cheek, that one would be stove in as well. I had a splendid mother-in-law in Cheshire who treated me well, but my surrogate mother-in-law was proving fractious. I might have to give her the Indian Mutiny treatment after all. If I used the forlorn 25pr. at Bedlington it might cheer It up a bit.

I arrived at Bid's late at night. She told me what had taken place and I assessed the situation and came to a quick decision and took charge. Without much discussion I bade Bid go and put on her coat and pack a bag. Luckily for me Bid went upstairs immediately, brought down a small case and, as the buses had stopped running we set out to walk from Knott-End to Hambleton. The aunt and uncle were very surprised when we left so abruptly.

It was a good walk, all of five miles I should think, but it was memorable and exhilarating. It had been a trying event but my wife was still by my side. We were young enough to take such trials in our stride; we had each other. So hand in hand through that quiet night, through deserted country lanes and past sleeping villages we trod lightly. Soemtimes laughing, sometimes pausing to hold each other and to kiss, we reached our destination eventually, for we were in no great hurry.

In the middle of the night we woke my mother, who greeted us warmly and took us in, as if such an arrival was the most commonplace of events. Shrewd lady that she was, she expressed no surprise at the drama which had been enacted previously, for later, it was always later, for my mother needed time to consider such matters, she revealed 'that she had seen it coming.' Very soon, Bid and I were lying close together in a feather bed in my own room, with the familiar furniture which had remained quite unchanged about us. It was a good feeling.

Bid came to join me on VE Day, which was in early May, and stayed until September. What a time we had. This happy period did much to compensate for the separation, the waiting and the uncertainty we had both had to face.

Bedlington is a mining village and should have been dull, dirty and uninteresting. It was none of these things, and furthermore the inhabitants were very kind and considerate to intruders such as we. We went regularly to the local cinema. We found an outdoor swimming pool tucked away in a picturesque setting in a wooded area. Bid and I swam about in it, wearing costumes which, according to the current fashion kept well within the bounds of respectability. Sea-bathing at Whitley Bay or at Blythe was another of our favourite activities. The Royal Ballet visited Newcastle and we enjoyed their production of *Coppelia*.

Sometimes we went to the Sergeants' Mess, where drinks and supper were served in an ante-room. Friendships were formed, particularly with one other young couple who had not been married long. At Morpeth we discovered a café where delicious teas of sandwiches and cakes aplenty could be got for half a crown each. Where could you get a tea nowadays for twelve and a half pence? My Sergeant's pay and allowances enabled us to live well.

There were river trips and country walks. When we were tired there were always hayfields to fling ourselves down in, when we could doze off amid country sounds and scents, with no need to worry about the arrival of shrieking missiles dropping on us out of the sky.

If we had considered the weather it was probably not the best of summers, for there are recollections of us running for shelter from sudden showers. Always we seemed to be running, always hand in hand, always laughing. Whatever the weather was like, it certainly did not worry us and we crammed a lot into those three months. It was the best of summers for us.

Somewhere in this playboy existence I must have managed to have satisfied Captain Tester and to have spent some time on preparation and lectures.

The climax of our mutual happiness at this time came when it was confirmed that Bid was expecting a child. Whether rightly or wrongly I very much wanted this baby at this time, for quite apart from the fact that I felt its arrival would establish the closest possible bond between us, there was a deeper psychological need to raise up a new life out of the ashes of destruction. For Bid I think it was more simple. She wanted what I wanted, was pleased because I was.

As the weeks wore on she suffered more and more from morning sickness, so we decided that it would be best to seek advice nearer home. In September I took her to Hambleton, and it was arranged that she should go into a nursing home in Blackpool when the time came. She went to stay with her mother in Cheshire but came back with me to my mother's for the Christmas of 1945. By this time I had been moved to Devizes in Wiltshire.

In the September when I had brought Bid from Bedlington, we had visited Baines Grammar School where we were treated with great courtesy, for good manners were still given great consideration and schoolmasters were still living examples to their pupils. We dined at the school and my old Headmaster, Mr F. J. Stafford, took us into his study and gave me some advice. Rather than take a degree course in English Literature, I decided to apply for admission to a Teachers' Training College which was a shorter course. I did not want to be away from home longer than I could help. Music would be one of my main studies.

It was whilst I was at Devizes that I went to Bristol and was interviewed and accepted for training, as soon as it could be arranged after I had left the Army. My new life and career was beginning to take shape and there were good prospects that I should be able to support my family with reasonable comfort.

On Sunday, 27th January, 1946 my mother sent a telegram which read:

'A son. Both well.'

By noon the next day I was in Blackpool, looking down at my tiny firstborn and greeting his mother with much tenderness. I should have been best man at Arthur's wedding, but I arrived at Stalmine just too late for the ceremony.

There is nothing much more to tell. Mother and son continued to thrive and went home to my mother.

After a short course on an Education Course at Welbeck Abbey I returned to Devizes from where I was sent on leave prior to my discharge on 27th June 1946.

It is ironical that I know more about how the officers fared than I do about the other ranks who were my close companions. Major Lucas was wounded in Italy fairly shortly after I was, and further to the north. He was shipped home and made such a good recovery that he continued his career as a soldier, becoming a Lieutenant-Colonel. He is now living in retirement. Major Babington, as stated previously, went to command 104th Field Battery RA, 30th Field Regiment RA when we were in North Africa. He and his Battery gained distinction on the Rapido in Italy. He became a Brigadier and is also retired. Mr Tallents left us when we were in Blackwater to train as Air OP. Later he went to North Africa and operated quite close to our position there. In Sicily he had the misfortune to drive a jeep over a mine. 'He woke up in hospital to find that he was minus a leg.' He died in the early 1980s. Captain Gethin, Commander of 'B' Troop, was killed in Italy before the final Cassino battle. Captain Peter stayed on with a Regular Commission and retired in 1964. Mr Hepworth became Adjutant, then Troop Commander and supported the Poles at Cassino. Later he joined the Malaysian Legal Service.

Sergeant Earle, he whom I called 'Grease', was wounded in the final phase of the Cassino battles. He died of his wounds in hospital not long afterwards. L/Bdr Cyrus Bell, 'Tex', came home unscathed in early 1946, having gone through Italy to Greece, still in 'A' Troop. He stayed with my mother for years and became 'Uncle Tex' to our two sons Geoffrey and John, and our daughter, Susan. He died in the late 1970s. L/Bdr Allman, my staunch limber-gunner, victim of human frailty, also came safe home and made a new life for himself. I met him once, years later when he seemed to have settled very happily. Alas he is also dead.

Battery Sergeant-Major Prior is still very much alive, and at the time of writing is rising eighty. His pals, Sergeant 'Smoky' Stoker and Sergeant 'Ginger' Rogers, who spent one and a half years in hospital, live near him on the south coast.

Of those others, 'Swaz' Burman, Ginger Hatton, 'Bam' Anstee, Sergeant-Artificer Bickle, Bdr Furlonger, Gunners L —, Slack and Smith, I know nothing. They emerge from time to time in my memory to flit across the stage, re-enacting some boisterous scene or other, unchanged in appearance after forty years, before they recede again into the shadows. No doubt there are many more such characters, including the elusive and mysterious 'Pete' of my North African Diary, asleep in my subconscious.

It is my own fault that I lost touch. When I was severed so abruptly and dramatically from my stark man's world, I felt bewildered and in a way unworthy to still count myself as one of those still left to slog it out in Italy. When I recovered from the shock and disappointment of being no longer fit for Active Service and wanted to communicate again, it was too late. My mates had come home and gone their several ways.

Since these concluding comments were written, a momentous occasion has occurred. Suddenly old links were re-established, forms emerged from the shadows. It came about that I attended a Regimental Reunion in London. Sad to say, there was only a token gathering, but it was still pleasurable to see faces one thought had disappeared forever, to relive experiences long gone. I met Colonel Lucas, who had led me in my searches by means of many postal exchanges. Dr Bill Wilson, our Regimental Medical Officer was present, bearing a Diary for 1944 with my name in it.

There was Sgt 'Smoky' Stoker, last seen as if through a mist, it will be remembered, in a setting much more dramatic than the Union Jack Club. I met Bdr H. Furlonger and Sgt Cook, 'Cookie', looking uncommonly fresh faced and upright, *still* insisting on addressing me as 'Young Bowman' as if the intervening years were as naught. Acquaintance was renewed with two of our drivers, both late of 'A' Troop. One was 'Taffy' C. H. Bonner, BEM, now Secretary of the London Branch of the Dunkirk Veterans Association, then notorious for his Napoleonic fixation with side-hats. The other was 'Tich' Greenhill, who shared a newspaper with me on our return from Dunkirk, as we strove to rid ourselves of *pendiculus pubis*.

After the Reunion a certain trepidation has become intermingled with my pleasure, for these my old comrades are the critics whom I really fear. From them no shortcomings or inaccuracies will be hidden. I can only plead that had I been able to draw on their experiences the book would have been more complete.

I had served seven years and one hundred and forty days. At the top of my final testimonial, under Military Conduct it says 'Exemplary'. The Cause of Discharge is given as 'Permanently unfit for any form of Military Service'.

I was a civilian once more, just another young man who had returned from tasting new experiences, fulfilling certain ambitions, who had been a little battered in the process, who had survived, much wiser and more competent I hoped to take up further challenges, to strive towards further goals yet unforeseen. The Regiment had been good to me. It would be fitting to conclude by saying that I was sorry to leave it, were it not for the fact that in one sense I never did.

EPILOGUE

The Regular Army bade farewell to the 25pr. field gun on 1st April, 1975, when gunners of 19th Field Regiment, RA, fired a salute at the Royal School of Artillery, Larkhill.

At the beginning of the Second World War there were only 78 such guns in existence and these had no carriages; at the end of the war about 12,000 had been manufactured.

The Gun is mounted at the entrance to the Royal School of Artillery. As befits one which has won its place in history it stands guard and bids a greeting to young members of the Regiment who have come for specialist training.

If you are passing, pause and look. It was my generation which saw its introduction and who put it to such effective use in all battle zones where troops of the British Empire were operating. It proved to be a considerable influence on the successful outcome of the war. Now the men who first brought the Gun into action, who cursed and sweated over it, who tended and worked it so assiduously, are not as agile and powerful as they were. Many died by it and many more were wounded in its shadow. We who lived are fast diminishing in number. But whole generations of gunners, skilled in the use of a succession of modern guns have followed us in an unbroken line, just as we stepped into the spaces vacated by our distinguished predecessors.

There will always be a job for our family of gunners. Fanatics still appear from time to time and have to be put down; dangerous sects emerge with malevolent intent. Those who preach pacificism so vehemently will be among the first to leap for shelter behind the safety of the guns.

We field gunners are not without pride or confidence or even conceit. Unashamedly we cling to these qualities, for we have earned them.

Our one battle honour is *Ubique*. It means 'Everywhere'. We have been everywhere, are everywhere. As we have been around for a long time now, it is pretty safe to speculate that we shall continue to keep an eye on things for some considerable time to come.

BIBLIOGRAPHY

The Badley Library, Royal School of Artillery, Larkhill
Public Record Office
Imperial War Museum
Gunners at War: Shelford Bidwell; Arrow Books
The Fourth Division 1939 to 1945: Hugh Williamson: Newman Neame
Iron Division: The History of the Third Division: Robin McNish: Ian Allen Ltd.
Monty: Nigel Hamilton: Book Club Associates
English History: A. J. P. Taylor: Book Club Associates
The Rise and Fall of the Third Reich: William L. Shires
Guderian Panzer General: Kenneth Macksey: MacDonald & James', London
Wellington as Military Commander: Michael Glover: Sphere Books
Bugles and a Tiger: John Masters: The Reprint Society, London
British Medical Journal Vol. 289: 22-29th December, 1984 (Penicillin — early trials in war casualties: Sir Ian Fraser)
The Reason Why: Cecil Woodham-Smith: Penguin